SOUTHERN LITERARY STUDIES

Fred Hobson, Editor

The Cass Mastern Material

THE CORE OF ROBERT PENN WARREN'S

All the King's Men

EDITED, WITH AN INTRODUCTION, BY

JAMES A. PERKINS

LOUISIANA STATE UNIVERSITY PRESS

BATON ROUGE

Manufactured in the United States of America
FIRST PRINTING

DESIGNER: Barbara Neely Bourgoyne
TYPEFACE: Adobe Minion, text; Brioso Pro, display
TYPESETTER: G&S Typesetters, Inc.
PRINTER AND BINDER: Thomson-Shore, Inc.

Library of Congress Cataloging-in-Publication Data

The Cass Mastern material : the core of Robert Penn Warren's "All the king's men" / edited, with an introduction, by James A. Perkins.
p. cm.—(Southern literary studies)
Includes bibliographical references and index.
ISBN 0-8071-3040-0 (hardcover : alk. paper)
1. Warren, Robert Penn, 1905– All the king's men—Sources. 2. United States—History—Civil War, 1861–1865—Literature and the war. 3. Warren, Robert Penn, 1905– —Knowledge—History. 4. Literature and history—United States. 5. Family in literature. 6. Ethics in literature I. Perkins, James A., 1941– II. Series.
PS3545.A748A7925 2005
813′.52—dc22

2004017915

The paper in this book meets the guidelines for permanence and durability of the Committee on Production Guidelines for Book Longevity of the Council on Library Resources. ♾

IN MEMORY OF

R. W. B. Lewis

(November 1, 1917–June 13, 2002)

who with energy, charm, and generosity
led me back to Robert Penn Warren
and to my own past

Contents

Preface

With the completion of this volume, I have finally produced a scholarly book that I enjoyed writing. There is no doubt that this book began with my first glimpse of the reading room at the Beinecke Rare Book and Manuscript Library at Yale University during an NEH Summer Seminar with R. W. B. Lewis in 1989. It was a clean, well-lighted place, and I was determined to sit there as often and for as long as I could.

While working there on the various dramatic version of *All the King's Men,* preparing the manuscript for *Robert Penn Warren's "All the King's Men": Three Stage Versions* that I edited with James A Grimshaw Jr. in 2000, I kept running into dramatic versions of chapter 4 of *All the King's Men,* the Cass Mastern story. I photocopied that material and kept it for another day.

Later, as I worked with multiple versions of the play and with the various other published versions of the Cass Mastern material, I kept wondering why Warren insisted, in introductions and interviews, that Jack Burden was Cass Mastern's grandnephew when anyone who had read the whole novel knew that Jack discovered, in the end, that his father was *really* Judge Irwin.

It was when I was reading page proofs for Noel Polk's "restored edition" of *All the King's Men* (2001), that I began to see that Warren may have insisted on the relationship between Cass Mastern and Jack Burden because it was the truth, a truth that has been overlooked by critics for more than half a century.

This realization led me into collaboration with a biologist and a lawyer and to a solution to the problem of Jack's paternity, which I published in an article presenting a radically new reading of *All the King's Men* and which I have repeated, in part, in the introduction to this volume.

Curiously, when I started this project, my goal was to provide critics with some material that might lead them to a new understanding and appreciation of *All the King's Men.* As it turns out, I have led myself there.

As is always the case in a project of this size, I have a number of people to thank: Charles T. Hazzelrigg, who introduced me to *All the King's Men* during my freshman year at Centre College in 1963; Robert Drake, who introduced me to Cleanth Brooks and Robert Penn Warren in the hallway outside his office in McClung Tower at the University of Tennessee; Mr. Brooks and Mr. Warren, who through their seminal texts *Understanding Poetry* and *Understanding Fiction* taught me the value of close reading; R. W. B. Lewis and the National Endowment for the Humanities who included me in an NEH Seminar on Warren at Yale in 1989; John Burt and the estate of Robert Penn Warren for sanctioning this book; Catherine Bennet, Lisa Lawrence, and the William Morris Agency for permission to publish "Cass Mastern's Wedding Ring" and an "An Untitled Play: A Drama of the American Civil War"; Philip Langner for permission to use the letters of Lawrence Langner; Patricia Willis, Nancy Kuhl, Stephan Jones, and the rest of the staff at the Beinecke Rare Book and Manuscript Library at Yale University, who made my trips to New Haven useful; Dorita Bolger and Connie Davis of the Westminster College library, who answered questions and gathered far-flung material; Patrick C. McCarthy for teaching me some genetics and Frank D. Allen Jr. for teaching me some law; Aimée Berger, Sue Kimball, Nancy Lewis, Raymond and Charlotte Beck, Randy and Cher Hendricks, William Bedford Clark, James Justus, and Noel Polk for various kinds of aid and support; everyone connected with Armellino's restaurant in Milford, Connecticut, for looking out for me; Frederick D. Horn and the members of the Westminster Faculty Development Committee for funding that supported this project at various stages; Carol Morrow, who assisted with the manuscript and solved my computer nightmares; Jillian Dobi, who helped with the index; and finally, my thanks to James A. Grimshaw Jr., Kay L. Coughenour, Eric Bentley, and Aaron Frankel for agreeing to participate in this project. (Frankel's very fine essay "Working in the Theater with Robert Penn Warren" was ultimately edited out of this volume. It appears in *RWP: An Annual of Robert Penn Warren Studies,* volume 2.) Finally I would like to thank John Easterly, Sylvia Frank Rodrigue, and especially George Roupe of Louisiana State University Press for seeing this project through.

The Cass Mastern Material

Introduction

James A. Perkins

When Jack Burden, the narrator of Robert Penn Warren's Pulitzer Prize–winning 1946 novel *All the King's Men,* reflects on Cass Mastern, the subject of his Ph.D. dissertation, he says that Cass Mastern "learned that the world is like an enormous spider web and if you touch it, however lightly, at any point, the vibration ripples to the remotest perimeter. . . ."[1]

What Jack Burden could not say was that he, Cass Mastern, Willie Stark, and Robert Penn Warren were all caught up in a great web of creativity, the center of which was the novel *All the King's Men.* For the most part this nexus involved the Willie Stark material. Warren began to develop this material with the verse play *Proud Flesh* (1937–40), written in collaboration with Francis Fergusson.[2] He continued in the novel *All the King's Men* (1943–46), the play *All the King's Men* (1947–48) produced by Erwin Piscator, the play *Willie Stark: His Rise and Fall* (1956–58) written in collaboration with Aaron Frankel, and finally in the play *All the King's Men* (1959), a rewrite with Mark Schoenberg of the 1947–48

1. Robert Penn Warren, *All the King's Men* (New York: Harcourt, 1946), 200; Robert Penn Warren *All the King's Men,* restored edition, ed. Noel Polk (New York: Harcourt, 2001), 266. In most cases, quotations from the text of *All the King's Men* will carry two page citations, the first for the 1946 "first edition" of the novel, edited by Lambert Davis, and the second for the "restored edition" edited by Noel Polk. Hereafter they will be distinguished in parenthetical references as "1946" and "2001."

2. Robert Penn Warren, letter to David Clay, November 8, 1941. This letter is reproduced here in its entirety in Appendix B. The letter is a gold mine of information about Warren's career at this time. Among other things, it provides a name for Warren's hitherto untitled second "unpublished" novel and states flatly that Warren as early as 1941 was planning to write a novel "based on Huey Long situation." The letter is a carbon copy located in the David Clay file in the Robert Penn Warren Papers in the Beinecke Rare Book and Manuscript Library at Yale University. Unless otherwise noted, all letters to Warren quoted herein can be found in this collection, known as YCAL MSS 51, denoting manuscript collection 51 in the Yale Collection of American Literature.

version. A full account of Warren's development of the Willie Stark material is presented in *Robert Penn Warren's "All the King's Men": Three Stage Versions*, edited by James A. Grimshaw Jr. and James A. Perkins and published by the University of Georgia Press in 2000.[3]

The present volume focuses on Robert Penn Warren and the Cass Mastern material. Warren discovered the character Cass Mastern during the writing of the novel *All the King's Men.* The character does not appear in the play *Proud Flesh.* As Warren recounted in "A Note to *All the King's Men*" in the summer 1953 *Sewanee Review,* "It was not until the spring of 1943 that I began again on the play [*Proud Flesh*]. I had taken the manuscript out of its cupboard with the intention of revising it, but immediately I found myself thinking of the thing as a novel. That idea wasn't entirely new."[4] What Warren might have been referring to in saying "[t]hat idea wasn't entirely new" was suggested in the November 8, 1941, letter to David Clay, a Vanderbilt classmate, who was then working at Harcourt Brace and who had approached Warren about changing publishers. Clay's overture was successful, and Warren published his next novel, *At Heaven's Gate* (referred to in this letter by the working title "And Pastures New"), with Harcourt Brace in 1943. On the second page of this letter Warren stated that he had two novels in mind, "Novel one, based on Huey Long situation, but not an exposé—on the theme of power versus values, means versus ends—some academic setting, but not central to novel. I plan to begin work on this next summer. Novel two, very short—an allegorical fantasy, about 50,000 words—What Says Don Martin—located in Mexico."

As it turned out, Warren evidently never wrote "What Says Don Martin," and he did not begin on the novel "based on Huey Long" until 1943. He was too busy wrapping up his novel *At Heaven's Gate* and writing his long critical essay on Coleridge's *The Rime of the Ancient Mariner* that was published in 1946 as an introduction to the Reynal and Hitchcock edition illustrated by Alexander Calder.

As Warren remembered it in the "Introduction to the 1974 English Edition," Cass Mastern emerged because: "I was afraid that my story would thin out into a narrative of mere intrigue, something like political shenanigans in a banana republic. I was afraid, too, that the narrator would become a mere narrator, nothing more than a technical convenience with no relation to the action.

3. James A. Grimshaw Jr. and James A. Perkins, eds., *Robert Penn Warren's "All the King's Men": Three Stage Versions* (Athens: University of Georgia Press, 2000), 1–18.

4. Robert Penn Warren, "A Note to *All the King's Men,*" *Sewanee Review* 61 (1953): 477.

In other words, to put it into a crude short-hand, I felt that the general story would lack any deep moral dimension, and the narrator any deep psychological dimension."[5]

In an interview with Ruth Fisher that first appeared in the May 1972 issue of *Four Quarters*, Warren gave a fuller account of the narrative function of the Cass Mastern material:

> The novel went along to a certain point in the full swing of action. The narrator of the novel got stuck (and I got stuck) with the problem of trying to make sense of his own feelings about his role in relation to Willie Stark, the political dictator in my novel. I could have stopped the action and made my narrator, Jack Burden, have a moral debate with himself: "I don't approve of all that's going on, and I must discuss this with myself, my God, and my kindly pastor, et cetera." He could, in other words have gone at the question abstractly. But this is not his character. He is, in fact, trying to live a life avoiding all moral issues. But anyway, the abstract way would have been death to the novel. At this point I suddenly had an idea. I gave Burden a Civil War relative (about whom he had been trying to do a Ph.D. dissertation)—Cass Mastern by name—and invented a story for Cass, in which Cass struggles for, and finds, moral awareness. The Cass story stands as a kind of mirror image for Jack, but not, I trust, merely as a device. Jack responds to the contrast, it has a part in his development. What I was trying to avoid was the abstract approach. I wanted to give the reader the sense of the meaning emerging from experiences. That anyway, is the essence of fiction—the image of meaning emerging from experience.[6]

From the beginning, Warren was fascinated with the story of Cass Mastern. The Cass Mastern material was first published as a short story titled "Cass Mastern's Wedding Ring" in the *Partisan Review*.[7] Some recognized its worth right away. In a letter to Warren dated November 10, 1944, James M. Reid wrote, "I have just read 'Cass Mastern's Wedding Ring' in *Partisan Review* and I want to tell you what a swell story it is. If the new novel is as good as this section of it, you will really have something." Warren then published the Cass Mastern material as chapter 4 of the novel *All the King's Men*. It should be noted here that, as Warren envisioned it, the Cass Mastern story was only the first half of chapter 4 in *All the*

5. Robert Penn Warren, "Introduction to the 1974 English Edition," in *All the King's Men* (London: Secker and Warberg, 1974), xiv.

6. Robert Penn Warren, interviewed by Ruth Fisher, "A Conversation with Robert Penn Warren," in *Talking with Robert Penn Warren*, ed. Floyd C. Watkins, John T. Hiers, and Mary Louise Weaks (Athens: University of Georgia Press, 1990), 179–80.

7. Robert Penn Warren, "Cass Mastern's Wedding Ring," *Partisan Review* 11 (Fall 1944): 375–407.

King's Men. In the "setting copy,"[8] sent by Warren to Lambert Davis, his editor at Harcourt, Brace, there are only nine chapters; the present chapters 4 and 5 are combined into one, chapter 4. In this combined structure, Burden's investigation of the Cass Mastern material is physically balanced by his investigation of Judge Irwin. His study of a person, his father's uncle, who *is* his relative, is thus balanced against his study of a person whom he later *comes to believe* to be his father. Never underestimate Warren's love of irony. Warren's irony concerning the relationship between Jack and Cass Mastern is more complex than it appears to be.

When Lambert Davis divided Warren's fourth chapter into two chapters, he destroyed this balance, isolated the Cass Mastern material, and may have caused some readers of the novel to consider the material extraneous. Clifford Dowdy certainly did, writing to Davis on August 3, 1946, "The Cass Mastern episode (which I had read as a story) seemed to me to have no place in the novel, though it was such a compelling story in itself, I can understand why it stayed in."[9]

It should also be noted that the story as it appeared in the *Partisan Review* differed from the version that finally appeared in the novel in one significant way. In the short story in the *Partisan Review* and in its subsequent printings, Warren identified Cass Mastern as the great-uncle of Jack Burden. Even in the much-edited Burnett version in *This Is My Best* (see details below), a headnote reads: "The narrator of *All the King's Men,* Jack Burden, a cousin [*sic*], two generations later, of Cass Mastern comes into possession of Cass's diary, and as a candidate for the Ph.D. in history attempts to use it, and other family documents, as the basis for his dissertation."[10] In the 1946 novel Cass is presented as "one of the two maternal uncles of Ellis Burden, the scholarly attorney. . . ." In the novel, Warren never says that Jack was the grand-nephew of Cass Mastern. It was not always so. As late as November 19, 1945, in the setting copy of the novel Warren was calling Cass Mastern Jack's relative. His editor Lambert Davis wrote: "The Cass Mastern

8. The setting copy for *All the King's Men* (YCAL MSS 51, Box 101, Folders 1869–76, Beinecke Rare Book and Manuscript Library, Yale University) contains 634 typed pages. Lambert Davis's division of the original chapter 4 into chapters 4 and 5 occurs on 257 of the setting copy.

9. Clifford Dowdy to Lambert Davis, August 3, 1946, Warren Papers, YCAL MSS 51, Box 91, F.1721.

10. Robert Penn Warren, headnote to "Cass Mastern," in *This Is My Best,* ed. Whit Burnett (Garden City, NY: Doubleday, 1970), 389. Warren's reference to Jack as a cousin of Cass Mastern is an error. Cass's sister, Lavinia Mastern, was the mother of Ellis Burden. Therefore, if Jack were Ellis Burden's son, Cass would be his great-uncle. See note 11.

passage has troubled me in the way in which it is introduced. Jack Burden is quite dead-pan, introducing this episode, in calling Cass his Great Uncle, and yet Cass is not his Great Uncle. The reader[,] finishing this story, can legitimately say he has been tricked."

When Warren answered this letter from Lambert Davis on November 24, 1945 (Warren's letter is included here in Appendix B), he wrote, in part: "I am delighted by the view you take of the novel. I have been waiting with breathless anxiety to hear from you. As for the things you mention: check on the matter of deception about the relationship of Cass Mastern to Jack. This is easily remedied. I can simply state the relation of Cass to the Scholarly Attorney and then let the chips fall where they will."[11] By establishing the relation of Cass Mastern to Ellis Burden and then letting "the chips fall where they will," Warren, the consummate New Critic, was creating a distinction without a difference. If Jack Burden is Ellis Burden's son, then saying that Cass Mastern is Ellis Burden's uncle is no different than saying Cass Mastern is Jack Burden's great-uncle.

Of course, at the end of the 1946 version of novel, as edited by Lambert Davis, the reader is led to believe, along with Jack Burden, that Jack's real father is not Ellis Burden, the scholarly attorney, but Judge Irwin, the man who commits suicide as the result of information Jack uncovers about the judge's past.[12]

11. Robert Penn Warren to Lambert Davis, November 24, 1945, Harcourt Brace Editorial Archive, Orlando, FL. See page 136 of the present volume.

12. The reader trying to determine how Warren could have it both ways on the subject of Jack burden's ancestry should consider the bedrock New Critical belief in the integrity, the separateness and the unity, of each individual work of art. I got my best exposure to this notion when I tried to argue with Cleanth Brooks that the Quentin Compson of *Sound and the Fury* was the same Quentin Compson as in *Absalom, Absalom!* and that Quentin created the idea of miscegenation in *Absalom, Absalom!* because he was the Quentin Compson of *Sound and the Fury* and he could not believe that a man could be shot for incest. Today we would refer to this as an intertextual reading. Mr. Brooks said it was trash. He said the two books are different works, each separate and unified, and there's an end to it. I don't believe that this is a particularly persuasive attitude, but it does explain how Warren could sometimes (in the short story) appear to refer to Cass Mastern as Jack Burden's great-uncle and at other times (in the novel) as something else. But Warren did not create this apparent contradiction. It was created by the way everyone (including me) read the novel for more than half a century.

After I created this New Critical way of balancing Warren's two statements about Jack's parentage, I came to realize that there weren't two authorial attitudes toward this subject. Warren consistently insisted that Cass Mastern was a relative of Jack Burden. Jack's mother insisted that Ellis Burden was not Jack's father (and therefore Cass was not his relative), and Lambert Davis as well as Jack (and the readers of the novel since 1946) believed her. I came to believe that Warren said that Cass Mastern was

The changes that Davis suggested in chapter 4 support Jack's acceptance of his mother's assertion and keep the casual reader from questioning the inconsistency of the information Warren has given about Jack's paternity.

As Warren recounted in his "Introduction to the 1974 English Edition," when the novel was published in England by Eyre and Spottiswoode in 1948, chapter 4, the Cass Mastern material was omitted because the "publisher had decided that the subject [the American Civil War] would not interest his public" (xiv). That may well have been part of the reason for the omission. Another part may have been the shortage of paper in England at the end of the war. A letter from R. Lynch at Eyre and Spottiswoode to Warren dated April 18, 1946, reads: "Mr. Graham Greene asks me to thank you for your letter of April 8th. We have written Miss Claudius to tell her that it will not be possible to publish your stories in book form until the end of 1947 owing to the extreme shortage of paper which we suffer from. We have retained the manuscript." And a letter from Graham Greene to Warren dated January 8, 1947, reads: "You will by now have received the complete proofs of ALL THE KING'S MEN. You will remember won't you that you were going to look at them with the eye to possible pruning for the English market?"

If Warren was attempting to reduce the size of the novel, the Cass Mastern material presented itself as an ideal target. In the finished novel, as it was published in the United States in 1946, the Cass Mastern material is a self-contained unit, chapter 4. There are only four mentions of Cass Mastern—in two cases a single sentence or phrase, in two others a short passage—outside of chapter 4. Three of them are in chapter 6 of the 1946 edition (chapter 7 of the restored edition). Two of these are quite brief. In the first, Jack observes that his own "nobility (or whatever it was) had had on my world almost as dire a consequence as Cass Mastern's sin had had on his" (1946, 315; 2001, 415). A sentence omitted from the 1946 version (so it appears only in the restored edition) discusses Jack's "Great Sleep": "I had once before experienced this—back when I was working on a dissertation on Cass Mastern for the Ph.D.—and so I knew the symptoms of its coming on" (427). The third and most important is a comparison of Jack's physiognomy to that of Cass Mastern:

> Anyway, Anne Stanton, age seventeen, had probably gone upstairs to be alone because she was, all of a sudden, in love. She was in love with a rather tall, somewhat gan-

---

Jack's great-uncle because it is true. I then created an underpinning for his assertion in the *Mississippi Quarterly* article referenced below.

> gly, slightly stooped, youth of twenty-one, with a bony horse face, a big, almost askew hook of a nose, dark unkempt hair, dark eyes (not burning and deep like those of Cass Mastern, his great uncle [this phrase appears only in the restored edition], but frequently vague or veiled, bloodshot in the mornings, brightening only with excitement), big hands that worked and twisted slowly in his lap, plucking at each other, and twisted big feet that were inclined to shamble—a youth not beautiful, not brilliant, not industrious, not good, not kind, not even ambitious, given to excesses and confusions, thrown between melancholy and random violence, between the cold mire and the hot flame, between curiosity and apathy, between humility and self-love, between yesterday and tomorrow. What she had succeeded in creating out of that unpromising lump of clay scooped up from the general earth, nobody was ever to know. (1946, 299; 2001, 393–94)

The final mention of Cass Mastern is in chapter 9/10:

> But I still had the money, and so I am spending it to live on while I write the book I began years ago, the life of Cass Mastern, whom once I would not understand but whom, perhaps, I now may come to understand. I suppose there is some humor in the fact that while I write about Cass Mastern I live in the house of Judge Irwin and eat bread bought with his money. For Judge Irwin and Cass Mastern do not resemble each other very closely. (If Judge Irwin resembles any Mastern it is Gilbert, the granite-headed brother of Cass.) (1946, 463–64; 2001, 608)

These passages are simply missing from the first two English editions.

When Lambert Davis became aware that Douglas Gerrold at Eyre and Spottiswoode was planning to excise Cass Mastern, he wrote to Warren on July 8, 1946, "I am interested particularly in his suggestion of cutting out the Cass Mastern section. You will recall it was at one time my suggestion too, but you felt that its symbolic value was too important in the story to warrant its omission."

It seems clear that Lambert Davis was reading a simpler novel than the one Warren had written. In the setting copy of the first half of chapter 4, which is now available to readers in Noel Polk's new edition of the novel, the narrator states clearly: "Cass Mastern was one of Jack Burden's father's two maternal uncles, a brother of his mother, Lavinia Mastern, a great-uncle to Jack Burden" (228). Jack, as a very self-conscious and postmodern narrator, in a passage omitted in the 1946 edition, covers himself for giving two different versions of the facts about another issue by saying:

> But to return to that day: the fact of my ignorance during the course of the events of the day creates a peculiar problem in narrative. Things as they came to me that day

> were only, or almost only, appearances, for I lacked knowledge of their logic. But if I narrate them in terms of the logic later perceived, that is, in terms of the principle in which inheres their reality, something is wrong, too. For in art as in life there is a sin against Appearance as well as against Reality. And there are no descending circles and only one flame in Hell. But it is a beauty.
>
> I shall keep distinct what I knew that day, and what I came subsequently to know. (535)

The setting copy, Warren's original version of Jack's narrative, forces the reader to see that Jack gives two distinct versions of his lineage and focuses on the fact that the secret of Jack's paternity lies solely with his mother. It is she who tells Jack that Judge Irwin was his father. It is she who told Judge Irwin and Ellis Burden (if in fact she did) that Judge Irwin is Jack's father. There is no other evidence in the novel to support her statement that Judge Irwin, rather than Ellis Burden, was Jack's father. As Frank D. Allen Jr., a retired government lawyer explained to me, the Civil Code, on which Louisiana law is founded, assumes that a child born in wedlock is the child of that marriage unless compelling evidence to the contrary is presented.[13]

There is compelling evidence in *All the King's Men,* but it is not to the contrary. Physical comparison is what we generally rely on as we look for family traits among consanguineous relatives. It is the method Lucy Stark asks Jack to use when she shows him Sibyl Frey's baby. "It looks like Tom," she says. "Don't you think so?" (1946, 450; 2001, 591). If we apply this method to the physical descriptions of the major characters in *All the King's Men,* we discover interesting patterns of evidence. In the descriptions of Jack, Jack's mother, Judge Irwin, and Ellis Burden there is enough evidence to preclude the possibility that Jack is the issue of Judge Irwin and Mrs. Burden.

Mrs. Burden is a blue-eyed blonde (1946, 137; 2001, 185); Judge Irwin has yellow eyes (1946, 130; 2001, 171), a tall skull (1946, 48; 2001, 83), and faded red hair (1946, 130; 2001, 171); Jack Burden is rather tall, somewhat gangly, has a bony horse face, dark unkempt hair, dark eyes (not burning and deep like the eyes of Cass Mastern), and big hands (1946, 299; 2001, 393–94); Ellis Burden has a shock of tangled black hair and eyes usually hidden by his glasses (1946, 121; 2001, 160); and Cass Mastern was tall (1946, 175; 2001, 234), had a long bony face, thick dark hair, dark, wide-set, deep eyes, and strong wrists and bony hands (1946, 171; 2001,

13. Much of the material in this section of the introduction appeared in a slightly different form in James A. Perkins, Patrick McCarthy, and Frank D. Allen Jr., "Human Genetics and *All the King's Men:* The Case of Jack Burden's Paternity," *Mississippi Quarterly* 55, no. 1 (winter 2002–03): 65–75.

228–29). Some of these details are more important than others. Eyes and hair are rather well understood and fairly predictable as genetic traits. According to a genetics textbook first published the same year as *All the King's Men,* "Eye color was the first normal Mendelian character recognized in man, when the Davenports (1907) and Hurst (1908) independently suggested that blue eyes are recessive to brown."[14]

Given what was known about human genetics in 1939, the year in which the main action of *All the King's Men* takes place, it is unlikely that Judge Irwin is Jack Burden's father. Recessive genes would express both Jack's mother's blonde hair and blue eyes. Likewise recessive genes would express Monty Irwin's red hair and yellow eyes (a variation of green eyes). Their combination would not likely express itself in Jack's dark hair and dark eyes. On the other hand, Jack's mother's recessive genes for blonde hair and blue eyes combined with Ellis Burden's dominant genes for dark hair and dark eyes would likely express themselves in Jack's dark hair and dark eyes. Patrick McCarthy, a biologist who teaches genetics wrote: "It's certainly safe to say that there is no chance that the Judge (light hair) and Jack's mother (light hair) could parent a dark-haired son, unless there was a *new* gene mutation coming from one of them."[15] I am indebted to McCarthy for any understanding of genetics that this introduction displays. He pointed out that H. J. Muller in 1922 (studying changes in fruit flies) began work that led to a Nobel Prize and later allowed J. V. Neel, in 1962 (long after *All the King's Men* was published), to establish mutation rates in humans at 4 per 100,000. Since Jack's dark hair and eyes would require two mutations in the same gamete (either sperm or egg), the rate of mutation would be 4/100,000 x 4/100,000, or 16 in 10 billion, or 1 in 625 million. Those would be the odds that the Judge is Jack's father.

I am not alone and not the first to notice the importance of Jack's paternity in the novel. Warren's friend and fellow close reader Robert Heilman wrote in a letter to Warren on October 7, 1946, shortly after the novel was finished, "Some day I want to ask you about the genealogical symbolism which I'm not sure about." There is no evidence that Heilman ever followed up on his perceptive observation. Had he done so, the critical view of the novel's final chapter might have been altered greatly.

Rather than the simple reversal found at the end of the 1946 version, the restored edition (which merely underlines the relationships already suggested by the 1946 edition) puts even more pressure on Jack's statement about Ellis Burden

14. Reginald Ruggles Gates, *Human Genetics,* vol. 1 (New York: Macmillan, 1946), 88.

15. Patrick McCarthy, E-mail message to the author, March 6, 2002.

near the end of the novel: "(Does he think that I am his son? I cannot be sure. Nor can I feel that it matters, for each of us is the son of a million fathers)" (1946, 462; 2001, 606). This, of course, is not true. Each of us has but one father, and the future that Jack claims to have at the end of *All The King's Men,* based on his having accepted the past, having accepted Judge Irwin as his father, is illusory and ironic. Jack, in fact, has denied his true past and accepted a past that he can live with. He has denied the old South of the slaveholder for the new South of the scalawag and sharper.

Warren clearly liked the material and wanted readers in the United Kingdom to see it. While he acceded to removing it from the first English edition of *All the King's Men,* he tried to get it (along with "The Statement of Ashby Wyndham," an excerpt from *At Heaven's Gate* that had already appeared as a story in the spring 1943 edition of the *Southern Review*) added to the planned English edition of *The Circus in the Attic.* On June 18, 1948, Ruby Miliar of the editorial department of Eyre and Spottiswoode informed Warren that the publisher preferred not to make major changes to the short story book and would not include "The Statement of Ashby Wyndham" and the Cass Mastern story in the volume.

Although chapter 4 and Cass Mastern were again absent from the second English edition, published by Eyre and Spottiswoode in 1960, and from the English paperback edition published in 1960 by Langborough, Warren restored the Cass Mastern material to the third English edition, published in 1974 by Secker and Warberg, with this "introductory" statement: "I have always felt that the section is central to the novel" (xiv). This was not the first time Warren made such an assertion about Cass Mastern. In his handwritten notes for the novel on a page marked "last chapter" Warren writes, "[L]iving in house—way of being able to carry past into present," and then below, "Cass is the connection."[16] If, in fact, what I have asserted here about Jack's father is true, then it is easier to see why Warren felt the Cass Mastern material was central to the novel.

Following its initial appearance in the *Partisan Review,* Warren republished the Cass Mastern material as a short story four more times during his life. Martha Foley chose it for *The Best American Short Stories of 1945.* Foley chose it again in 1975 for *200 Years of Great American Short Stories.* Warren chose it for inclusion in Whit Burnett's *This Is My Best* in 1970. On November 21, 1968, when Burnett wrote Warren asking for a submission, he was unsure in what genre to represent

16. Robert Penn Warren, "Last chapter," YCAL MSS 51, Box 98, Folder 1834, Beinecke Library, Yale University.

Warren. "Both Hallie and I look on you as a novelist," he wrote, "but on many of the ballots was written, in one phrase or another: 'He should be with the poets.' Poet, critic, novelist, the choice is your own—but we are all looking forward to what it will be, and what you will add to it in your comments."

Warren responded by sending the short story "Cass Mastern's Wedding Ring," which proved to be too long. On March 7, 1969, Burnett sent Warren an edited version that entirely omitted Jack Burden from the tale to save space. In his cover letter, Burnett wrote, "If you think this does the piece harm, however, I would be happy to have five or six poems or anything else you think you can say represents you, in one form or another, at your 'best.'"

Like Warren's excision of chapter 4 and other mentions of Cass Mastern from the first two English editions of *All the King's Men,* Burnett's excision of Jack Burden from his version of the Cass Mastern story was a fairly simple process. Chapter 4 is essentially a frame tale with Jack Burden's attempt to write his dissertation about Cass Mastern acting as the frame. In the tale itself, most of the mentions of Jack Burden are parenthetical insertions.

Despite Burnett's editing, and despite his invitation to send "poems or anything else you think represents you," Warren stayed with "Cass Mastern's Wedding Ring" as his "best."

Again in 1987, Warren's life-long friend and editor Albert Erskine chose it for inclusion in *A Robert Penn Warren Reader.* Warren, by then already terminally ill with bone cancer, was not involved in the selections, but he finally signed off on what Erskine did. Clearly Warren liked the story.

He was not alone in this feeling. Charles H. Bonner in his *Robert Penn Warren* praised the piece: "The Cass Mastern episode, chapter 4 of the novel, is a superb evocation of the ante-bellum South and a bravura piece of imaginative historical reconstruction without equal in American literature."[17] William Faulkner in a letter dated July 25, 1946, to Lambert Davis, the editor he shared with Warren at Random House, wrote: "The Cass Mastern story is a beautiful and moving piece. That was his novel. The rest of it I would throw away."[18] And the drama critic Eric Bentley wrote in a critical essay on Warren's first three novels in the *Kenyon Review:* "What of the Cass Mastern story (the interlude that constitutes Warren's fourth chapter)? It has frivolously been suggested that Warren put it in because it

17. Charles H. Bonner, *Robert Penn Warren* (New York: Twayne, 1964), 94.

18. William Faulkner to Lambert Davis, July 25, [1946], in *Selected Letters of William Faulkner,* ed. Joseph Blotner (New York: Random House, 1977), 239.

was too good to be left out; and I gather that the London publisher will omit it on grounds of irrelevance. Thematically, however, it is central."[19] In a July 13, 1946, letter to Warren, his old friend Cleanth Brooks wrote, "The story of Cass Mastern was a stroke of genius. It furnishes you with a very powerful lever—which you use admirably."[20] Brooks expanded on that cryptic statement in a speech he made on *All the King's Men* at the Flora Levy Lecture in the Humanities at the University of Southwestern Louisiana in 1988:

> Warren, by the way, has found an excellent means for relating his hero's personal plight to the general plight of the culture—its moral confusion and its lack of direction. It has to do with why Jack cannot finish his dissertation for the Ph.D. . . .
>
> Why couldn't Jack write the life of Cass Mastern? He had all the facts. There they were in Mastern's personal papers. He couldn't because he couldn't make any sense of that life. Such a tender conscience, such deep remorse for having committed a breach of honor—to get oneself killed for such matters as these? To a man of the 20th Century, to the young man that Jack Burden has come to be, it doesn't make sense and so the dissertation was put on the shelf to gather dust.[21]

The Cass Mastern episode in the novel *All the King's Men* acts as an interpolated exemplum in much the same way that the Willie Proudfit tale in *Night Rider* and the statements of Ashby Wyndham in *At Heaven's Gate* act. In all three of these novels, Warren introduced complex subplots, stories of former events, that tend to act as foils against which it becomes easier to discern the issues at conflict in the main plots of the novels. In his seminal 1981 volume, *The Achievement of Robert Penn Warren,* James H. Justus discussed the function of these exempla as well as they are ever likely to be discussed:

> In the first novel, only the hero of the interpolated story, Willie Proudfit, can be said to have passed from the negative state of violence and confusion to a positive state of self-knowledge; the overall vision is nihilistic. In the second novel, the self-knowledge of Ashby Wyndham is so unremittingly radical and fundamentalist that it virtually debases the self rather than lifting it up as a model of growth for others; but the protago-

19. Eric Bentley, "The Meaning of Robert Penn Warren's Novels," *Kenyon Review* 10 (summer 1938): 415.

20. Cleanth Brooks to Robert Penn Warren, July 13, 1946, in *Cleanth Brooks and Robert Penn Warren: A Literary Correspondence,* ed. James A. Grimshaw Jr. (Columbia: University of Missouri Press, 1998), 110.

21. Cleanth Brooks, "*All the King's Men:* The Local and the Universal," undated typescript, Warren Papers, YCAL MSS 51, Box 102, F.1886, [12–13].

> nist, Jerry Calhoun, though he has by the end of the novel endured humiliation and defeat, at least survives, taken in hand by a loving and humble father in whose care lies the possibility of regeneration. Cass Mastern in *All the King's Men* constitutes a plausible model for his twentieth-century kinsman, who in his own story survives spiritual drift and betrayal (his own and others) long enough to pick up the pieces of a casually violent life.[22]

In all three cases Warren printed these exempla as separate stories in magazines prior to the publication of the novels from which they came: "The Statement of Ashby Wyndham," *Sewanee Review* 51 (Spring 1943), 183–236; "How Willie Proudfit Came Back," *Southern Review* 4 (Autumn 1938), 299–321; "Cass Mastern's Wedding Ring," *Partisan Review* 11 (fall 1944), 375–407. James A. Grimshaw Jr. in his Warren bibliography lists the Willie Proudfit tale as a story rather than as an excerpt. It seems likely that it existed in the form published in the *Southern Review* and was later revised and worked into the novel *Night Rider.* Conversely, it seems likely that "The Statement of Ashby Wyndham" and "Cass Mastern's Wedding Ring" developed through the writing of the novels in which they appear.[23]

The story itself, "Cass Mastern's Wedding Ring," as it appears in the present volume is taken from the *Partisan Review,* where it was first published. It is a complex story, a frame tale, constructed by Jack Burden, who had attempted to write a dissertation about his paternal great-uncle Cass Mastern. Cass Mastern is brought to Mississippi by his brother (who is fifteen years older than he) and put to work helping Gilbert run his plantation Valhalla. Cass is at best a poor farmer, but he is interested in the education he is getting from Mr. Lawson, "a tubercular and vague young man from Princeton." He is sent by his brother to Transylvania College in Lexington, Kentucky. In Lexington Cass is welcomed into the home of Duncan Trice and his wife Annabelle. Cass and Annabelle have an affair. Duncan discovers the affair and commits suicide. He makes his death look like an accident but leaves his wedding ring under his wife's pillow so that she will know the truth. The house slave Phebe finds the ring and brings it to Mrs. Trice,

22. James H. Justus, *The Achievement of Robert Penn Warren* (Baton Rouge: Louisiana State University Press, 1981), 162–63. Justus in this passage and Joseph Blotner in his foreword to the 1996 edition of *All the King's Men* (ix) both refer to Cass Mastern as a relative of Jack Burden. Neither of them has written on Jack's paternity. It would be interesting to know whether these references are anything more than a convenient way of identifying Cass Mastern.

23. For an alternate version of the composition of the Cass Mastern story, see Jonathan S. Cullich, "From 'Jack Burden' to 'I,'" in *Making History: The Biographical Narratives of Robert Penn Warren* (Baton Rouge: Louisiana State University Press, 2000), 99–126.

who realizes immediately that Phebe knows the truth. Annabelle gives the ring to Cass and indicates that Phebe knows their secret. Mrs. Trice cannot stand the idea of Phebe's gaze, so she sells her to a slave dealer headed for New Orleans. When Cass learns what Annabelle has done, he tries to find Phebe. This attempt causes the relationship between Cass and Annabelle to end. She returns to Washington, and Cass goes back to Mississippi. There he frees his slaves and tries to run his plantation with them as hired help. It is at this point that he begins to write the diary out of which his story is reconstructed. Finally he sends his freed slaves north into what he is sure will be a worse life than the one from which he has released them. When the Civil War comes, Cass enlists as an infantryman from Mississippi. He carries a rifle though he is determined never to fire it at the enemy. Also he wears Duncan Trice's wedding ring on a string around his neck, just as the Ancient Mariner (the title character of the work Warren had written an introduction to just before his began work on *All the King's Men*) wore the albatross, the symbol of his sin, around his neck. This is the wedding ring of the title, "Cass Mastern's Wedding Ring." Cass, of course, was never married. It is not his ring. As I said earlier, never underestimate Warren's love of irony.

During this period Cass writes the occasional letters to his brother that become another source for his story. He seeks his own death at Shiloh, Corinth, Chickamauga, Knoxville, and Chattanooga. He is wounded outside Atlanta, rots slowly to death in an Atlanta hospital, and is buried in an unmarked grave. Just before his death he dictates a final letter to his brother. The story then follows Gilbert's life, based on ancillary material Jack Burden was able to find, to his death in 1914 and recounts how the diary, the letters, and the ring came into Burden's hands. All told, the story and its frame cover a period from Gilbert's birth in about 1820 till roughly 1939. But it focuses on the period from Cass Mastern's birth in 1830 through his introduction to Annabelle Trice in 1852, the death of Duncan Trice in 1854, and the beginning of the Civil War in 1861 to his death in 1864. At the very least, it is a story with many settings, and it covers a long period of time.

Warren was a writer who was always at something. He wrote in almost every genre imaginable (perhaps only travel literature is missing from his oeuvre). From 1946 and the publication of *All the King's Men* until the film version of the novel was complete, the Cass Mastern material was set aside for other more pressing projects. In 1947 Harcourt Brace published Warren's collection of short stories, *The Circus in the Attic, and Other Stories.* In 1949 the same house published the first edition of Brooks and Warren's *Modern Rhetoric.* And in 1950 Henry Holt published the second edition of Brooks and Warren's *Understanding Poetry.* Throughout this period, Warren was at work on a new novel, *World*

Enough and Time, which was published by Random House in 1950, as well as the long verse narrative that would finally appear as *Brother to Dragons: A Tale in Verse and Voices* in 1953. He was involved, but not deeply, with the Erwin Piscator's stage version of *All the King's Men,* which played in 1948 at the President Theatre in New York City. This dramatic version of the novel, like the three others in *Robert Penn Warren's "All the King's Men": Three Stage Versions* and like director Robert Rossen's film version of *All the King's Men,* omits the Cass Mastern material completely.

Shortly after Rossen began filming of *All the King's Men* in 1948, he contacted the William Morris Agency with the proposal that he and Warren write a stage play based on the material he had left out of the movie, the Cass Mastern story. Writing a stage play based on the Cass Mastern material presented a unique problem to Warren. He had sold the rights to the novel *All the King's Men* and the play *Proud Flesh* to Columbia Pictures, and presumably they would also own rights to the characters developed in those works despite the fact that Rossen omitted them from the film script. So Warren was in a position of having to "write around" some of his own best work. Although he had created several very memorable scenes in chapter 4—the scene where Cass becomes aware of the power and beauty of Annabelle's eye as she lights the candles and the scene, after Duncan Trice's death, in which Annabelle gives Cass the ring—Warren had to be careful to avoid copying himself too closely.

On March 16, 1949, Helen Strauss of the William Morris Agency wrote to Warren, who was about to go to Hollywood to begin his collaboration with Rossen. "I'm not so sure that something can't be done about the motion picture rights of Cass Mastern," she said, "and I am writing to Moe Slackin about this to see if something can't be worked out with Columbia Pictures but this is a very long shot and I would not depend too much on it." In addition to the possible legal problems with Columbia Pictures, Harcourt, Brace was also claiming rights to the "character Cass Mastern," since they had published the novel. Strauss warned Warren in a letter dated June 27, 1949, "I'm afraid, with your situation at Harcourt, Brace, they will go to all lengths to stop the play if you don't concede that they have rights in the character Cass Mastern."

Apparently during the final week of June and the first week of July 1949 in Hollywood, Warren spent almost as much time dancing with lawyers and agents as he spent working on the play with Rossen. The Warrens remained in California till early September 1949. On September 12, 1949, Warren wrote Brooks: "Forgive my terrible delay. I've been driven hard on the work here for one thing, and for another I postponed from day to day in hope that I would have some decided progress on the revision to report to you. Actually I've done very little, damned little. There simply wasn't the time. I finished the draft of the play only this week—this past week—and the revision of the novel isn't finished yet."[24]

The draft that Warren and Rossen finished was titled *The Wedding Ring,*[25] and it opened with this note on chronology:

> The action of this play begins on the afternoon of October 17, 1859. On the night before, John Brown, the radical Abolitionist, with the fame of his border fighting in Kansas and the blood of his massacre at Pottawatomie still hot upon him, had raided the town of Harper's Ferry, Virginia, with the intention of freeing slaves and arming them from the United States arsenal there. On October 18, Robert E. Lee, then a Colonel in the United States Army, captured Brown and his surviving men and turned them over to the authorities. On December 2 John Brown was hanged for treason. Although the Secession Conventions was not assembled until February 4, 1861, and the firing on Fort Sumpter in the harbor of Charleston, South Carolina, did not occur until April 13 of that year, the raid of John Brown initiates, symbolically at least, the tragic conflict. This play, then, is a historical play, but I hope that if it means anything it means that history is never over. For history is only the image of our present anguish and the hope—the only hope we have—for our future victory.

The first draft of the play ends with Cass Mastern dead at the hands of a slave trader to whom he has gone in search of Phebe. Cass takes offense when a French slave dealer assumes he is looking for a light-skinned mistress. Cass rushes him, and the slave dealer pulls a sword from a cane and runs Cass through. The seeds of this ending are found in the novel in the wound Cass receives from a Bowie knife–wielding redneck at the Lewis C. Robards barracoon.

After completing *World Enough and Time,* Warren spent part of every day working with Rossen on the play. By the end of the summer, he felt that it would be ready for a road tryout late in the summer of 1950 and a New York opening in October.[26] Shortly after the serious collaboration began, Rossen became a subject of the House Un-American Activities Committee investigation of Hollywood

24. Grimshaw, *A Literary Correspondence,* 172. The novel Warren was revising was *World Enough and Time.*

25. That this is the first draft of the play is speculation on my part. As Bo Grimshaw and I observed in our discussion of the three stage versions of *All the King's Men,* the number of drafts and their order of composition are difficult if not impossible to determine. Many of the physical details surrounding the texts were lost by the time William K. Finley catalogued the Warren papers. There is internal evidence to suggest an order of composition. It remains for some other highly specialized and dedicated scholar to establish the correct order of composition.

26. Joseph Blotner, *Robert Penn Warren: A Biography* (New York: Random House, 1997), 253.

and the movie industry, and he fled to Mexico. Strauss wrote to Warren on May 29, 1951: "I received a call from Bob Rossen, who is still in Mexico City at the Reforma Hotel. I doubt whether his plans include a return to the United States. I think we really ought to call off this deal, particularly in view of his current publicity. Enclosed is a clipping from The New York Times." The clipping, from the Tuesday, May 29, 1951, *Times* is a story titled "Columbia Will End Pact with Rossen." It details the allegations against Rossen and states that Columbia Pictures was negotiating with Rossen to buy back Rossen's interest in two of the pictures he had directed for Columbia, *All the King's Men* and *The Brave Bulls.*

Apparently by the middle of 1951 the collaboration between Warren and Rossen was terminated; however, despite the legal problems presented by the Cass Mastern material, Warren continued to struggle with the play for another ten years. And it was a struggle. The story is a difficult one to shape for the stage. It is presented through fragments of the diary and the letters of a man, Cass Mastern, who has been dead some seventy-five years by the time the story is told. And the story is being told and interpreted by a man, Jack Burden, who finally gives up trying to tell the story because he can't understand it.

When I began this project, I thought Warren's attempts to craft this material for the stage were rather unsuccessful, because I was assuming that Warren was attempting to make a dramatic adaptation of the story "Cass Mastern's Wedding Ring." I should have learned from working with the various stage versions of the Willie Stark material that Warren reimagines his works when he moves from draft to draft, let alone from one genre to another. Even when I was interviewing Eric Bentley, I asked questions that presupposed that the plays were not very good.

After I read the essay in this volume by James A. Grimshaw Jr. and Kay L. Coughenour, I began to realize that when Warren limited the setting of his play to the Trice's home and reduced the time frame to a period from Cass Mastern's introduction into that home to his departure from it, after the death of Duncan Trice and the sale of Phebe, he necessarily changed the story he was telling. Drama is very much like real estate. In real estate, location is everything. In drama, setting is very important. The play is no longer about Cass Mastern and his guilt and conflict. It is rather the story of Bella Trice and the circumscribed social system she finds herself in as an attractive, vibrant, young wife in the mid-nineteenth-century South.

The decade of the 1950s was one of Warren's most productive ever. A number of events coalesced to bring great changes to his life. In 1950 Warren was appointed Professor of Playwriting at Yale University. As my collaborator James A.

Grimshaw Jr. and I said in our introduction to *Robert Penn Warren's "All the King's Men": Three Stage Versions,*

> At the time Warren joined the faculty of the School of Drama in 1950, the only plays he had written were *Proud Flesh* and an early version of *All the King's Men,* which Erwin Piscator directed for the Dramatic Workshop of the New School at the President Theatre in New York in 1948. Warren studied drama, especially English Renaissance drama, and he had the tutelage of several eminent critics, including Francis Fergusson, Eric Bentley, and his long-time friend Cleanth Brooks, as he found his way into the genre. But his appointment at Yale probably was the result of Yale's desire to have a Pulitzer Prize–winning author on the staff and the result of Brooks's and Warren's desire to reunite the team that had already produced *An Approach to Literature* (1936), *Understanding Poetry* (1938), *Understanding Fiction* (1943), and *Modern Rhetoric* (1949).[27]

The present volume provides new information about Warren's process of dramatic collaboration. There is an interview with the critic and dramatist Eric Bentley. Bentley and Warren met when both of them were teaching at the University of Minnesota. Bentley was aware of the power of the Cass Mastern material from the moment he read *All the King's Men.* On September 3, 1946, he wrote to Warren: "Stark as you create him for us, Long as rumor and myth have handed him down to us—he is so interesting that it's hard for your reader to be interested in anything else, in Burden's private history. And so one doesn't quite realize how good, for instance, the Cass Mastern story is. . . ."

As early as September 5, 1950, Bentley was trying to get Warren's permission to publish the Cass Mastern play in a series of drama anthologies under the general title *From the Modern Repertoire.* He read what he called "Version A" of the play and on September 12, 1950, sent Warren three pages of suggested revisions (see Appendix B). Warren later rewrote the script that Bentley saw into a two-act version that ended with Cass headed South on the slow steamer *Arethuse,* trying to get to New Orleans in time to buy back Phebe, who is on the faster *Star of New Orleans* with the slave trader Monsieur Larue. Mark Trice has a vision that in the future Cass may join the infantry as a common soldier and walk into battle never firing his gun. The play ends with a wild Bella snuffing candles and ranting (not unlike Molly Bloom) of her love for Cass.

Later, in 1955, Bentley listened to a tape of and read a newer version of the Cass Mastern play and sent Warren two more pages of suggestions for revision (see Appendix B). Warren was very good at accepting criticism and applying it con-

27. Grimshaw and Perkins, *Three Stage Versions,* 8.

structively. A subsequent version of the play shows him incorporating many of Bentley's suggestions.

In 1951 Warren divorced his wife of twenty-one years, Emma Brescia Warren. In 1952 he married the writer Eleanor Clark. On July 27, 1953, Warren's first child, a daughter, Rosanna, was born. And on July 19, 1955, Warren's son Gabriel was born. These changes in Warren's personal life may have been catalysts in his writing life. For ten years, from 1945 till 1954, Warren hit a dry patch in his poetry writing. As he remembered it in an interview with Richard B. Sale, "I didn't finish a single short poem for ten years, from '45—God, it must have been '44 or '45, along there—until '54. I didn't finish a single poem, not one. I was working on a long poem during that time, *Brother to Dragons,* but I didn't finish it then. I must have started fifty short poems. Not one panned out. I threw them all away, and some of them were going okay. I couldn't finish them; they died on me. For ten years every one of them died."[28]

While Warren was not writing short poems in the first third of the decade of the fifties, he was nonetheless active as a writer. In addition to working on the novel *Band of Angels,* he began a return to poetry with *Brother to Dragons: A Tale in Verse and Voices.* He was also putting together books that would help ensure the financial well-being of his new family. In 1950, he and Brooks published a revised edition of *Understanding Poetry* and *A Handbook of Modern Rhetoric.* In 1953 they published *An Anthology of Stories from "The Southern Review."* In 1954 Warren and Albert Erskine published *Short Story Masterpieces,* and the following year, they produced *Six Centuries of Great Poetry.* Warren may have felt financially secure by 1956, or he may have wanted more freedom to write. Whatever his reason, he resigned his position at the Yale School of Drama in 1956.

During the rest of the decade, Warren's creative pace continued. He wrote the poems for *Promises: Poems, 1954–1956,* which was published in 1957. These were the first short poems Warren had written in fourteen years. Following the Supreme Court decision in *Brown v. Board of Education* in 1954, Warren traveled through several southern states to gage public opinion on how the issue would play out. The interviews Warren conducted on these travels were first published in *Life* magazine and later collected as *Segregation: The Inner Conflict in the South* (1956). Warren worked with Aaron Frankel on *Willie Stark: His Rise and Fall,* a new dramatic version of *All the King's Men,* from 1956 through 1958. Shortly after that, he was working with Mark Schoenberg on a revision of the 1947 version of

28. Robert Penn Warren, interviewed by Richard B. Sale, "An Interview in New Haven with Robert Penn Warren," in Watkins, Hiers, and Weaks, *Talking with Robert Penn Warren,* 179–80.

the play *All the King's Men.* This collaboration led to a production at the Seventy-Fourth Street Theatre in 1959 and publication by Random House in 1960. He published *Selected Essays* in 1958, *The Cave* in 1959, *You, Emperors, and Others: Poems, 1957–1960* in 1960, and *Wilderness* and *The Legacy of the Civil War* in 1961. Also in 1961, Warren rejoined his old friend Cleanth Brooks as a member of the Department of English at Yale University.

During this period he also continued to edit texts and collections. In 1957 he and Erskine published *A New Southern Harvest.* Brooks and Warren published a second edition of *Modern Rhetoric* in 1958, a second edition of *Understanding Fiction* in 1959, and *The Scope of Fiction* in 1960.

Toward the end of the 1950s, Warren again turned to the Cass Mastern material. This time he was working with Vincent J. Donehue who was considering directing *Listen to the Mockingbird,* as the Cass Mastern play was then titled. On July 28, 1960, Lawrence Langner of the Theatre Guild wrote to Warren trying to set up a script conference between Warren and Donehue. As had other collaborators Warren worked with—Francis Fergusson, Eric Bentley, and Aaron Frankel—Donehue had a number of suggestions for improving the dramatic nature of the play. On March 11, 1960, he outlined his suggestions in a long letter to Warren (see Appendix B). On July 25, 1960, in a letter Langner sent on to Warren, Donehue wrote to Langner, "I am very eager to meet with you and Robert Penn Warren about *Listen to the Mocking Bird* and to see the progress he has made on the rewrites." On July 28, in a letter he copied to Warren, Langner answered: "Thanks for your letter of July 25. Robert Penn Warren made some very considerable improvements in the rewriting of the play, as you will note from the new copy which is sent herewith. I thought it would be a good idea for you to read this through, and you will note that he has done a great deal to improve the play, especially as regards making the meaning of the play clearer, and also as regards certain arrangements, etc. . . . I think the character of Cass has been made more important and interesting and many other good things have happened."

The final version of the play, the one published here, ends with Cass leaving the Trice home in search of Phebe and with Mark Trice saying: "I can see him marching with them, bearing in his knowledge what share he may of the burden they bear in their ignorance. I can see him marching into battle—oh, not Gilbert Mastern's fine captain—only one of the ranks, with a rifle—marching into battle but never firing a bullet. Waiting until some bullet finds him" ("Untitled Play," 128).

Mark Trice, a character Warren added to the stage version, is a cousin to Duncan Trice and a professor at Transylvania. He is the character Jack Burden would have become if he had been able to understand Cass Mastern and finish his dissertation. After Bella Trice calls Mark a coward, Gilbert Mastern describes him in terms that shed light on Jack Burden: "No, ma'am. It's just he knows the truth, ma'am. *(Locating his beaver on the table, picking it up)* Yes, Professor Trice is the kind of man who knows the truth about everything. He even knows the truth about you. *(Pause)* He even knows the truth about himself. *(Pause)* It's just he never knows what to do about it" ("Untitled Play," 126).

While the changes to the play seemed to go well, the planned production ran into other problems. On May 12, 1960, Langner wrote to Warren, "I have been somewhat troubled about the title, 'Listen to the Mocking Bird,' as there was a very poor play done under this title a year and a half ago, by one of the Chodorovs, with Eve Gallienne and a large company in New Haven, Boston, Cleveland, and Washington, and while in Washington, fortunately for all concerned (in my opinion) the scenery caught fire and not only put an end to the play, but also to the theatre in which it played." So the play that had at one time been called "The Wedding Ring" and later was titled "Listen to the Mockingbird" came finally to be known as "An Untitled Play: A Drama of the American Civil War." Later in the same letter, Langner discusses the play: "As to the play itself [yours—inserted in pen], there is some need to try to get the work done as soon as possible, because Vincent Donehue is very much in demand, and we would like to send the play to different actors and actresses. I told Vincent that you liked his suggestions, and he was pleased; also that you are working on the last act."

Warren was evidently pushing for the production of his play but was concerned about leaving Vermont, where he was working on his novel. On August 1, 1960, Langner wrote: "Even if we had the play entirely ready and a good cast lined up, it would still not be possible to secure a New York theatre for the first half of the present season. Plays are lined up and waiting. We, ourselves, have a very heavy schedule for the fall. Therefore, unless Vinnie has some urgent reason for wanting to bring you in during August, I would say, wait until after Labor Day. I know how bad it is to interrupt work on a novel, and unless there is some urgency about which I am not aware, I would certainly prefer to postpone the meeting." Then on September 29, 1960, Langner wrote to Warren: "I had a note from Vinnie Donehue, and he is eager to meet with us. I will get in touch with you the first of next week to arrange a meeting for the middle or the end of the week."

In spite of the interest and enthusiasm of Langner and Donehue, and in spite of a dozen years of hard work by Warren, the play was never produced during Warren's lifetime. Donehue was a very active director. He directed *Sunrise at Campobello* on Broadway, for which he received a Tony Award, in 1958. In 1959 he directed *The Sound of Music* on Broadway. In 1960, the year he was trying to work out an arrangement to do Warren's Cass Mastern play, he directed the Mary Martin version of *Peter Pan* on television and the film version of *Sunrise at Campobello.* The next year, 1961, he directed *Daughter of Silence* on Broadway.

Although Warren carefully followed Donehue's suggestions and incorporated them into the text presented here (the text presented here is not meant to be a facsimile of Warren's final draft of the play but is presented in standard dramatic format, and I have corrected any typos and misspellings that I believe would have been caught in proof), by 1961, he seems to have lost interest in the project. He had not taught drama at Yale since 1956; he was back at Yale in the Department of English, and as was usual, he was keeping up with a punishing amount of writing. His longtime literary agent at the William Morris Agency, Helen Strauss, had this comment on Warren the dramatist: "Warren's aspirations as a dramatist remained frustrated, but like many another client, he did have a brief infatuation with the idea of writing for the motion picture screen. Fortunately, it came early and he recovered."[29]

Eric Bentley made what is probably the clearest assessment of Warren the dramatist in his March 28, 1955, letter to Warren, after he had listened to and read a revised version of the Cass Mastern play: "To me, there is a lack of dramatic progression in the long speeches. They hang in the air. I say this after a certain experience with your work. You were right to de-theatricalize DRAGONS, because your mind tends to a philosophical poetry, a rhetoric which is non-theatrical. Some of the passages in PROUD FLESH were non-theatrical in the same way. They didn't have the drive and thrust *forwards into the action* which I require from theatre—poetry."

The play remained buried in the archives of the Beinecke Library at Yale University until it was put on by Grimshaw and Coughenour of Texas A&M University–Commerce in the Region VI Kennedy Center American College Theater Festival, hosted by Texas Women's University in Denton in October 1998. This production did not use the script reproduced in this volume but an earlier version, and Grimshaw and Coughenour's essay and Coughenour's director's notes reference that earlier version of the play.

29. Helen Strauss, *A Talent for Luck: An Autobiography* (New York: Random House, 1979), 133. Strauss is referring to Warren's collaboration with Max Schulmann on a film treatment called "Don't Bury Me at All" that Strauss carried to Hollywood without success. Her tone seems like that of a successful agent who would like to see her charges focus on what they do best.

I hope that this collection of material—the Cass Mastern material along with the interview, letters, and essays that accompany it—when read in conjunction with Noel Polk's restored edition of *All the King's Men* and *Robert Penn Warren's "All the King's Men": Three Stage Versions* will shed new light on plots and characters in Warren's rich and complex Pulitzer Prize–winning novel.

Cass Mastern's Wedding Ring

Robert Penn Warren

Long ago Jack Burden was a graduate student, working for his Ph.D. in American History, in the State University of his native state. This Jack Burden (of whom the present Jack Burden, *Me,* is a legal, biological, and perhaps even metaphysical continuator) lived in a slatternly apartment with two other graduate students, one industrious, stupid, unlucky, and alcoholic, and the other idle, intelligent, lucky, and alcoholic. At least they were alcoholic for a period after the first of the month, when they received the miserable check paid them by the University for their miserable work as assistant teachers. The industry and ill luck of one cancelled out against the idleness and luck of the other and they both amounted to the same thing, and they drank what they could get when they could get it. They drank because they didn't really have the slightest interest in what they were doing now and didn't have the slightest hope for the future. They could not even bear the thought of pushing on to finish their degrees, for that would mean leaving the University (leaving the first-of-the-month drunks, the yammer about "work" and "ideas" in smoke-blind rooms, the girls who staggered slightly and giggled indiscreetly on the dark stairs leading to the apartment) to go to some normal school on a sun-baked cross-roads or a junior college long on Jesus and short on funds, to go to face the stark reality of drudgery and dry-rot and prying eyes and the slow withering of the green wisp of dream which had, like some window-plant in an invalid's room, grown out of a bottle. Only the bottle hadn't had water in it. It had had something which looked like water, smelled like kerosene, and tasted like carbolic acid: one-run corn whisky.

Jack Burden lived with them, in the slatternly apartment among the unwashed dishes in the sink and on the table, the odor of stale tobacco smoke, the dirty shirts and underwear piled in corners. He even took a relish in the squalor, in the privilege of letting a last crust of buttered toast fall to the floor to lie undisturbed until the random heel should grind it into the mud-colored carpet, in the spectacle of the fat roach moving across the cracked linoleum of the bathroom floor while he steamed in the tub. Once he had brought his mother to the apartment for tea, and she had sat on the edge of the overstuffed chair, holding a cracked cup and talking with a brittle and calculated charm out of a face which was obviously being held in shape by a profound exercise of will. She saw a roach venture out from the kitchen door. She saw one of Jack Burden's friends crush an ant on the inner lip of the sugar bowl and flick the carcass from his finger. The nail of the finger itself was not very clean. But she kept right on delivering the charm, out of the rigid face. He had to say that for her.

But afterwards, as they walked down the street, she had said: "Why do you live like that?"

"It's what I'm built for, I reckon," Jack Burden said.

"With those people," she said.

"They're all right," he said, and wondered if they were, and wondered if he was.

His mother didn't say anything for a minute, making a sharp, bright clicking on the pavement with her heels as she walked along, holding her small shoulders trimly back, carrying her famished-cheeked, blue-eyed, absolutely innocent face slightly lifted to the pulsing sunset world of April like a very expensive present the world ought to be glad even to have a look at. And back then, fifteen years ago, it was still something to look at, too. Sometimes Jack Burden (who was *Me* or what *Me* was fifteen years ago) would be proud to go into a place with her, and have people stare the way they would, and just for a minute he would be happy. But there is a lot more to everything than just walking into a hotel lobby or restaurant.

Walking along beside him, she said meditatively: "That dark-haired one—if he'd get cleaned up—he wouldn't be bad looking."

"That's what a lot of other women think," Jack Burden said, and suddenly felt a nauseated hatred of the dark-haired one, the one who had killed the ant on the sugar bowl, who had the dirty nails. But he had to go on, something in him made him go on: "Yes, and a lot of them don't even care about cleaning him up. They'll take him like he is. He's the great lover of the apartment. He put the sag in the springs of that divan we got."

"Don't be vulgar," she said, because she definitely did not like what is known as vulgarity in conversation.

"It's the truth," he said.

She didn't answer, and her heels did the bright clicking. Then she said, "If he'd throw those awful clothes away—and get something decent."

"Yeah," Jack Burden said, "on his seventy-five dollars a month."

She looked at him now, down at his clothes. "Yours are pretty awful, too," she said.

"Are they?" Jack Burden demanded.

"I'll send you money for some decent clothes," she said.

A few days later the check came and a note telling him to get a "couple of decent suits and accessories." The check was for two hundred and fifty dollars. He did not even buy a necktie. But he and the two other men in the apartment had a wonderful blow-out, which lasted for five days, and as a result of which the industrious and unlucky one lost his job, and the idle and lucky one got too sociable and, despite his luck, contracted what is quaintly known as a social disease. But nothing happened to Jack Burden, for nothing ever happened to Jack Burden, who was invulnerable. Perhaps that was the curse of Jack Burden: he was invulnerable.

So, as I have said, Jack Burden lived in the slatternly apartment with the two other graduate students, for even after being fired the unlucky, industrious one still lived in the apartment. He simply stopped paying anything but he stayed. He borrowed money for cigarettes. He sullenly ate the food the others brought in and cooked. He lay around during the day, for there was no reason to be industrious any more, ever again. Once at night, Jack Burden woke up and thought he heard the sound of sobs from the living room, where the unlucky, industrious one slept on a wall-bed. Then one day the unlucky, industrious one was not there. They never did know where he had gone, and they never heard from him again.

But before that they lived in the apartment, in an atmosphere of brotherhood and mutual understanding. They had this in common: they were all hiding. The difference was in what they were hiding from. The two others were hiding from the future, from the day when they would get degrees and leave the University. Jack Burden, however, was hiding from the present. The other two took refuge in the present. Jack Burden took refuge in the past. The other two sat in the living room and argued and drank or played cards or read, but Jack Burden was sitting, as like as not, back in his bed room before a little pine table, with the notes and papers and books before him, scarcely hearing the voices. He might come out and take a drink or take a hand of cards or argue or do any of the other things they did, but what was real was back in that bed room on the pine table.

What was back in the bed room on the pine table?

A large packet of letters, eight tattered, black-bound account books tied together with faded red tape, a photograph, 5 x 8 inches, mounted on cardboard and stained in its lower half by water, and a plain gold ring, mansized, with some engraving in it, on a loop of string. The past. Or that part of the past which had gone by the name of Cass Mastern.

Cass Mastern was one of Jack Burden's father's two maternal uncles, a brother of his mother, Lavinia Mastern, a great-uncle to Jack Burden. The other great-uncle was named Gilbert Mastern, who died in 1914, at the age of ninety-four or five, rich, a builder of railroads, a sitter on boards of directors, and left the packet of letters, the black account books, and the photograph, and a great deal of money to a grandson (and not a penny to Jack Burden). Some ten years later the heir of Gilbert Mastern, recollecting that his cousin Jack Burden, with whom he had no personal acquaintance, was a student of history, or something of the sort, sent him the packet of letters, the account books, and the photograph, asking if he, Jack Burden, thought that the enclosures were of any "financial interest" since he, the heir, had heard that libraries sometimes would pay a "fair sum for old papers and ante-bellum relics and keep-sakes." Jack Burden replied that, since Cass Mastern had been of no historical importance as an individual, it was doubtful that any library would pay more than a few dollars, if anything, for the material, and asked for instructions as to the disposition of the parcel. The heir replied that under the circumstances Jack Burden might keep the things for "sentimental reasons."

So Jack Burden made the acquaintance of Cass Mastern, his great-uncle, who had died in 1864 at a military hospital in Atlanta, who had been only a heard but forgotten name to him, and who was the pair of dark, wide-set, deep eyes which burned out of the photograph, through the dinginess and dust and across more than fifty years. The eyes, which were Cass Mastern, stared out of a long, bony face, but a young face with full lips above a rather thin, curly black beard. The lips did not seem to belong to that bony face and the burning eyes.

The young man in the picture, standing visible from the thighs up, wore a loose-fitting, shapeless jacket, too large in the collar, short in the sleeves, to show strong wrists and bony hands clasped at the waist. The thick dark hair, combed sweepingly back from the high brow, came down long and square-cut, after the fashion of time, place, and class, almost to brush the collar of the coarse, hand-me-down-looking jacket, which was the jacket of an infantryman in the Confederate Army.

But everything in the picture, in contrast with the dark, burning eyes, seemed accidental. That jacket, however, was not accidental. It was worn as the result of calculation and anguish, in pride and self-humiliation, in the conviction that it would be worn in death. But death was not to be that quick and easy. It was to come slow and hard, in a stinking hospital in Atlanta. The last letter in the packet was not in Cass Mastern's hand. Lying in the hospital with his rotting wound, he dictated his farewell letter to his brother, Gilbert Mastern. The letter, and the last of the account books in which Cass Mastern's journal was kept, were eventually sent back home to Mississippi, and Cass Mastern was buried somewhere in Atlanta, nobody had ever known where.

It was, in a sense, proper that Cass Mastern—in the gray jacket, sweat-stiffened, and prickly like a hair shirt, which it was for him at the same time that it was the insignia of a begrudged glory—should have gone back to Georgia to rot slowly to death. For he had been born in Georgia, he and Gilbert Mastern and Lavinia Mastern, Jack Burden's grandmother, in the red hills up toward Tennessee. "I was born," the first page of the first volume of the journal said, "in a log cabin in north Georgia, in circumstances of poverty, and if in later years I have lain soft and have supped from silver, may the Lord not let die in my heart the knowledge of frost and of coarse diet. For all men come naked into the world, and in prosperity 'man is prone to evil as the sparks fly upward.'" The lines were written when Cass was a student at Transylvania College, up in Kentucky, after what he called his "darkness and trouble" had given place to the peace of God. For the journal began with an account of the "darkness and trouble"—which was a perfectly real trouble, with a dead man and a live woman and long nailscratches down Cass Mastern's bony face. "I write this down," he said in the journal, "with what truthfulness a sinner may attain unto that if ever pride is in me, of flesh or spirit, I can peruse these pages and know with shame what evil has been in me, and may be in me, for who knows what breeze may blow upon the charred log and fan up the flame again?"

The impulse to write the journal sprang from the "darkness and trouble," but Cass Mastern apparently had a systematic mind, and so he went back to the beginning, to the log cabin in the red hills of Georgia. It was the older brother, Gilbert, some fifteen years older than Cass, who lifted the family from the log cabin. Gilbert, who had run away from home when a boy and gone West to Mississippi, was well on the way to being "a cotton-snob" by the time he was twenty-seven or eight, that is, by 1850. The penniless and no doubt hungry boy walking barefoot onto the black soil of Mississippi was to become, ten or twelve years later, the master sitting the spirited roan stallion (its name was Powhatan—that from the journal) in front of the white veranda. How did Gilbert make his first dollar? Did he cut the throat of a traveler in the cane-brake? Did he black boots at an inn? It is not recorded. But he made his fortune, and sat on the white veranda and voted Whig. After the war, when the white veranda was a pile of ashes and the fortune was gone, it was not surprising that Gilbert, who had made one fortune with his bare hands, out of the very air, could now, with all his experience and cunning and hardness (the hardness harder now for the four years of riding and short rations and disappointment), snatch another one, much greater than the first. If in later years he ever remembered his brother Cass and took out the last letter, the one dictated in the hospital in Atlanta, he must have mused over it with a tolerant irony. For it said: "Remember me, but without grief. If one of us is lucky, it is I. I shall have rest and I hope in the mercy of the Everlasting and in His blessed election. But you, my dear brother, are condemned to eat bread in bitterness and build on the place where the charred embers and ashes are and to make bricks without straw and to suffer in the ruin and guilt of our dear land and in the common guilt of man. In the next bed to me there is a young man from Ohio. He is dying. His moans and curses and prayers are not different from any others to be heard in this tabernacle of pain. He marched hither in his guilt as I in mine. And in the guilt of his land. May a common Salvation lift us both from the dust. And dear brother, I pray God to give you strength for what is to come." Gilbert must have smiled, looking back, for he had eaten little bread in bitterness. He had had his own kind of strength. By 1870 he was again well off. By 1875 he was rich. By 1880 he had a fortune, was living in New York, was a name, a thick, burly man, slow of movement, with a head like a block of bare granite. He had lived out of one world into another. Perhaps he was even more at home in the new than in the old. Or perhaps the Gilbert Masterns are always at home in any world. As the Cass Masterns are never at home in any world.

But to return: Jack Burden came into possession of the papers from the grandson of Gilbert Mastern. When the time came for him to select a subject for his dissertation for his Ph.D., his professor suggested that he edit the journal and letters of Cass Mastern, and write a biographical essay, a social study based on those and other materials. So Jack Burden began his first journey into the past.

It seemed easy at first. It was easy to reconstruct the life of the log cabin in the red hills. There were the first letters back from Gilbert, after he had begun his rise (Jack Burden managed to get possession of the other Gilbert Mastern papers of the period before the Civil War). There was the known pattern of that life, gradually altered toward comfort as Gilbert's affluence was felt at that distance. Then, in one season, the mother and father died, and Gilbert returned to burst, no doubt, upon Cass and Lavinia as an unbelievable vision, a splendid imposter in black broadcloth, varnished boots, white linen, heavy gold ring. He put Lavinia in a school in Atlanta, bought her trunks of dresses, and kissed her goodbye. ("Could you not have taken me with you, dear Brother Gilbert? I would have been ever so dutiful and affectionate a sister," so she wrote to him, in the copy-book hand, in brown ink, in a language not her own, a language of school-room propriety. "May I not come to you now? Is there no little task which I"— But Gilbert had other plans. When the time came for her to appear in his house she would be ready.) But he took Cass with him, a hobbledehoy now wearing black and mounted on a blooded mare.

At the end of three years Cass was not a hobbledehoy. He had spent three years of monastic rigor at *Valhalla,* Gilbert's house, under the tuition of a Mr. Lawson and of Gilbert himself. From Gilbert he learned the routine of plantation management. From Mr. Lawson, a tubercular and vague young man from Princeton, New Jersey, he learned some geometry, some Latin, and a great deal of Presbyterian theology. He liked the books, and once Gilbert (so the journal said) stood in the doorway and watched him bent over the table and then said, "At least you may be good for *that.*"

But he was good for more than that. When Gilbert gave him a small plantation, he managed it for two years with such astuteness (and such luck, for both season and market conspired in his behalf) that at the end of the time he could repay Gilbert a substantial part of the purchase price. Then he went, or was sent, to Transylvania. It was Gilbert's idea. He came into the house on Cass's plantation one night to find Cass at his books. He walked across the room to the table where the books lay, by which Cass now stood. Gilbert stretched out his arm and tapped the open book with his riding crop. "You might make something out of that," he said. The journal reported that, but it did not report what book it was that Gilbert's riding crop tapped. It is not important what book it was. Or perhaps it is important, for something in our mind, in our imagination, wants to know the fact. We see the red, square, strong hand ("My brother is strong-made and florid") protruding from the white cuff, grasping the crop[,] which in that grasp looks fragile like a twig. We see the flick of the little leather loop on the open page, a flick brisk, not quite contemptuous, but we cannot make out the page.

In any case, it probably was not a book on theology, for it seems doubtful that Gilbert, in such a case, would have used the phrase "make something out of that." It might have been a page of the Latin poets, however, for Gilbert would have discovered that, in small doses, they went well with politics or the law. So Transylvania College it was to be, suggested, it developed, by Gilbert's neighbor and friend, Mr. Davis, Mr. Jefferson Davis, who had once been a student there. Mr. Davis had studied Greek.

At Transylvania, in Lexington, Cass discovered pleasure. "I discovered that there is an education for vice as well as for virtue, and I learned what was to be learned from the gaming table, the bottle, and the racecourse, and from the illicit sweetness of the flesh." He had come out of the poverty of the cabin and the monastic regime of *Valhalla* and the responsibilities of his own little plantation; and he was tall and strong and, to judge from the photograph, well favored, with the burning dark eyes. It was no wonder that he "discovered pleasure"—or that pleasure discovered him. For, though the journal does not say so, in the events leading up to the "darkness and trouble," Cass seems to have been, in the beginning at least, the pursued rather than the pursuer.

The pursuer is referred to in the journal as "She" and "Her." But I learned the name. "She" was Annabelle Trice, Mrs. Duncan Trice, and Mr. Duncan Trice was a prosperous young banker of Lexington, Kentucky, who was an intimate of Cass Mastern and apparently one of those who led him into the paths of pleasure. I learned the name by going back to the files of the Lexington newspapers for the middle 1850's to locate the story of a death. It was the death of Mr. Duncan Trice. In the newspaper it was reported as an accident. Duncan Trice had shot himself by accident, the newspaper said, while cleaning a pair of pistols. One of the pistols, already cleaned, lay on the couch where he had been sitting, in his library, at the time of the accident. The other, the lethal instrument, had fallen to the floor. I had known, from the journal, the nature of the case, and when I had located the special circumstances, I had learned the identity of "She." Mr. Trice, the newspaper said, was survived by his widow, née Annabelle Puckett, of Washington, D.C.

Shortly after Cass had come to Lexington, Annabelle Trice met him. Duncan Trice brought him home, for he had received a letter from Mr. Davis, recommending the brother of his good friend and neighbor, Mr. Gilbert Mastern. (Duncan Trice had come to Lexington from Southern Kentucky, where his own father had been a friend of Samuel Davis, the father of Jefferson, when Samuel lived at Fairview and bred racers.) So Duncan Trice brought the tall boy home, who was no longer a hobbledehoy, and set him on a sofa and thrust a glass into his hand and called in his pretty, husky-voiced wife, of whom he was so proud, to greet the stranger. "When she first entered the room, in which the shades of approaching twilight were gathering though the hour for the candles to be lit had scarcely come, I thought that her eyes were black, and the effect was most striking, her hair being of such a fairness. I noticed, too, how softly she trod and with a gliding motion which, though she was perhaps of a little less than moderate stature, gave an impression of regal dignity—

> *et avertens rosea cervice refulsit*
> *ambrosiaeque comae divinum vertice odorem*
> *spiravere, pedes vestis defluxit ad imos,*
> *et vera incessu patuit dea.*

So the Mantuan said, when Venus appeared and the true goddess was revealed by her gait. She came into the room and was the true goddess as revealed in her movement, and was, but for Divine Grace (if such be granted to a parcel of corruption such as I), my true damnation. She gave me her hand and spoke with a tingling huskiness which made me think of rubbing my hand upon a soft deep-piled cloth, like velvet, or upon a fur. It would not have been called a musical voice such as is generally admired. I know that, but I can only set down what effect it worked upon my own organs of hearing."

Was she beautiful? Well, Cass set down a very conscientious description of every feature and proportion, a kind of tortured inventory, as though in the midst of the "darkness and trouble," at the very moment of his agony and repudiation, he had to take one last backward look even at the risk of being turned into a pillar of salt. "Her face was not large though a little given to fullness. Her mouth was strong but the lips were red and moist and seemed to be slightly parted or about to part themselves. The chin was short and firmly moulded. Her skin was of a great whiteness, it seemed then before the candles were lit, but afterwards I was to see that it had a bloom of color upon it. Her hair, which was in a remarkable abundance and of great fairness[,] was drawn back from her face and worn in large coils low down to the neck. Her waist was very small and her breasts, which seemed naturally high and round and full, were the higher for the corsetting. Her dress, of a dark blue silk, I remember, was cut low to the very downward curve of the shoulders, and in the front showed how the breasts were lifted like twin orbs."

Cass described her that way. He admitted that her face was not beautiful. "Though agreeable in its proportions," he added. But the hair was beautiful, and "of astonishing softness, upon your hand softer and finer than your thought of silk." So even in that moment, in the midst of the "darkness and trouble," the recollection intrudes into the journal of how that abundant, fair hair had slipped across his fingers. "But," he added, "her beauty was her eyes."

He had remarked how, when she first came in, into the shadowy room, her eyes had seemed black. But he had been mistaken, he was to discover, and that discovery was the first step toward his undoing. After the greeting ("she greeted me with great simplicity and courtesy and bade me again take my seat"), she remarked on how dark the room was and how the autumn always came to take one unawares. Then she touched a bell-pull and a negro boy entered. "She commanded him to bring light and to mend the fire, which was sunk to ash, or near so. He came back presently with a seven-branched candlestick which he put upon the table back of the couch on which I sat. He struck a lucifer but she said 'Let me light the candles.' I remember it as if yesterday. I was sitting on the couch. I had turned my head idly to watch her light the candles. The little table was between us. She leaned over the candles and applied the lucifer to the wicks, one after another. She was leaning over, and I saw how the corset lifted her breasts together, but because she was leaning the eyelids shaded her eyes from my sight. Then she raised her head a little and looked straight at me over the new candle flames, and I saw all at once that her eyes were not black. They were blue, but a blue so deep that I can only compare it to the color of the night sky in autumn when the weather is clear and there is no moon and the stars have just well come out. And I had not known how large they were. I remember saying that to myself with perfect clearness, 'I had not known how large they were,' several times, slowly, like a man marvelling. Then I knew that I was blushing and I felt my tongue dry like ashes in my mouth and I was in the manly state.

"I can see perfectly clearly the expression on her face even now, but I cannot interpret it. Sometimes I have thought of it as having a smiling hidden in it, but I cannot be sure. (I am only sure of this: that man is never safe and damnation is ever at hand, O God and my Redeemer!) I sat there, one hand clenched upon my knee and the other holding an empty glass, and I felt that I could not breathe. Then she said to her husband, who stood in the room behind me, 'Duncan, do you see that Mr. Mastern is in need of refreshment?'"

The year passed. Cass, who was a good deal younger than Duncan Trice, and as a matter of fact several years younger than Annabelle Trice, became a close companion of Duncan Trice and learned much from him, for Duncan Trice was rich, fashionable, clever, and high-spirited ("much given to laughter and full-blooded"). Duncan Trice led Cass to the bottle, the gaming table and the race-course, but not to "the illicit sweetness of the flesh." Duncan Trice was passionately and single-mindedly devoted to his wife. ("When she came into a room, his eyes would fix upon her without shame, and I have seen her avert her face and blush for the boldness of his glance when company was present. But I think that it was done by him unawares, his partiality for her was so great.") No, the other young men, members of the Trice circle, led Cass first to the "illicit sweetness." But despite the new interests and gratifications, Cass could work at his books. There was even time for that, for he had great strength and endurance.

So the year passed. He had been much in the Trice house, but no word beyond the "words of merriment and civility" had passed between him and Annabelle Trice. In June, there was a dancing party at the house of some friend of Duncan Trice. Duncan Trice, his wife, and Cass happened to stroll at some moment into the garden and to sit in a little arbor, which was covered with a jasmine vine. Duncan Trice returned to the house to get punch for the three of them, leaving Annabelle and Cass seated side by side in the arbor. Cass commented on the sweetness of the scent of jasmine. All at once, she burst out ("her voice low-pitched and with its huskiness, but in a vehemence which astonished me"), "Yes, yes, it is too sweet. It is suffocating. I shall suffocate." And she laid her right hand, with the fingers spread, across the bare swell of her bosom above the pressure of the corset.

"Thinking her taken by some sudden illness," Cass recorded in the journal, "I asked if she were faint. She said no, in a very low, husky voice. Nevertheless I rose, with the expressed intention of getting a glass of water for her. Suddenly she said, quite harshly and to my amazement, because of her excellent courtesy, 'Sit down, sit down, I don't want water!' So somewhat distressed in mind that unwittingly I might have offended, I sat down. I looked across the garden where in the light of the moon several couples promenaded down the paths between the low hedges. I could hear the sound of her breathing beside me. It was disturbed and irregular. All at once she said, 'How old are you, Mr. Mastern?' I said twenty-two. Then she said, 'I am twenty-nine.' I stammered something, in my surprise. She laughed as though at my confusion, and said 'Yes, I am seven years older than you, Mr. Mastern. Does that surprise you, Mr. Mastern?' I replied in the affirmative. Then she said, 'Seven years is a long time. Seven years ago you were a child, Mr. Mastern.' Then she laughed, with a sudden sharpness, but quickly stopped herself to add, 'But I wasn't a child. Not seven years ago, Mr. Mastern.' I did not answer her, for there was no thought clear in my head. I sat there in confusion, but in the middle of my confusion, I was trying to see what she would have looked like as a child. I could call up no image. Then her husband returned from the house."

A few days later Cass went back to Mississippi to devote some months to his plantation, and, under the guidance of Gilbert, to go once to Jackson, the capital, and once to Vicksburg. It was a busy summer. Now Cass could see clearly what Gilbert intended: to make him rich and to put him into politics. It was a flattering and glittering prospect, and one not beyond reasonable expectation for a young man whose brother was Gilbert Mastern ("My brother is a man of great taciturnity and strong mind, and when he speaks, though he practices no graces and ingratiations, all men, especially those of the sober sort who have responsibility and power, weigh his words with respect.") So the summer passed, under the strong hand and cold eye of Gilbert. But toward the end of the season, when already Cass was beginning to give thought to his return to Transylvania, an envelope came addressed to him from Lexington, in an unfamiliar script. When Cass unfolded the single sheet of paper a small pressed blossom, or what he discovered to be such, slipped out. For a moment he could not think what it was, or why it was in his hand. Then he put it to his nostrils. The odor, now faint and dusty, was the odor of jasmine.

The sheet of paper had been folded twice, to make four equal sections. In one section, in a clean, strong, not large script, he read: "Oh, Cass!" That was all.

It was enough.

One drizzly autumn afternoon, just after his return to Lexington, Cass called at the Trice house to pay his respects. Duncan Trice was not there, having sent word that he had been urgently detained in the town and would be home for a late dinner. Of that afternoon, Cass wrote: "I found myself in the room alone with her. There were shadows, as there had been that afternoon, almost a year before, when I first saw her in that room, and when I had thought that her eyes were black. She greeted me civilly, and I replied and stepped back after having shaken her hand. Then I realized that she was looking at me fixedly, as I at her. Suddenly, her lips parted slightly and gave a short exhalation, like a sigh or suppressed moan. As of one accord, we moved toward each other and embraced. No words were passed between us as we stood there. We stood there for a long time, or so it seemed. I held her body close to me in a strong embrace, but we did not exchange a kiss, which upon recollection has since seemed strange. But was it strange? Was it strange that some remnant of shame should forbid us to look each other in the face? I felt and heard my heart racing within my bosom, with a loose feeling as though it were unmoored and were leaping at random in a great cavity within me, but at the same time I scarcely accepted the fact of my situation. I was somehow possessed by incredulity, even as to my identity, as I stood there and my nostrils were filled with the fragrance of her hair. It was not to be believed that I was Cass Mastern, who stood thus in the house of a friend and benefactor. There was no remorse or horror at the turpitude of the act, but only the incredulity which I have referred to. (One feels incredulity at observing the breaking of a habit, but horror at the violation of a principle. Therefore what virtue and honor I had known in the past had been an accident of habit and not the fruit of will. Or can virtue be the fruit of human will? The thought is pride.)

"As I have said, we stood there for a long time in a strong embrace, but with her face lowered against my chest, and my own eyes staring across the room and out a window into the deepening obscurity of the evening. When she finally raised her face, I saw that she had been silently weeping. Why was she weeping? I have asked myself that question. Was it because even on the verge of committing an irremediable wrong she could weep at the consequence of an act which she felt powerless to avoid? Was it because the man who held her was much younger than she and his embrace gave her the reproach of youth and seven years? Was it because he had come seven years too late and could not come in innocence? It does not matter what the cause. If it was the first, then the tears can only prove that sentiment is no substitute for obligation, if the second, then they only prove that pity of the self is no substitute for wisdom. But she shed the tears and finally lifted her face to mine with those tears bright in her large eyes, and even now, though those tears were my ruin, I cannot wish them unshed, for they testify to the warmth of her heart and prove that whatever her sin (and mine) she did not step to it with a gay foot and with the eyes hard with lust and fleshly cupidity.

"The tears were my ruin, for when she lifted her face to me some streak of tenderness was mixed into my feelings, and my heart seemed to flood itself into my bosom to fill that great cavity wherein it had been leaping. She said, 'Cass'—the first time she had ever addressed me by my Christian name. 'Yes,' I replied. 'Kiss me,' she said very simply, 'you can do it now.' So I kissed her. And thereupon in the blindness of our mortal blood and in the appetite of our hearts we performed the act. There in that very room with the servants walking with soft feet somewhere in the house and with the door to the room open and with her husband expected, and not yet in the room the darkness of evening. But we were secure in our very recklessness, as though the lustful heart could give forth a cloud of darkness in which we were shrouded, even as Venus once shrouded Aeneas in a cloud so that he passed unspied among men to approach the city of Dido. In such cases as ours the very recklessness gives security as the strength of the desire seems to give the sanction of justice and righteousness.

"Though she had wept and had seemed to perform the act in a sadness and desperation, immediately afterward she spoke cheerfully to me. She stood in the middle of the room pressing her hair into place, and I stumblingly ventured some remark about our future, a remark very vague for my being was still confused, but she responded, 'Oh, let us not think about it now,' as though I had broached a subject of no consequence. She promptly summoned a servant and asked for lights. They were brought and thereupon I inspected her face to find it fresh and unmarked. When her husband came, she greeted him familiarly and affectionately, and as I witnessed it my own heart was wrenched, but not, I must confess, with compunction. Rather with a violent jealousy. When he spoke to me, so great was my disturbance that I was sure that my face could but betray it."

So began the second phase of the story of Cass Mastern. All that year, as before, he was often in the house of Duncan Trice, and as before he was often with him in field sports, gambling, drinking, and race-going. He learned, he says, to "wear his brow unwrinkled," to accept the condition of things. As for Annabelle Trice, he says that sometimes looking back, he could scarcely persuade himself that "she had shed tears." She was, he says, "of a warm nature, reckless and passionate of disposition, hating all mention of the future (she would never let me mention times to come), agile, resourceful, and cheerful in devising to gratify our appetites, but with a womanly tenderness such as any man might prize at a sanctified hearthside." She must indeed have been agile and resourceful, for to carry on such a liaison undetected in that age and place must have been a problem. There was a kind of summer house at the foot of the Trice garden, which one could enter unobserved from an alley. Some of their meetings occurred there. A half-sister of Annabelle Trice, who lived in Lexington, apparently assisted the lovers or winked at their relationship, but, it seems, only after some pressure by Annabelle, for Cass hints at "a stormy scene." So some of the meetings were there. But now and then Duncan Trice had to be out of town on business, and on those occasions Cass would be admitted, late at night, to the house, even during a period when Annabelle's mother and father were staying there; so he actually lay in the very bed belonging to Duncan Trice.

There were, however, other meetings, unplanned and unpredictable moments snatched when they found themselves left alone together. "Scarce a corner, cranny, or protected nook or angle of my friend's trusting house did we not at one time or another defile, and that even in the full and shameless light of day," Cass wrote in the journal, and when Jack Burden, the student of history, went to Lexington and went to see the old Trice home he remembered the sentence. The town had grown up around the house, and the gardens, except for a patch of lawn, were gone. But the house was well maintained (some people named Miller lived there and by and large respected the place) and Jack Burden was permitted to inspect the premises. He wandered about the room where the first meeting had taken place and she had raised her eyes to Cass Mastern above the newly lighted candles and where, a year later, she had uttered the sigh, or suppressed moan, and stepped to his arms; and out into the hall, which was finely proportioned and with a graceful stair; and into a small, shadowy library; and to a kind of back hall, which was a well "protected nook or angle" and had, as a matter of fact, furniture adequate to the occasion. Jack Burden stood in the main hall, which was cool and dim, with dully glittering floors, and in the silence of the house, recalled that period, some seventy years before, of the covert glances, the guarded whispers, the abrupt rustling of silk in the silence (the costume of the period certainly had not been designed to encourage casual vice), the sharp breath, the reckless sighs. Well, all of that had been a hell of a long time before, and Annabelle Trice and Cass Mastern were long since deader than mackerel, and Mrs. Miller, who came down to give Jack Burden a cup of tea (she was flattered by the "historical" interest in her house, though she didn't guess the exact nature of the case), certainly was not "agile" and didn't look "resourceful" and probably had used up all her energy in the Ladies Altar Guild of Saint Luke's Episcopal Church and in the D.A.R.

The period of the intrigue, the second phase of the story of Cass Mastern, lasted all of one academic year, part of the summer (for Cass was compelled to go back to Mississippi for his plantation affairs and to attend the wedding of his sister Lavinia, who married a well-connected young man named Willis Burden), and well through the next winter, when Cass was back in Lexington. Then, on March 19, 1854, Duncan died, in his library (which was a "protected nook or angle" of his house), with a lead slug nearly the size of a man's thumb in his chest. It was quite obviously an accident.

The widow sat in church, upright and immobile. When she once raised her veil to touch at her eyes with a handkerchief, Cass Mastern saw that the cheek was "pale as marble but for a single flushed spot, like the flush of fever." But even when the veil was lowered he detected the fixed, bright eyes glittering "within that artificial shadow."

Cass Mastern, with five other young men of Lexington, cronies and boon companions of the dead man, carried the coffin. "The coffin which I carried seemed to have no weight, although my friend had been of large frame and had inclined to stoutness. As we proceeded with it, I marvelled at the fact of its lightness, and once the fancy flitted into my mind that he was not in the coffin at all, that it was empty, and that all the affair was a masquerade or mock-show carried to ludicrous and blasphemous length, for no purpose, as in a dream. Or to deceive me, the fancy came. I was the object of the deception, and all the other people were in league and conspiracy against me. But when that thought came, I suddenly felt a sense of great cunning and a wild exhilaration. I had been too sharp to be caught so. I had penetrated the deception. I had the impulse to hurl the coffin to the ground and see its emptiness burst open and to laugh in triumph. But I did not, and I saw the coffin sink beneath the level of the earth on which we stood and receive the first clods.

"As soon as the sound of the first clods striking the coffin came to me, I felt a great relief, and then a most overmastering desire. I looked toward her. She was kneeling at the foot of the grave, with what thoughts I could not know. Her head was inclined slightly and the veil was over her face. The bright sun poured over her black-clad figure. I could not take my eyes from the sight. The posture seemed to accentuate the charms of her person and to suggest to my inflamed senses the suppleness of her members. Even the funereal tint of her costume seemed to add to the provocation. The sunshine was hot upon my neck and could be felt through the stuff of my coat upon my shoulders. It was preternaturally bright so that I was blinded by it and my eyes were blinded and my senses swam. But all the while I could hear, as from a great distance, the scraping of the spades upon the piled earth and the muffled sound of earth falling into the excavation."

That evening Cass went to the summer house in the garden. It was not by appointment, simply on impulse. He waited there a long time, but she finally appeared, dressed in black "which was scarce darker than the night." He did not speak, or make any sign as she approached, "gliding like a shadow among shadows," but remained standing where he had been, in the deepest obscurity of the summer house. Even when she entered, he did not betray his presence. "I can not be certain that any premeditation was in my silence. It was prompted by an overpowering impulse which gripped me and sealed my throat and froze my limbs. Before that moment, and afterwards, I knew that it is dishonorable to spy upon another, but at the moment no such considerations presented themselves. I had to keep my eyes fixed upon her as she stood there thinking herself alone in the darkness of the structure. I had the fancy that since she thought herself alone I might penetrate into her being, that I might learn what change, what effect, had been wrought by the death of her husband. The passion which had seized me to the very extent of paroxysm that afternoon at the very brink of my friend's grave was gone. I was perfectly cold now. But I had to know, to try to know. It was as though I might know myself by knowing her. (It is the human defect—to try to know oneself by the self of another. One can only know oneself in God and in His great eye.)

"She entered the summer house and sank upon one of the benches, not more than a few feet from my own location. For a long time I stood there, peering at her. She sat perfectly upright and rigid. At last I whispered her name, as low as might be. If she heard it, she gave no sign. So I repeated her name, in the same fashion, and again. Upon the third utterance, she whispered, 'yes,' but she did not change her posture or turn her head. Then I spoke more loudly, again uttering her name, and instantly, with a motion of wild alarm she rose, with a strangled cry, and her hands lifted toward her face. She reeled, and it seemed that she would collapse to the floor, but she gained control of herself and stood there staring at me. Stammeringly, I made my apology, saying that I had not wanted to startle her, that I had understood her to answer yes to my whisper before I spoke, and I asked her, 'Did you not answer to my whisper?'

"She replied that she had.

"'Then why were you distressed when I spoke again?' I asked her.

"'Because, I did not know that you were here,' she said.

"'But,' I said, 'you say that you had just heard my whisper and had answered to it, and now you say that you did not know I was here.'

"'I did not know that you were here,' she repeated, in a low voice, and the import of what she was saying dawned upon me.

"'Listen,' I said, 'when you heard the whisper—did you recognize it was my voice?'

"She stared at me, not answering.

"'Answer me,' I demanded, for I had to know.

"She continued to stare, and finally replied hesitantly, 'I do not know.'

"'You thought it was—' I began, but before I could utter the words she had flung herself upon me, clasping me in desperation like a person frantic with drowning, and ejaculated: 'No, no, it does not matter what I thought, you are here, you are here!' And she drew my face down and pressed her lips against mine to stop my words. Her lips were cold, but they hung upon mine.

"I too was perfectly cold, as of a mortal chill. And the coldness was the final horror of the act which we performed, as though two dolls should parody the shame and filth of man to make it doubly shameful.

"After, she said to me, 'Had I not found you here tonight, it could never have been between us again.'

"'Why?' I demanded.

"'It was a sign,' she said.

"'A sign?' I asked.

"'A sign that we cannot escape, that we—' and she interrupted herself, to resume, whispering fiercely in the dark, 'I do not want to escape—it is a sign—whatever I have done is done.' She grew quiet for a moment, then she said, 'Give me your hand.'

"I gave her my right hand. She grasped it, dropped it, and said, 'The other, the other hand.'

"I held it out, across my own body, for I was sitting on her left. She seized it with her own left hand, bringing her hand upward from below to press my hand flat against her bosom. Then, fumblingly, she slipped a ring upon my finger, the finger next to the smallest.

"'What is that?' I asked.

"'A ring,' she answered, paused, and added, 'It is his ring.'

"Then I recalled that he, my friend, had always worn a wedding ring, and I felt the metal cold upon my flesh. 'Did you take it off of his finger?' I asked, and the thought shook me.

"'No,' she said.

"'No?' I questioned.

"'No,' she said, 'he took it off. It was the only time he ever took it off.'

"I sat beside her, waiting for what, I did not know, while she held my hand pressed against her bosom. I could feel it rise and fall. I could say nothing.

"Then she said, 'Do you want to know how—how he took it off?'

"'Yes,' I said in the dark, and waiting for her to speak, I moved my tongue out upon my dry lips.

"'Listen,' she commanded me in an imperious whisper, 'that evening after—after it happened—after the house was quiet again, I sat in my room, in the little chair by the dressing table, where I always sit for Phebe to let down my hair. I had sat there out of habit, I suppose, for I was numb all over. I watched Phebe preparing the bed for the night.' (Phebe was her waiting maid, a comely yellow wench somewhat given to the fits and sulls.) 'I saw Phebe remove the bolster and then look down at a spot where the bolster had lain, on my side of the bed. She picked something up and came toward me. She stared at me—and her eyes, they are yellow, you look into them and you can't see what is in them—she stared at me—a long time—and then she held out her hand, clenched shut and she watched me—and then—slow, so slow—she opened up the fingers—and there lay the ring on the palm of her hand—and I knew it was his ring but all I thought was, it is gold and it is lying in a gold hand. For Phebe's hand was gold—I had never noticed how her hand is the color of pure gold. Then I looked up and she was still staring at me, and her eyes were gold, too, and bright and hard like gold. And I knew that she knew.'

"'Knew?' I echoed, like a question, for I knew, too, now. My friend had learned the truth—from the coldness of his wife, from the gossip of servants—

and had drawn the gold ring from his finger and carried it to the bed where he had lain with her and had put it beneath her pillow and had gone down and shot himself but under such circumstances that no one save his wife would ever guess it to be more than an accident. But he had made one fault of calculation. The yellow wench had found the ring.

"'She knows,' she whispered, pressing my hand hard against her bosom, which heaved and palpitated with a new wildness. 'She knows—and she looks at me—she will always look at me.' Then suddenly her voice dropped, and a wailing intonation came into it: 'She will tell. All of them will know. All of them in the house will look at me and know—when they hand me the dish—when they come into the room—and their feet don't make any noise!' She rose abruptly, dropping my hand. I remained seated, and she stood there beside me, her back toward me, the whiteness of her face and hands no longer visible, and to my sight the blackness of her costume faded into the shadow, even in such proximity. Suddenly, in a voice which I did not recognize for its hardness, she said in the darkness above me, 'I will not abide it, I will not abide it!' Then she turned, and with a swooping motion leaned to kiss me upon the mouth. Then she was gone from my side and I heard her feet running up the gravel of the path. I sat there in the darkness for a time longer, turning the ring upon my finger."

After that meeting in the summer house, Cass did not see Annabelle Trice for some days. He learned that she had gone to Louisville, where, he recalled, she had close friends. She had, as was natural, taken Phebe with her. Then he heard that she had returned, and that night, late, went to the summer house in the garden. She was there, sitting in the dark. She greeted him. She seemed, he wrote later, peculiarly cut off, remote, and vague in manner, like a somnambulist or a person drugged. He asked about her trip to Louisville, and she replied briefly that she had been down the river to Paducah. He remarked that he had not known that she had friends in Paducah, and she said that she had none there. Then, all at once, she turned on him, the vagueness changing to violence, and burst out, "You are prying—you are prying into my affairs—and I will not tolerate it." Cass stammered out some excuse before she cut in to say, "But if you must know, I'll tell you. I took her there."

For a moment Cass was genuinely confused. "Her?" he questioned. "Phebe," she replied, "I took her to Paducah, and she's gone."

"Gone—gone where?"

"Down the river," she answered, repeated, "down the river," and laughed abruptly, and added, "and she won't look at me any more like that."

"You sold her?"

"Yes, I sold her. In Paducah, to a man who was making up a coffle of negroes for New Orleans. And nobody knows me in Paducah, nobody knew I was there, nobody knows I sold her, for I shall say she ran away into Illinois. But I sold her. For thirteen hundred dollars."

"You got a good price," Cass said, "even for a yellow girl as sprightly as Phebe." And, as he reports in the journal, he laughed with some "bitterness and rudeness," though he does not say why.

"Yes," she replied, "I got a good price. I made him pay every penny she was worth. And then do you know what I did with the money, do you?"

"No."

"When I came off the boat at Louisville, there was an old man, a nigger, sitting on the landing stage, and he was blind and picking on a guitar and singing 'Old Dan Tucker.' I took the money out of my bag and walked to him and laid it in his old hat."

"If you were going to give the money away—if you felt the money was defiled—why didn't you free her?" Cass asked.

"She'd stay right here, she wouldn't go away, she would stay right here and look at me. Oh, no, she wouldn't go away, for she's the wife of a man the Motley's have, their coachman. Oh, she'd stay right here and look at me and tell, tell what she knows, and I'll not abide it!"

Then Cass said: "If you had spoken to me I would have bought the man from Mr. Motley and set him free, too."

"He wouldn't have sold," she said, "the Motleys won't sell a servant."

"Even to be freed?" Cass continued, and she cut in, "I tell you I won't have you interfering with my affairs, do you understand that?" And she rose from his side and stood in the middle of the summer house, and, he reports, he saw the glimmer of her face in the shadow and heard her agitated breathing. "I thought you were fond of her," Cass said.

"I was," she said, "until—until she looked at me like that."

"You know why you got that price for her?" Cass asked, and without waiting for an answer, went on: "Because she's yellow and comely and well-made. Oh, the drovers wouldn't take her down chained in a coffle. They wouldn't wear her down. They'll take her down the river soft. And you know why?"

"Yes, I know why," she said, "and what is it to you? Are you so charmed by her?"

"That is unfair," Cass said.

"Oh, I see, Mr. Mastern," she said, "oh, I see, you are concerned for the honor of a black coachman. It is a very delicate sentiment, Mr. Mastern. Why—" and she came to stand above him as he still sat on the bench, "why did you not show some such delicate concern for the honor of your friend? Who is now dead."

According to the journal, there was, at this moment, "a tempest of feeling" in his breast. He wrote: "Thus I heard put into words for the first time the accusation which has ever, in all climes, been that most calculated to make wince a man of proper nurture or natural rectitude. What the hardened man can bear to hear from the still small voice within, may yet be when spoken by any external tongue an accusation dire enough to drain his very cheeks of blood. But it was not only that accusation in itself, for in very truth I had supped full of that horror and made it my long familiar. It was not merely the betrayal of my friend. It was not merely the death of my friend, at whose breast I had leveled the weapon. I could have managed somehow to live with those facts. But I suddenly felt that the world outside of me was shifting and the substance of things, and that the process had only begun of a general disintegration of which I was the center. At that moment of perturbation, when the cold sweat broke on my brow, I did not frame any sentence distinctly to my mind. But I have looked back and wrestled to know the truth. It was not the fact that a slave woman was being sold away from the house where she had had protection and kindness and away from the arms of her husband into debauchery. I knew such things had happened in fact, and I was no child, for after my arrival in Lexington and my acquaintance with the looser sort of companions, the sportsmen and the followers of the races, I had myself enjoyed such diversions. It was not only the fact that the woman for whom I had sacrificed my friend's life and my honor could, in her new suffering, turn on me with a cold rage and the language of insult so that I did not recognize her. It was, instead, the fact that all of these things—the death of my friend, the betrayal of Phebe, the suffering and rage and great change of the woman I had loved—all had come from my single act of sin and perfidy, as the boughs from the bole and the leaves from the bough. Or to figure the matter differently, it was as though the vibration set up in the whole fabric of the world by my act had spread infinitely and with ever increasing power and no man could know the end. I did not put it into words in such fashion, but I stood there shaken by a tempest of feeling."

When Cass had somewhat controlled his agitation, he said, "To whom did you sell the girl?"

"What's it to you?" she answered.

"To whom did you sell the girl?" he repeated.

"I'll not tell you," she said.

"I will find out," he said. "I will go to Paducah and find out."

She grasped him by the arm, driving her fingers deep into the flesh, "like talons," and demanded, "Why—why are you going?"

"To find her," he said. "To find her and buy her and set her free." He had not premeditated this. He heard the words, he wrote in the journal, and knew that that was his intention. "To find her and buy her and set her free," he said, and felt the grasp on his arm released and then in the dark suddenly felt the rake of her nails down his cheek, and heard her voice in a kind of "wild sibilance" saying, "If you do—if you do—oh, I'll not abide it—I will not!"

She flung herself from his side and to the bench. He heard her gasp and sob, "a hard, dry sob like a man's." He did not move. Then he heard her voice, "If you do—if you do—she looked at me that way, and I'll not abide it—if you do—" Then after a pause, very quietly: "If you do, I shall never see you again."

He made no reply. He stood there for some minutes, he did not know how long, then he left the summer house, where she still sat, and walked down the alley.

The next morning he left for Paducah. He learned the name of the trader, but he also learned that the trader had sold Phebe (a yellow wench who answered to Phebe's description) to a "private party" who happened to be in Paducah at the time but who had gone on down river. His name was unknown in Paducah. The trader had presumably sold Phebe so that he would be free to accompany his coffle when it had been made up. He had now headed, it was said, into south Kentucky, with a few bucks and wenches, to pick up more. As Cass had predicted, he had not wanted to wear Phebe down by taking her in the coffle. So getting a good figure of profit in Paducah, he had sold her there. Cass went south as far as Bowling Green, but lost track of his man there. So, rather hopelessly, he wrote a letter to the trader, in care of the market at New Orleans, asking for the name of the purchaser and any information about him. Then he swung back north to Lexington.

At Lexington he went down to West Short Street, to the Lewis C. Robards barracoon, which Mr. Robards had converted from the old Lexington Theatre a few years earlier. He had a notion that Mr. Robards, the leading trader of the section, might be able, through his down-river connections, to locate Phebe, if enough of a commission was in sight. At the barracoon there was no one in the office except a boy, who said that Mr. Robards was down river but that Mr. Simms was "holding things down" and was over at the "house" at an "inspection." So Cass went next door to the house. (When Jack Burden was in Lexington investigating the life of Cass Mastern, he saw the "house" still standing, a two-storey brick building of the traditional residential type, roof running lengthwise, door in center of front, window on each side, chimney at each end, lean-to in back. Robards had kept his "choice stock" there and not in the coops, to wait for "inspection.")

Cass found the main door unlocked at the house, entered the hall, saw no one, but heard laughter from above. He mounted the stairs and discovered, at the end of the hall, a small group of men gathered at an open door. He recognized a couple of them, young hangers-on he had seen about town and at the track. He approached and asked if Mr. Simms was about. "Inside," one of the men said, "showing." Over the heads, Cass could see into the room. First he saw a short, strongly made man, a varnished looking man, with black hair, black neck-cloth, large bright black eyes, and black coat, with a crop in his hand. Cass knew immediately that he was a French "speculator," who was buying "fancies" for Louisiana. The Frenchman was staring at something beyond Cass's range of vision. Cass moved farther and could see within.

There he saw the man whom he took to be Mr. Simms, a nondescript fellow in a plug hat, and beyond him the figure of a woman. She was a very young woman, some twenty years old perhaps, rather slender, with skin slightly darker than ivory, probably an octoroon, and hair crisp rather than kinky, and deep dark liquid eyes, slightly bloodshot, which stared at a spot above and beyond the Frenchman. She did not wear the ordinary plaid osnaburg and kerchief of the female slave up for sale, but a white, loosely cut dress, with elbow-length sleeves, and skirts to the floor and no kerchief, only a band to her hair. Beyond her, in the neatly furnished room ("quite genteel," the journal called it, while noting the barred windows), Cass saw a rocking chair and little table, and on the table a sewing basket with a piece of fancy needle-work lying there with the needle stuck in it, "as though some respectable young lady or householder had dropped it casually aside upon rising to greet a guest." Cass recorded that somehow he found himself staring at the needlework.

"Yeah," Mr. Simms was saying, "yeah." And grasped the girl by the shoulder to swing her slowly around for a complete view. Then he seized one of her wrists and lifted the arm to shoulder level and worked it back and forth a couple of times to show the supple articulation, saying, "yeah." That done, he drew the arm forward, holding it toward the Frenchman, the hand hanging limply from the wrist which he held. (The hand was, according to the journal, "well moulded, and the fingers tapered.") "Yeah," Mr. Simms said, "look at that-air hand. Ain't no lady got a littler, teensier hand. And round and soft, yeah?"

"Ain't she got nuthen else round and soft?" one of the men at the door called, and the others laughed.

"Yeah," Mr. Simms said, and leaned to take the hem of her dress, which with a delicate flirting motion he lifted higher than her waist, while he reached out with his other hand to wad the cloth and draw it into a kind of "awkward girdle" about her waist. Still holding the wad of cloth he walked around her, forcing her to turn (she turned "without resistance and as though in a trance") with his motion until her small buttocks were toward the door. "Round and soft, boys," Mr. Simms said, and gave her a good whack on the near buttock to make the flesh tremble. "Ever git yore hand on anything rounder ner softer, boys?" he demanded. "Hit's a cushion, I declare. And shake like sweet jelly."

"God-a-mighty and got on stockings," one of the men said.

While the other men laughed, the Frenchman stepped to the side of the girl, reached out to lay the tip of his riding crop at the little depression just above the beginning of the swell of the buttocks. He held the tip delicately there for a moment, then flattened the crop across the back and moved it down slowly, evenly across each buttock, to trace the fullness of the curve. "Turn her," he said in his foreign voice.

Mr. Simms obediently carried the wad around, and the body followed in the half revolution. One of the men at the door whistled. The Frenchman laid his crop across the woman's belly as though he were a "carpenter measuring something or as to demonstrate its flatness," and moved it down as before, tracing the structure, until he came to rest across the thighs, below the triangle. Then he let his hand fall to his side, with the crop. "Open your mouth," he said to the girl.

She did so, and he peered earnestly at her teeth. Then he leaned and whiffed her breath. "It is a good breath," he admitted, as though grudgingly.

"Yeah," Mr. Simms said, "yeah, you ain't a-finden no better breath."

"Have you any others?" the Frenchman demanded. "On hand?"

"We got 'em," Mr. Simms said.

"Let me see," the Frenchman said, and moved toward the door with, apparently, the "insolent expectation" that the group there would dissolve before him. He went out into the hall, Mr. Simms following. While Mr. Simms locked the door, Cass said to him, "I wish to speak to you, if you are Mr. Simms."

"Huh?" Mr. Simms said ("grunted" according to the journal), but looking at Cass became suddenly civil for he could know from dress and bearing that Cass was not one of the casual hangers-on. So Mr. Simms admitted the Frenchman to the next room to inspect its occupant, and returned to Cass. Cass remarked in the journal that trouble might have been avoided if he had been more careful to speak in private, but he wrote that at the time the matter was so much upon his mind that the men who stood about were as shadows to him.

He explained his wish to Mr. Simms, described Phebe as well as possible, gave the name of the trader in Paducah, and offered a liberal commission. Mr. Simms seemed dubious, promised to do what he could, and then said, "But nine outa ten you won't git her, Mister. And we got sumthen here better. You done seen Delphy, and she's nigh white as airy woman, and a sight more juicy, and that gal you talk about is nuthen but yaller. Now Delphy—"

"But the young gemmun got a hankeren fer yaller," one of the hangers-on said, and laughed, and the others laughed too.

Cass struck him across the mouth. "I struck him with the side of my fist," Cass wrote, "to bring blood. I struck him without thought, and I recollect the surprise which visited me when I saw the blood on his chin and saw him draw a bowie from his shirt-front. I attempted to avoid his first blow, but received it upon my left shoulder. Before he could withdraw, I had grasped his wrist in my right hand, forced it down so that I could also use my left hand, which still had some strength left at that moment, and with a turning motion of my body I broke his arm across my right hip, and then knocked him to the floor. I recovered the bowie from the floor, and with it faced the man who seemed to be the friend of the man who was now prostrate. He had a knife in his hand, but he seemed disinclined to pursue the discussion."

Cass declined the assistance of Mr. Simms, pressed a handkerchief over his wound, walked out of the building and toward his lodgings, and collapsed on West Short Street. He was carried home. The next day he was better. He learned that Mrs. Trice had left the city, presumably for Washington. A couple of days later his wound infected, and for some time he lay in delirium between life and death. His recovery was slow, presumably retarded by what he termed in the journal his "will toward darkness." But his constitution was stronger than his will, and he recovered, to know himself as the "chief of sinners and a plague-spot on the body of the human world." He would have committed suicide except for the fear of eternal damnation for that act, for though "hopeless of Grace I yet clung to the hope of Grace." But sometimes the very fact of damnation because of suicide seemed to be the very reason for suicide: he had brought his friend to suicide and the friend, by that act, was eternally damned; therefore he, Cass Mastern, should, in justice, insure his own damnation by the same act. "But the Lord preserved me from self-slaughter for ends which are His and beyond my knowledge."

Mrs. Trice did not come back to Lexington.

He returned to Mississippi. For two years he operated his plantation, read the Bible, prayed, and, strangely enough, prospered greatly, almost as though against his will. In the end he repaid Gilbert his debt, and set free his slaves. He had some notion of operating the plantation with the same force on a wage basis. "You fool," Gilbert said to him, "be a private fool if you must, but in God's name don't be a public one. Do you think you can work them and them free? One day work, one day loaf. Do you think you can have a passell of free niggers next door to a plantation with slaves? If you did have to set them free, you don't have to spend the rest of your natural life nursing them. Get them out of this country, and take up law or medicine. Or preach the Gospel and at least make a living out of all this praying." Cass tried for more than a year to operate the plantation with his free negroes, but was compelled to confess that the project was a failure. "Get them out of the country," Gilbert said to him. "And why don't you go with them? Why don't you go North?"

"I belong here," Cass replied.

"Well, why don't you preach Abolition right here?" Gilbert demanded. "Do something, do anything, but stop making a fool of yourself trying to raise cotton with free niggers."

"Perhaps I shall preach Abolition," Cass said, "someday. Even here. But not now. I am not worthy to instruct others. Not now. But meanwhile there is my example. If it is good, it is not lost. Nothing is ever lost."

"Except your mind," Gilbert said, and flung heavily from the room.

There was a sense of trouble in the air. Only Gilbert's great wealth and prestige and scarcely concealed humorous contempt for Cass saved Cass from ostracism, or worse. ("His contempt for me is a shield," Cass wrote. "He treats me like a wayward and silly child who may learn better and who does not have to be taken seriously. Therefore my neighbors do not take me seriously.") But trouble did come. One of Cass's negroes had a broad-wife on a plantation near by. After she had had some minor trouble with the overseer, the husband stole her from the plantation and ran away. Toward the Tennessee border the pair were taken. The man, resisting officers, was shot; the woman was brought back. "See," Gilbert said, "all you have managed to do is get one nigger killed and one nigger whipped. I offer my congratulations." So Cass put his free negroes on a boat bound up river, and never heard of them again.

"I saw the boat head out into the channel, and watched the wheels churn against the strong current, and my spirit was troubled. I knew that the negroes were passing from one misery to another, and that the hopes they now carried would be blighted. They had kissed my hands and wept for joy, but I could take no part in their rejoicing. I had not flattered myself that I had done anything for them. What I had done I had done for myself, to relieve my spirit of a burden, the burden of their misery and their eyes upon me. The wife of my dead friend had found the eyes of the girl Phebe upon her and had gone wild and had ceased to be herself and had sold the girl into misery. I had found their eyes upon me and had freed them into misery, lest I should do worse. For many cannot bear their eyes upon them, and enter into evil and cruel ways in their desperation. There was in Lexington a decade and more before my stay in that city, a wealthy lawyer named Fielding L. Turner, who had married a lady of position from Boston. This lady, Caroline Turner, who had never had blacks around her and who had been nurtured in sentiments opposed to the institution of human servitude, quickly became notorious for her abominable cruelties performed in her fits of passion. All persons of the community reprehended her floggings, which she performed with her own hands, uttering meanwhile little cries in her throat, according to report. Once while she was engaged in flogging a servant in an apartment on the second floor of her palatial home, a small negro boy entered the room and began to whimper. She seized him and bodily hurled him through the window of the apartment so that he fell upon a stone below and broke his back to become a cripple for his days. To protect her from the process of law and the wrath of the community, Judge Turner committed her to a lunatic asylum. But later the physicians said her to be of sound mind and released her. Her husband in his will left her no slaves, for to do so would, the will said, be to doom them to misery in life and a speedy death. But she procured slaves, among them a yellow coachman named Richard, mild of manner, sensible, and of plausible disposition. One day she had him chained and proceeded to flog him. But he tore himself from the chains that held him to the wall and seized the woman by the throat and strangled her. Later he was captured and hanged for murder, though many wished that his escape had been contrived. This story was told me in Lexington. One lady said to me: 'Mrs. Turner did not understand negroes.' And another: 'Mrs. Turner did it because she was from Boston where the Abolitionists are.' But I did not understand. Then, much later, I began to understand. I understood that Mrs. Turner flogged her negroes for the same reason that the wife of my friend sold Phebe down the river: she could not bear their eyes upon her. I understand, for I can no longer bear their eyes upon me. Perhaps only a man like my brother Gilbert can in the midst of evil retain enough of innocence and strength to bear their eyes upon him and to do a little justice in the terms of the great injustice."

So Cass, who had a plantation with no one to work it, went to Jackson, the capital of the state, and applied himself to the law. Before he left, Gilbert came to him and offered to take over the plantation and work it with a force of his people from his own great place on a share basis. Apparently he was still trying to make Cass rich. But Cass declined, and Gilbert said: "You object to my working it with slaves, is that it? Well, let me tell you, if you sell it, it will be worked with slaves. It is black land and will be watered with black sweat. Does it make any difference then, which black sweat falls on it?" And Cass replied that he was not going to sell the plantation. Then Gilbert, in an apoplectic rage, bellowed: "My God, man, it is land, don't you understand, it is land, and land cries out for man's hand!" But Cass did not sell. He installed a caretaker in the house, and rented a little land to a neighbor for pasture.

He went to Jackson, sat late with his books, and watched trouble gathering over the land. For it was the autumn of 1858 when he went to Jackson. On January 8, 1861, Mississippi passed the Ordinance of Secession. Gilbert had opposed secession, writing to Cass: "The fools, there is not a factory for arms in the state. Fools not to have prepared themselves if they have foreseen the trouble. Fools, if they have not foreseen it, to act thus in the face of facts. Fools not to temporize now and, if they must, prepare themselves to strike a blow. I have told responsible men to prepare. All fools." To which Cass replied: "I pray much for peace." But later, he wrote: "I have talked with Mr. French, who is, as you know, the Chief of Ordnance, and he says that they have only old muskets for troops, and those but flintlocks. The agents have scraped the state for shotguns, at the behest of Governor Pettus. Shotguns, Mr. French said, and curled his lips. And what shotguns, he added, and then told me of a weapon contributed to the cause, an old musket barrel strapped with metal to a piece of cypress rail crooked at one end. An old slave gave this treasure to the cause, and does one laugh or weep?" (One can guess what Gilbert would have done, reading the letter.) After Jefferson Davis had come back to Mississippi, having resigned from the Senate, and had accepted the command of the troops of Mississippi with the rank of Major-General, Cass called upon him, at the request of Gilbert. He wrote to Gilbert: "The General says that they have given him 10,000 men, but not a stand of modern rifles. But the General also said, they have given me a very fine coat with fourteen brass buttons in front and a black velvet collar. Perhaps we can use the buttons in our shotguns, he said, and smiled."

Cass saw Mr. Davis once more, for he was with Gilbert on the steamboat *Natchez* which carried the new President of the Confederacy on the first stage of his journey from his plantation, "Brierfield," to Montgomery. "We were on old Mr. Tom Leather's boat," Cass wrote in the journal, "which had been supposed to pick up the President at a landing a few miles below Brierfield. But Mr. Davis was delayed in leaving his house and was rowed out to us. I leaned on the rail and saw the little black skiff proceeding toward us over the red water. A man waved from the skiff to us. The captain of the *Natchez* observed the signal, and gave a great blast of his boat's whistle which made our ears tingle and shivered out over the expanse of waters. Our boat stopped and the skiff approached. Mr. Davis was received on board. As the steamboat moved on, Mr. Davis looked back and lifted his hand in salute to the negro servant (Isaiah Montgomery whom I had known at Brierfield) who stood in the skiff, which rocked in the wash of the steamboat, and waved his farewell. Later, as we proceeded upriver toward the bluffs of Vicksburg, he approached my brother, with whom I was standing on the deck. We had previously greeted him. My brother again, and more intimately, congratulated Mr. Davis, who replied that he could take no pleasure in the honor. I have, he said, always looked upon the Union with a superstitious reverence and have freely risked my life for its dear flag on more than one battlefield, and you, gentlemen, can conceive the sentiment now in me that the object of my attachment for many years has been withdrawn from me. And he continued, I have in the present moment only the melancholy pleasure of an easy conscience. Then he smiled, as he did rarely. Thereupon he took his leave of us and retired within. I had observed how worn to emaciation was his face by illness and care, and how thin the skin lay over the bone. I remarked to my brother that Mr. Davis did not look well. He replied, a sick man, it is a fine how-de-do to have a sick man for a president. I responded that there might be no war, that Mr. Davis hoped for peace. But my brother said, make no mistake, the Yankees will fight and they will fight well and Mr. Davis is a fool to hope for peace. I replied, all good men hope for peace. At this my brother uttered an indistinguishable exclamation and said, what we want now that they've got into this is not a good man but a man who can win, and I am not interested in the luxury of Mr. Davis' conscience. Then my brother and I continued our promenade in silence, and I reflected that Mr. Davis was a good man. But the world is full of good men, I reflect as I write these lines, and yet the world drives hard into darkness and the blindness of blood, even as now late at night I sit in this hotel room in Vicksburg, and I am moved to ask the meaning of our virtue. May God hear our prayer!"

Gilbert received a commission as colonel in a cavalry regiment. Cass enlisted as a private in the Second Mississippi Rifles. "You could be a captain," Gilbert said, "or a major. You've got brains enough for that. And," he added, "damned few of them have." Cass replied that he preferred to be a private soldier, "marching with other men." But he could not tell his brother why, or tell his brother that, though he would march with other men and would carry a weapon in his hand, he would never take the life of an enemy. "I must march with these men who march," he wrote in the journal, "for they are my people and I must partake with them of all bitterness, and that more fully. But I cannot take the life of another man. How can I who have taken the life of my friend, take the life of an enemy, for I have used up my right to blood?" So Cass marched away to war, carrying the musket which was, for him, but a meaningless burden, and wearing on a string, against the flesh of his chest, beneath the fabric of the gray jacket, the ring which had once been Duncan Trice's wedding ring and which Annabelle Trice, that night in the summer house, had slipped onto his finger as his hand lay on her bosom.

Cass marched to Shiloh, between the fresh fields, for it was early April, and then into the woods that screened the river. (Dogwood and redbud would have been out then.) He marched into the woods, heard the lead whistle by his head, saw the dead men on the ground, and the next day came out of the woods and moved in the sullen withdrawal toward Corinth. He had been sure that he would not survive the battle. But he had survived, and moved down the crowded road "as in a dream." And he wrote: "And I felt that henceforward I should live in that dream." The dream took him into Tennessee again—Chickamauga, Knoxville, Chattanooga, and the nameless skirmishes, and the bullet for which he waited did not find him. He became known as a man of extreme courage. At Chickamauga, when his company wavered in the enemy fire and seemed about to break in its attack, he moved steadily up the slope and could not understand his own inviolability. And the men regrouped, and followed. "It seemed strange to me," he wrote, "that I who in God's will sought death and could not find it, should in my seeking lead men to it who did not seek." When Colonel Hickman congratulated him, he could "find no words" for answer.

But if he had put on the gray jacket in anguish of spirit and in hope of expiation, he came to wear it in pride, for it was a jacket like those worn by the men with whom he marched. "I have seen men do brave things," he wrote, "and they ask for nothing." More and more into the journals crept the comments of the professional soldier, between the prayers and the scruples—criticism of command (of Bragg after Chickamauga), satisfaction and an impersonal pride in manoeuvre or gunnery ("the practice of Marlowe's battery excellent"), and finally the admiration for the feints and delays executed by Johnston's virtuosity on the approaches to Atlanta, at Buzzard's Roost, Snake Creek Gap, New

Hope Church, Kenesaw Mountain ("there is always a kind of glory, however stained or obscured, in whatever man's hand does well, and General Johnston does well").

Then, outside Atlanta, the bullet found him. He lay in the hospital and rotted slowly to death. But even before the infection set in, when the wound in the leg seemed scarcely serious, he knew that he would die. "I shall die," he wrote in the journal, "and shall be spared the end and the last bitterness of war. I have lived to do no man good, and have seen others suffer for my sin. I do not question the Justice of God, that others have suffered for my sin, for it may be that only by the suffering of the innocent does God affirm that men are brothers, and brothers in His Holy Name. And in this room with me now, men suffer for sins not theirs, as for their own. It is a comfort to know that I suffer only for my own." He knew not only that he was to die, but that the war was over. "It is over. It is all over but the dying, which will go on. Though the boil has come to a head and has burst, yet must the pus flow. Men shall yet come together and die in the common guilt of man and in the guilt that sent them hither from far places and distant firesides. But God in His Mercy has spared me the end. Blessed be His Name."

There was no more in the journal. There was only the letter to Gilbert, written in the strange hand, dictated by Cass after he had grown too weak to write. "Remember me, but without grief. If one of us is lucky, it is I . . . "

Atlanta fell. In the last confusion, the grave of Cass Mastern was not marked. Someone at the hospital, a certain Albert Calloway, kept Cass's papers and the ring which he had carried on the cord around his neck, and much later, after the war in fact, sent them to Gilbert Mastern with a courteous note. Gilbert preserved the journal, the letters from Cass, the picture of Cass, and the ring on its cord, and after Gilbert's death, the heir finally sent the packet to Jack Burden, the student of history and the grand-nephew of Cass and Gilbert Mastern. So they came to rest on the little pine table in Jack Burden's bedroom in the slatternly apartment which he occupied with the two other graduate students, the unlucky, industrious, and alcoholic one, and the lucky, idle, and alcoholic one.

Jack Burden lived with the Mastern papers for a year and a half. He wanted to know all of the facts of the world in which Cass and Gilbert Mastern had lived, and he did know many of the facts. And he felt that he knew Gilbert Mastern. Gilbert Mastern had kept no journal, but he felt that he knew him, the man with the head like the block of bare granite, who had lived through one world into another and had been at home in both. But the day came when Jack Burden sat down at the pine table and realized that he did not know Cass Mastern. He did not have to know Cass Mastern to get the degree; he only had to know the facts about Cass Mastern's world. But without knowing Cass Mastern, he could not put down the facts about Cass Mastern's world. Not that Jack Burden said that to himself. He simply sat there at the pine table, night after night, staring at the papers before him, twisting the ring on its cord, staring at the photograph, and writing nothing. Then he would get up to get a drink of water, and would stand in the dark kitchen, holding an old jelly glass in his hand, waiting for the water to run cold from the tap.

An Untitled Play

A Drama of the American Civil War

ROBERT PENN WARREN

CHARACTERS

IN ORDER OF APPEARANCE

Major Gilbert Mastern, a rich Mississippi planter

Cass Mastern, his younger brother

Bella Trice, a fashionable young woman of Lexington, Kentucky

Abbott Coldwater, her younger brother

Duncan Trice, husband to Bella, a landowner

Guests, neighbors to the Trices

Mark Trice, cousin to Duncan Trice, a professor at the Transylvania University

Phebe, a slave, personal servant to Bella

Old Alec, an old freedman

Mr. Wilton, one of the guests

Larue, a slave trader, from Louisiana

Negro Houseboy, a slave

ACT I

SCENE 1

SCENE: *The drawing room of the* TRICE *house, on an estate near Lexington, Kentucky. It is a handsome establishment, but with an air of use, a hint of rurality, in its elegance. The most prominent object is a large, full-length portrait of a young woman on the wall, slightly to stage right—a figure standing in a formal garden, leaning pensively and romantically on an urn, a greyhound at her feet. As will be discovered, this is a portrait of* BELLA TRICE. *Below the portrait a little to stage left of it, is a great vase with boughs of colored autumn leaves. At stage right a door is indicated to give toward a garden and garden house. Forward, a window is indicated. To stage left a stair descends. Beyond, but more toward center, there is an arch, and beyond it a sense of space. On a little table near the stairs is a beaver hat, upside down. In the drawing room, there is ordinary furniture, with a large couch prominent below the portrait.*

TIME: *A late afternoon in October, 1859.*

AT RISE: GILBERT *and* CASS MASTERN *are talking closely, under the portrait of* BELLA TRICE, *while near the stairs and beyond the arch a group of people are chatting gaily, several men and women, all in riding habit.* BELLA TRICE *is in this group, gay but not conspicuous.* GILBERT—GIL—*is a man verging toward forty, but in a sense an ageless man, stocky and strong, with a bald granite skull, sharp active eyes, an impassive face.* He *is dressed in severe black. His whole impression is of reserved and sardonic force.* CASS, *his brother, with whom* HE *is now earnestly engaged, is a tall, raw-boned youth of some twenty-two, dark and brooding, a mixture of shyness, clumsiness, and natural physical grace.* HE *wears gray pantaloons, a dark tailcoat, a blue waistcoat with sprigs.* HE *seems uneasy in his clothes. As* THEY *talk, there is the far-off sound of a banjo, very faint, coming and going. The tune is "Listen to the Mockingbird."*

GIL: Well, why don't you want to stay here?

CASS: I don't know, Brother—it's just—

GIL: I'll stay around a few days before I go on to Washington. Till you get the hang of things.

CASS: I could get a room in town. After you go, I mean. Maybe I could study better in a room in town. Near the university.

GIL: God-a-Mighty, a boarding house! *(Picking up a knick-knack, hefting it in his hand)* See that. Look. You know what it is?

CASS: No, Brother.

GIL: Well, it's Sevres. Foreign. French. Did you know that?

CASS: No, sir.

GIL: You ought to know such things. It comes in handy, sometimes. And you won't find out such things in some boarding house smelling of sow-belly and cabbage. (HE *notices the disarrayed stock at his brother's neck*) Fix your stock! *(As* CASS *awkwardly adjusts the stock)* Gad, boy, I took you out of that shack, I gave you a plantation and a hundred niggers, I hired a man to teach you Latin, and you still can't tie your stock. If you stay around here, you at least might learn to tie your stock.

CASS: But—

GIL: What are you afraid of?

CASS: It's not that, it's—

GIL: *(Leaning at him)* Listen, I'm richer'n any of 'em. Seven plantations. Seven. Eight, till I gave you that little piss-ant one so you could learn something. I was rich before I was thirty. But any fool can make money. Money doesn't mean much if you don't have taste and judgment. Did you know that?

CASS: Yes, sir.

GIL: Well, this is a house of taste and judgment. That's why Jefferson Davis has arranged for you to be a guest here. To learn taste and judgment. *(With a sharp appraising glance at the room)* What are you afraid of? (*With the same sharp appraisal directed at* CASS) You're my brother, and stronger than any of 'em. This Trice—sure, he's rich, but he couldn't have even made his own money. Had everything given to him. *(Again assessing the room, till his eye comes to rest on the portrait)* Yes, everything. *(Caught by the portrait)* See that picture. See how proud and correct she is.

CASS: Yes. Yes, sir.

GIL: When I was your age, I was starving. I walked down the road and a carriage would come by and I'd step in the ditch like a nigger and the mud splashed on me, and I'd look up and see one of them sitting proud and correct. *(Nods toward the portrait)* Me, Gilbert Mastern, down in the ditch. (*Unconscious, his hand reaches out to take a bough of the autumn leaves from the great vase. Unconsciously the other hand strips off the leaves, as* HE *stares up, and begins to tap his leg with a riding crop.* HE *turns suddenly back to* CASS) But you know one thing—no matter how proud and correct, not one of 'em can be proud and correct on her back. Did you know that?

CASS: Yes, sir.

GIL: You don't know a damned thing about it. But— (BELLA *enters, having managed to extricate herself from her new arrivals, not in riding dress, who have just entered.* SHE *is in riding dress, not tall, but her fine carriage makes her seem so.* SHE *is a little over thirty, blonde and charming, vivacious but not nervous, aware of her womanly obligation to delight those around her, but at moments a shade of sadness can drop over her face and* SHE *seems caught into distance*)

BELLA: Oh, forgive me! I was greeting new guests. I thought Duncan was with you—the dear old wretch. Oh, it's disgraceful enough, not even to be at home when you arrive, to be gallivanting off somewhere on a horse, but now—

GIL: We should have informed you more precisely.

BELLA: Oh, I shall die of shame! (Abbott Coldwater, *the brother of* BELLA, *enters.* HE *is an attractive, athletic young man, about the age of* CASS, *confident, easy, spoiled, but charming in manner.* HE *is in old, well-used riding dress, which* HE *wears as naturally as his skin.* HE *clearly admires his sister, proud of her. Now* HE *moves swiftly to her, taking her by the shoulder, shaking her affectionately*)

ABBOTT: Lord, Bella, that jump you took! You're crazy, but it was wonderful.

BELLA: *(Laying a finger to his lips, and* HE *kisses it)* Hush! Besides, you haven't met the Masterns. (*To* GIL) Major Mastern, this is my wicked baby brother Abbott—eh, Abbey-Boy, are you wicked? *(Tousling his hair lightly)*

ABBOTT: *(Shaking hands with* GIL, *but casting a glance of mock reproach at her over his shoulder)* Oh, Bella.

BELLA: *(As* ABBOTT *and* CASS *shake hands and* ABBOTT *murmurs the civilities,* SHE *touches* CASS *on the arm)* But maybe you'll reform him, Mr. Mastern. It looks like I just can't raise him right. Oh, I've been trying ever since he used to fall out of the apple tree and I'd have to kiss where it hurt and rock him in my arms—but oh, he is so wicked! (DUNCAN TRICE *enters, a letter in his hand, lifting it to the* GUESTS *who follow him.* HE *is little over forty, a handsome, well-fed, florid, faintly vacuous man, likeable, complacent, genial.* HE *often stands close to his wife's side, and is sometimes seen to suppress an impulse to touch her arm or shoulder*)

DUNCAN: I've found it! *(Waving the letter)* Ah, Major Mastern, we'll make your ears burn a little. Ladies and gentlemen, this is a letter from Mr. Jefferson Davis, Major Mastern's neighbor in Mississippi, whom we must thank for the present pleasure and honor. *(Clearing his throat, officially)* Oyez, oyez, to all presents—ergo, seriatim, Q.E.D., so help you God, to wit—

ALL: Read! Read!

DUNCAN: *(Reading weightily)* Major Mastern is a powerful man of our state, nay, of our section, fit for the gravest councils, strong in all affairs of business and the public weal. A soldier of address and staunchness, he was a major in the Mexican War, and at the assault at Buena Vista, under the gruelling fire of the enemy—

BELLA: *(Waving her hand to stop her husband)* Come, come, I'll put Major Mastern under the gruelling fire of these ladies' eyes! (GIL *is surrounded by the ladies*)

ABBOTT: (*With wonderment, inspecting* CASS) So you lived near Natchez? What about that Natchez-Under-the-Hill? Is it like they say?

CASS: I don't know.

ABBOTT: You never tried to even find out?

CASS: I had to stay in the country.

ABBOTT: All the time!

CASS: Four years. At Valhalla—my brother's place. You see, he got me a tutor. To help me study.

ABBOTT: Study! Listen— (*Putting a friendly and insinuating arm about the shoulder of* CASS) —you stay around here, and I'll show you something to study. Trust old Abbey-Boy. Down at Monsieur Vincent's place in town, there's a— *(The voice sinks, low and confidential.* GIL *is saying something to bring gales of laughter from the ladies.* MARK TRICE *enters in haste.* HE *is about forty-five to fifty years old, tall and slender, gracefully careless in manner, a man at home in the world, meticulously and severely dressed.* HE *has a small beard, flecked with gray, no moustache.* HE *wears spectacles.* BELLA *notices his arrival)*

BELLA: (*To* CASS) Oh, look, there's Cousin Mark—Duncan's cousin—Professor Trice. Professor at the Transylvania University. He is the one who arranged everything for you here, he's— (*Interrupting herself, waving to* MARK) Oh, Mark, come here— *(Seeing his face as* HE *steps toward her)* Mark, what's the matter?

MARK: *(To the assembly)* Ladies and gentlemen, I bring shocking news. *(Silence)* There is an insurrection. At Harper's Ferry, in Virginia. Last night—

FIRST GUEST: An insurrection. The blacks? You mean the slaves, the—

MARK: John Brown—the John Brown of Kansas— *(General murmur and stir)* — he struck the town last night. He has occupied the United States arsenal, to arm the slaves. There have been deaths in the fighting.

SECOND GUEST: That Brown . . . that common horse thief!

GIL: I beg your pardon, sir . . . a most uncommon horse thief. *(In quick pantomime* DUNCAN *is introducing* MARK *to* GIL, *while the* THIRD GUEST *is speaking)*

THIRD GUEST: Remember the massacre! At Pottawatomie. He took men out at night—innocent men out of their beds—and chopped them down with sabers. In cold blood.

FIRST GUEST: Here—it could be here next.

SECOND GUEST: There are men left in Kentucky.

THIRD GUEST: To defend ourselves! And our sacred institutions.

DUNCAN: What do you think, Major Mastern?

GIL: I'm a practical man. I believe in defending my—my hide. And my property. *(Hesitating drily)*

THIRD GUEST: Bravo!

GIL: *(With sardonic side glance)* But I do not see any institution as sacred. An institution is—is sacred—just so long as it gets something done. Our institution—our labor system, shall I say?—happens to suit us at the moment. The North does not find it profitable. They find it more profitable to put small white children in cotton mills at a starving wage, and then kick them out to starve in good earnest as soon as they are sick or old.

FIRST GUEST: It's worse than slavery!

GIL: It is merely a labor system. It will last as long as profitable.

THIRD GUEST: But our system—we must defend it!

GIL: As long as it works. When it ceases to work, I shall get a system worth defending.

MARK: Hear! Hear!

THIRD GUEST: *(To* MARK, *with asperity)* But Abolitionists sometimes argue thus. Oh, that's subtle, that's—

FIRST GUEST: Abolitionists! Will we allow them to run wild? If there must be blood—if throats must be cut, white and black— (BELLA, *alarmed at the violence of the* GUEST, *interrupts gaily. Meanwhile,* PHEBE *has entered, and stands in the background, staring at the* FIRST GUEST. PHEBE *is a handsome mulatto, about the age of her mistress, prettily dressed, clearly the type of favored personal servant. Behind her the lights come up in the space beyond the arch to show a silver punch bowl, etc.*)

BELLA: Oh, politics, politics—and we ladies are pining away in our beauty, and never a word but old politics! *(At this the* FIRST GUEST *has caught* PHEBE'S *gaze upon him, and turns away, embarrassed by his previous violence. Now there is the banjo again, closer, and an old ragged* NEGRO MAN *appears below the indicated window at the edge of the garden, stage right. In a cracked old voice* HE *is singing:)*

OLD ALEC: I am dreaming now of Hallie,
Dear Hallie, sweet Hallie.
She's lying now in the valley,
And the mockingbird is singing where she lies.
Oh, listen to the mockingbird, etc.

(The GUESTS *are listening)*

ABBOTT: Just Old Alec. He's a freedman—somebody set him free in his will—(*Explaining to* GIL) and all he can do is wander around with that old banjo. *(Stepping to the window, tossing down a coin, which* OLD ALEC *expertly scoops up while* HE *doffs his ragged hat)*

OLD ALEC: Thank 'ee, thank 'ee—

ABBOTT: Go round to the kitchen. Make 'em give you some supper. *(Meanwhile* DUNCAN *is greeting a new arrival, whom* HE *now escorts to the group)*

DUNCAN: Mr. Wilton has good news! Good news, ladies and gentlemen.

WILTON: Colonel Lee—Robert E. Lee, that is—has arrived at Harper's Ferry. With a regiment of Marines. Brown is surrounded in the engine house. Many of his men are taken, or dead. He is nearly alone—

ABBOTT: Hurrah! Colonel Lee will finish him off! (*To* GIL) Sir, did you know Colonel Lee in Mexico?

GIL: Yes.

FIRST GUEST: Won't he finish off that Brown?

GIL: Colonel Lee is a very sober and competent man. And— *(Pause)* —he has a thousand Marines.

BELLA: *(Who has returned to the group, addressing* CASS, *trying courteously to draw him into the conversation)* You, Mr. Mastern, what do you think?

CASS: I—why, I wasn't thinking anything.

BELLA: Oh, yes—I could tell by your face.

CASS: Well, nothing—nothing worth anything.

BELLA: *(Pressing)* But what.

CASS: I was just thinking—thinking how he is alone—how he—

BELLA: How who is alone?

CASS: That old man—Brown.

THIRD GUEST: That blackguard and traitor!

CASS: (*Caught in his own thoughts, not hearing the* GUEST) He is alone, and an old man—oh, I know, he is a murderer—but he is there—in that place, alone—and a thousand Marines around, and—

THIRD GUEST: Thank God for that!

CASS: Yes—yes—but—

BELLA: Mr. Mastern.

CASS: Yes, ma'am.

BELLA: Those men outside, those men surrounding him, they are men like you, Mr. Mastern. Like us all.

CASS: Yes, ma'am. But the men inside—Brown—we are like them, too, and . . .

THIRD GUEST: Begging your pardon, I am not!

DUNCAN: But that's all far off in Virginia! Come, gentlemen, come. Bring the ladies. Let us take some refreshment. *(Leading back beyond the arch)* There's nothing like a little refreshment, now. This punch, the recipe is from Georgia. Mr. Sutton brought it from Savannah, and—

BELLA: (*Lingering with* CASS) What you said, Mr. Mastern—what made you say it? About that Brown, I mean?

CASS: I didn't mean to make an argument. It just popped out. I'm sorry.

BELLA: I know you aren't an Abolitionist. Not with your brother a great planter, and a friend of Jefferson Davis, and all.

CASS: Oh, no, ma'am!

BELLA: I just wondered if you were a little like Cousin Mark—not exactly an Abolitionist, Heaven's Name forbid—but he has some peculiar ideas. I was just wondering if you had some peculiar ideas. Like Mark.

CASS: Oh, no, ma'am.

BELLA: Forgive me—please forgive me—but somehow I just had to ask why you said what you did.

CASS: I don't rightly know. Just he is old. Old and surrounded—oh, I know he's wicked, and a murderer, but— *(Pausing)* Didn't you ever see anybody like that? Surrounded, old, cut off?

BELLA: No—no—

CASS: No?

BELLA: *(Suddenly)* Yes. Yes, once. Long back—on the street, in Louisville—he was old—old and sick, propped against a wall, and some children, they were staring at him. Yes, and I was a child and I wanted to stare and my father, he pulled me on. He said, "Come on, come on, Bella—this is no place for you." And I began to cry, but he said, "Come on, come on."

CASS: Then you know. What I mean—I mean you can think how it would be with him—whatever he is—alone and cut off—

BELLA: *(Suddenly inward)* Alone—yes. Cut off—yes. Yes.

CASS: Don't you see what I mean? I can't say it exactly, but— *(As* SHE *is studying his face, as though trying to determine the import of what* HE *has said,* ABBOTT *steps up and slaps* CASS *on the shoulder)*

ABBOTT: Hey, Bella, you're making this old fellow die of thirst! Look, his tongue is hanging out. Like a hound on a dead scent and ticks in his ears. *(As* ABBOTT *takes* CASS *by the arm to draw him away,* BELLA *catches sight of* PHEBE, *with a platter in one hand, secretly wiping away a tear with the other)*

BELLA: (*Rushing to* PHEBE) Why, Phebe! Dear little Phebe—dear little goose, why, you're crying!

PHEBE: I'm sorry—I didn't mean to—

BELLA: What is the matter, dear goose?

PHEBE: Jason—it's Jason—

BELLA: Can't he come? Why, it is Friday night, isn't it—his night to come? Does Miss Hartmann need him tonight? *(Laying a hand lovingly on* PHEBE'S *arm, shaking her)* Oh, you sweet goose—she'll let him come tomorrow. You silly goose, you've been married a whole year and you act like this. Just wait till you're an old married woman like me, and—

PHEBE: *(Suddenly sobbing, almost dropping the platter, which* BELLA *takes and sets aside)* Oh, I'm sorry, Miss Bella—to make a fuss—with all these people—but Jason—he's my husband, and— *(She can't go on)*

BELLA: What? And what?

PHEBE: Gonna sell him. Sell him off.

BELLA: Sell him! It's ridiculous! Miss Hartmann would never sell him. She's so proud of him, she'd die first. Why, he's the finest coachman in Kentucky!

PHEBE: But it's norated 'mongst the people, how Miss Becky's gonna sell the place and all the people. All this war talk, gonna sell her place and go to her sister in Ca'lina. And ma'am—oh, ma'am— *(Seizing* BELLA'S *hand)*

BELLA: Don't cry, Phebe, dear. Oh, I can't bear to see you cry!

PHEBE: Oh, Miss Bella—if you'd only buy him—buy Jason!

BELLA: *(With sudden decision, excitement taking her)* Hurry! Go tell Jim to saddle a horse. No, not Celeste—I've jumped her so much today. Saddle Daybreak. And a horse for you. Yes, yes, you come with me.

PHEBE: What?—

BELLA: Quick—we'll go now— *(Gaily, conspiratorially, her hand on* PHEBE'S *arm)* we'll buy Jason—now— *(As* PHEBE *looks about at the* GUESTS *instinctively aware of her duties)* Let the wretches starve! Hurry! Oh, dear Phebe, won't it be wonderful to have Jason here? *(As* PHEBE *turns to go)* Oh, he's the finest coachman in Kentucky—Hurry! *(Before* PHEBE *has taken more than another step,* DUNCAN, *followed by* CASS *and* GIL, *has approached* BELLA. PHEBE *stops, watching anxiously, aware that something is about to fall across the plan)*

DUNCAN: (*To* BELLA) My dear, I have bad news.

BELLA: (*Not noticing* CASS *and* GIL) I'm sorry—I've got to go—

DUNCAN: Go? Go where?

BELLA: To buy Jason. Miss Hartmann is selling off and—

DUNCAN: But for Heaven's sake, my dear. You're so impulsive. Nobody's selling off this time of day. If you decided you want Jason, yes, by all means—but tomorrow—the day after—

BELLA: But it's Phebe—it's for Phebe—he's her husband and she's frightened and—

DUNCAN: (*Spying* PHEBE) Now look at Phebe. She's a very sensible girl. Aren't you, Phebe? Yes, Phebe knows that nothing will happen tonight. (PHEBE *steps back, picks up her platter and in a numbed way holds it out to a* GUEST) Besides, my dear, your guests—Mr. Mastern must leave. He says he must, and—

BELLA: *(Turning abruptly toward* CASS, *taking a step toward him, sudden concern in face and manner, and confusion)* Oh—oh, I'm sorry—I truly am—

DUNCAN: *(Puzzled)* But my dear—oh, it's my fault, I should have said Major Mastern. *(As* BELLA *slowly turns)* Yes, it's Major Mastern. He must change his plans. He must go.

BELLA: *(Adopting a tone of gay, polite hyperbole, in contrast to her previous manner)* Treason! Treason! Bar the doors! *(Pausing, making a charming tentative gesture toward him)* But seriously, dear sir, we cannot permit it. Leave! Why you've only just arrived. This very hour. What would our friend Mr. Davis say if we let you leave?

GIL: Madame, if I consulted my inclinations things would be different. But the world is not always tailored to my inclinations. In fact, if I may say so, I go to Washington in the hope of tailoring the world a little more closely after my fashion.

MARK: But you are going by the cars. And the line—the B&O isn't it?—it runs through the Ferry, and the fighting, it's there.

GIL: All the more reason to get through. With that fool business at the Ferry there's no telling what worse damned foolishness—begging your pardon Madame—will be cooking in Washington.

DUNCAN: But a day to two—wait, for you may not get through now.

GIL: There's always a way. If you put your mind to it.

BELLA: But I will not permit it. All the ladies of Lexington have waited for your coming. Eyes are brighter today, Major Mastern. Hearts are beating faster. Oh, cruel sir—

GIL: I am unworthy of your kindness. But, Madame—

DUNCAN: Enough, my dear. Major Mastern knows his necessity.

BELLA: *(Spying* CASS *coming up)* Well, we'll hold your brother as earnest money for your return.

DUNCAN: *(Slapping* CASS *on the shoulder)* Yes, my boy, we'll hang on to you. Better one Mastern than none! *(To his wife)* But, my dear, if Major Mastern insists on this unhappy decision, he must have need of a few words with his brother. Come, my dear. *(When* THEY *have left the brothers)* My dear, I've invited Jim Talbutt and Sue and Sam Fairlea and Colonel Allen to drop back for dinner, and— *(His voice trails apologetically off)*

BELLA: Why how delightful! How did you ever think of it? *(As* HE *flushes with relief and pleasure,* SHE *affects a girlish enthusiasm)* And Jim Talbutt will tell us all about that straight flush, or whatever it was, and— (SHE *gaily imitates a man playing cards)* —Sam Fairlea will tell us what he said that time to Daniel Webster— *(Sticking one finger into an imaginary waistcoat, placing her left hand behind her back in the stance of a statesman, pulling a grave face)* —and the Colonel will lead that cavalry charge under the gruelling fire of those awful Mexicans down in Mexico— *(Imitating a man in a saddle, rising in the stirrups, waving a saber, then stopping herself, studying her husband's confused face, reaching out to comfort him)* Oh, poor, dear old Dunc!

DUNCAN: I'm sorry, Bella. I thought you liked them.

BELLA: But I do. I love them. It's just—

DUNCAN: Just what?

BELLA: Oh, nothing. *(Shrugging, turning away)* It's just— *(As* GUESTS *come up, taking leave, her vivacity returns, and there is the leave-taking in pantomime, as the exchange between* GILBERT *and* CASS *emerges)*

GIL: Apply yourself to your studies. Take necessary pleasure. It purges the blood and sharpens the wits. You will find the arrangements easy. Ask other gentlemen. But study your Greek. Mr. Davis studied his Greek right here at the Transylvania University. I did not have the opportunity of studying the tongues, but I know that Greek sounds good in a speech. Latin sounds good, but Greek sounds better. (GUESTS *are coming up to say goodbye to the* MASTERNS, *in pantomime, as* DUNCAN, *momentarily alone with his wife, is speaking to her*)

DUNCAN: Oh, it's so many things I don't know about. That jump you took today. God, you scared me! *(To a* GUEST *coming up)* I was just saying that Bella scared me, taking that jump.

GUEST: Not five men in the county would have tried it.

BELLA: *(Lighting up)* Oh, my beautiful Celeste! She'd take anything. *(The* GUEST *kisses her hand and goes)*

DUNCAN: What made you do it? Promise, not ever again. Never. *(Another* GUEST *up to her, and the voice of* GIL *comes out)*

GIL: This is a handsome house. But every roof covers some fools. But a wise man can learn from fools. And a strong man can use foolishness. Remember that. And remember that I have plans for you. Don't you know that?

CASS: Yes, sir.

GIL: You are my brother. I will make you great. (DUNCAN, *with a hand on his wife's arm, has been speaking earnestly with her. But* SHE *suddenly jerks back*)

BELLA: Oh, Duncan, I'm all right. (*Catching sight of* GIL, *who has just finished with* CASS) Look, our guests! (*Approaching* GIL) Oh, Major Mastern, you do us a grave wrong. *(As* HE *bows and kisses her hand)* But we shall return good for evil. We'll take good care of your brother.

GIL: I humbly trust in your great kindness, Madame. *(Accompanied by* DUNCAN, GIL *marches in a military fashion to the little table where his hat, the beaver, lies, picks it up, wheels, puts it over his heart, bows stiffly)* I thank you for all courtesies. (DUNCAN *escorts* GIL *out. There is a sound of loitering laughter beyond, from other* GUESTS. BELLA *stands for a moment looking toward the sound of laughter, seemingly unaware of the presence of* CASS, *a melancholy shrouding her face. With a start* SHE *turns to* CASS)

BELLA: How stupid of me! Letting you stand there.

CASS: That's all right.

BELLA: *(Going to the big couch, seating herself there)* Be seated, I pray you.

CASS: *(Seeming not to hear her, looking out the door where* GIL *has gone, suddenly coming to)* Oh, I'm sorry—I was just— (HE *stops*)

BELLA: Thinking? (SHE *pats the couch for him to sit down, an imperious, graceful little gesture*) What were you thinking, Mr. Mastern? *(As* HE *looks at her, hesitates and then sits, but far away from her)* I don't want to pry, Mr. Mastern. I truly don't. *(Suddenly laughing)* Oh, but I truly do want to. Forgive me.

CASS: You aren't prying.

BELLA: Oh, but I am! What was it you were thinking about?

CASS: About something long back.

BELLA: Back in Mississippi? On the plantation? Or Natchez at a ball?

CASS: No. No. In Georgia.

BELLA: Georgia?

CASS: Yes, when Gilbert left.

BELLA: When he left?

CASS: Yes, long back. Back in Georgia. He was big, about grown. He just didn't come in one night from the field. You couldn't blame him. There wasn't anything for him there. Just the shack, and—

BELLA: Shack?

CASS: Yes, we lived there, in the piney woods, and the land all ruined, anyway. He was gone, and I—I was just a sprig and—

BELLA: A sprig?

CASS: Yes, a sprig—a young one, a boy, a— *(Stopping, embarrassed, as* SHE *finishes for him)*

BELLA: —sprig. *(Stopping meditatively)*

CASS: About four or five years old. And I thought I couldn't stand it, having my big brother gone. So I ran to the woods. I just stood there in the pine trees, in the dark. I cried, I reckon. *(Turning apologetic, as* HE *chokes from the memory)* You know how it is. I was young then.

BELLA: Then?

CASS: Then my father died. It was hard for a widow to make out, I was so little. It was long after when the letter came from Gilbert. He'd been to war, in Mexico. He was brave, and they made him a major. But he was rich already—I mean he had made his way. He was already a friend of Mr. Davis. He had been—

BELLA: The letter? What about the letter?

CASS: Oh, yes, long afterwards he wrote the letter to my mother. I could read it to her.

BELLA: Weren't her eyes good?

CASS: Yes, her eyes were good. But my mother—she, she never learned to read. Not there, in the piney woods.

BELLA: *(After a long pause)* How did you learn?

CASS: A preacher. A Presbyterian preacher. The letter came, and I was so proud to read it to her. And he sent five hundred dollars. He said he would come see her sometime. She cried for joy.

BELLA: And he came?

CASS: Yes. But—

BELLA: But what?

CASS: It wasn't in time.

BELLA: In time for what?

CASS: For her. She was dead.

BELLA: Dead. Too late.

CASS: Yes. But he put up a tombstone. Then he took me away. He didn't even shut the door. He looked back at the shack—it wasn't better than a shack—and said, "Let it rot down!"

BELLA: Oh, she never saw him. He came too late. And to leave her there in the woods. In the piney woods. And that door open and the wind blowing. Blowing into her house. And the rain— *(Pausing)* Oh, it's too pitiful. Isn't it pitiful? *(Leaning toward him, demanding)*

CASS: Yes. Yes, ma'am. Now—even now I wake up in the night. I think of that door left open.

BELLA: It's terrible. Oh, I can't bear it, I really can't— *(Looking at him, with intent questioning)* You—how do you bear it?

CASS: Bear it?

BELLA: Yes, how can you?

CASS: *(Puzzled)* I—I don't know. I never thought. I reckon you just bear what you bear. Just do what you have to do. There wasn't anything else to do. But ride away. Ride away. And remember, I reckon.

BELLA: You—you— *(Studying him)* —you were just a boy. Just a boy. And— (SHE *suddenly stops, shivers as though at a cold gust. The room has grown darker, light fading over the garden at stage right.* SHE *rises abruptly*) How dark it is getting! It comes so quickly. The dark is like autumn, autumn comes so quick to surprise you, and in autumn the dark comes so quickly. Look how dark it is getting. *(As* SHE *stands there,* PHEBE *enters carrying a large seven-branched candelabra and sets it on the table at the end of the couch, stage right. As* SHE *is about to light the candles, her mistress interrupts, impulsively)* Give me the lucifer! (PHEBE *hands her the match;* BELLA *strikes it, and leans over the candles facing the end of the couch. As* SHE *deliberately lights the candles, one by one, her eyes are downcast.* PHEBE *has gone out.* CASS *is staring at* BELLA *with greater and greater intensity, drawn, as it were by her veiled, downcast eyes, which give him liberty by being averted from him. When the last candle is lighted* SHE *abruptly lifts her eyes to find him staring directly into her face, leaning unconsciously toward her. For a moment neither moves. The match burns down to her fingers, and* SHE *drops it, uttering a little soft cry.* SHE *steps back, making an obvious effort to disengage herself.* MARK, SHE *discovers, has been standing just within the arch.* SHE *turns to him, as though with relief*) Oh, Mark, Mr. Mastern here—he was telling me something—the most interesting thing.

MARK: *(Coming forward with courteous attention)* Yes, of course.

BELLA: He was telling me—how—how— (SHE *seems to have lost something.* CASS *rises abruptly from the couch, just as Duncan, rubbing his hands, and Abbott come back, smiling.* DUNCAN *stops as* CASS *begins to speak, not really to* MARK*— not really to anyone present*)

CASS: It was nothing. Nothing of any interest. Just something that happened a long time ago. When I lived in Georgia.

ABBOTT: Gosh, I thought it was Mississippi—on the plantation.

CASS: No, Georgia. It was Georgia. And a long time ago.

End Act I, Scene 1

ACT I

SCENE 2

SCENE: *Drawing room of the Trice house.*

TIME: *An evening in early December, 1859.*

AT RISE: BELLA *is seated on the couch, at her embroidery. To stage left, at a little table near the end of the couch,* ABBOTT *and* MARK *are seated with books and papers. At another table, at stage right,* DUNCAN *is dealing himself poker hands, or idly shuffling the cards. On the table stands a glass, from which* HE *takes an occasional sip.* CASS *sits in a chair a little forward of* DUNCAN *and more to stage right, reading.*

DUNCAN: Listen to that rain! *(As* BELLA *obediently lifts her head to listen)* If it would just let up, we could still go to town.

BELLA: Oh, Duncan, when Cousin Mark has come all this way on a night like this to help Abbott—help him stay in the university.

DUNCAN: He just failed an examination.

BELLA: You're an angel, Mark, you really are.

MARK: *(Giving the boy an affectionate chuck in the ribs)* This ox is in the ditch. *(Meanwhile* DUNCAN *has wandered around the back of the couch and is toying with his wife's hair, as* SHE *moves her head in a slight, slow, luxurious fashion.* CASS *is covertly watching over his book)*

DUNCAN: Mark, you all hurry, we might get up a little game right here.

BELLA: Oh, let them study!

DUNCAN: *(Again trying to fondle his wife's hair, as* SHE *draws from him, then coming around, picking up a book on the way to sit beside her)* We'll just study a little bit, ourselves, you and me. *(Clearing his throat, pedagogically, pretending to read)* History: In 1492 Columbus sailed the ocean blue. Mathematics: A straight line is the shortest distance between two points. Hum-m— *(Leaning at her, as though to kiss her)* Latin: *Amo,* I love; *amas,* you love; *amat,* he loves; *amamus,* we love— *(Laughing, straightening up)* Latin!—I like Latin best. *(Reaching over to take her hand)*

BELLA: But it's a dead language.

DUNCAN: But not for me, my dear. But not for me. (HE *bows to kiss her hand.* SHE *shows pleasure in the moment, then becomes aware of the gaze of* CASS, *and lowers her eyes, drawing her hand away. As* DUNCAN *looks up in surprise,* SHE *rises, goes to the window, pulls a curtain aside, and stares out to the dark and rain. Both* DUNCAN *and* CASS *are staring at her, then detect each other in the act and look aside*)

BELLA: We could go! All right—we could go.

DUNCAN: *(Rising)* That's my Bella!

BELLA: No! No, it's raining.

DUNCAN: Sure—but you just said—

BELLA: It's just the rain. It makes me nervous. Being locked up all day. Of course, we can't go now. *(She crosses to her husband, lays a hand on his arm)* I'm sorry, old Dunc. I'm sorry I'm so jumpy or something. *(As* SHE *goes back to the couch and picks up her embroidery,* CASS *is watching her.* DUNCAN *casts his gaze aimlessly about the room until it falls upon* CASS. HE *picks up the cards and steps toward* CASS, *shuffling them.* HE *deals out a hand)*

DUNCAN: Well! Look at that. Suppose you held this hand, Cass. And somebody raised. Look there, boy. Many a fellow has lost a plantation and a passel of black folks because he—

ABBOTT: (*Looking up from his book to* MARK) I honestly don't see the point of studying this stuff.

MARK: Moral philosophy? Ah, the nature of the Good!

ABBOTT: Heck, everybody already understands what good is. (*Catching* MARK's *smile, and turning to* DUNCAN) Don't they, Duncan?

DUNCAN: Sure—good is what if you don't do they put you in jail.

MARK: Or don't invite you to dinner.

BELLA: Don't be absurd, Cousin Mark. Almost everybody invites you. Even now, with all this war talk. And everybody would love to, if—Oh, you know what I mean!

MARK: That the good is what people happen to agree with. *(Picking up a book from the table, balancing it on fingertips)* The Athenians didn't happen to agree with Socrates, so they gave him the hemlock.

BELLA: We aren't talking about Socrates. We're talking about you.

MARK: *(Laughing) Touché,* dearest Bella! We professors just play at being Socrates. Then we go out of the classroom and get invited to dinner—roast beef and chicken and pudding and claret and port. And never a drop of hemlock. But who can be Socrates without a little ration of hemlock? But Socrates— *(Picking up the book and turning again to* ABBOTT*)* —and the examination for the young philosopher who knows what the good is. Yes, sir— what is Socrates' idea of virtue? *(As* BELLA *goes back to her embroidery and* DUNCAN *wanders)*

ABBOTT: I reckon that's what I missed.

MARK: Cass, do you know what Socrates said?

CASS: Didn't he say that virtue is knowledge?

MARK: Yes.

CASS: But nobody can teach you. You—you have to remember it from the time before you were born. When you were not of this world.

BELLA: *(Catching the phrase, lifting her head, speaking as to herself)* When—when you were not—of this world—

CASS: (*Still to* MARK) And unless you remember—unless the gods inspire you to remember—then all you have is just opinion, the opinion of people.

BELLA: Oh, I'm sick of people!

DUNCAN: What, Bella! What? *(Coming to her, laying his hands on her shoulders)*BELLA: *(Withdrawing, picking up her embroidery)* Oh, nothing—nothing. *(Baffled,* DUNCAN *moves away.* MARK *has turned to* ABBOTT, *explaining, "Now what Socrates meant is. . . ."* DUNCAN *now stares out at the rain.* CASS *is still standing at one end of the couch, stealing a glance down at her as* SHE *leans at her work. Not looking up,* SHE *speaks)* You know—sometimes I feel like that.

CASS: Like what?

BELLA: Like Socrates said. As though I were remembering something. Something from long before. From another world— *(Lifting her head, but not turning toward him)* Yes, just for a second, it's like a promise, a wonderful promise, and it's going to come true. *(Swinging her face toward him)* Do you know what I mean? Do you? And just for a second you feel on the verge of something wonderful, something you've always sort of known but never seen—and now it's going to come true—and— *(There is a sudden noise in the hall, and* GUESTS *are admitted, four members of the first scene. One is flushed and slightly the worse for drink. They pay their respects to* Bella, *etc.* Duncan *is clearly delighted, and* Abbott *brightens at the reprieve from moral philosophy)*

First Guest: The rain is slacking up.

Second Guest: We're going to town. We'll have a little congress— *(Nodding at the cards on the table)*

Duncan: *(To* Bella, *somewhat apologetically)* They say the rain's slacking, and—

Bella: Oh, Duncan!

Duncan: (*To the* Guests) Well— *(With sudden inspiration)* Look here—we can just play here!

First Guest: Sure, Dunc. *(There is a general movement toward the room beyond the arch, but* Duncan *turns back)*

Duncan: Come on, Mark. I'll show you something Socrates didn't know.

Mark: *(Laughing)* Well, I don't guess I deserve to, then.

Bella: *(As* Abbott *leaps up)* Oh, Abbey-Boy, you are so wicked!

Duncan: Come on, Cass. *(As* Cass, *who has risen for the greetings, hesitates,* Duncan *slaps him on the shoulder)* Don't let me bully you, boy. Go back to your old book. (He *slaps* Cass *again on the shoulder, and leads the* Guests *away. Beyond the arch they can be seen at their game, playing in pantomime, and drinking wine.* Cass *has resumed his studying.* Bella *is at her embroidery. There is an occasional burst of rain at the window.* Mark *sits musing)*

Bella: I'm truly ashamed. After you came all this way just to help Abbott.

Mark: Now I can sit here and watch a lady embroider and pretend I'm not an old bachelor.

Bella: What makes you think you are old?

Mark: *(Gaily)* Because I feel so wise.

Bella: If you got married you wouldn't feel so old.

Mark: Or so wise?

Bella: Why don't you get married, Cousin Mark?

Mark: Don't you know I am wed already?

Bella: She must be awfully unattractive. You never let anybody see her.

Mark: Poor lady, she would never make a great social success.

BELLA: What's the poor dear's name?

MARK: Truth, that's her name.

BELLA: Ho, no, pretending to be Socrates again!

MARK: No, just making a poor joke at my own expense. Listen, I'll tell you. You remember Jacob in the Bible, how he served seven years for the beautiful Rachel, and then found they had foisted off poor, homely Leah on him? I'm like Jacob. I worked seven years for Truth for wife, and then guess what I found on my pillow on the wedding morn? The face of poor Leah, the poor homely sister of Truth.

BELLA: And what's her name?

MARK: Some people call her Miss Pedantry. I call her Self-Conceit. Anyway, she has moles like a witch and a squint in one eye, and she never sits with her embroidery. And—

BELLA: And what?

MARK: And she is a very cold bed-fellow.

BELLA: Poor Cousin Mark! Why don't you get married?

MARK: I just never got around to it in time. Then, all at once, I seemed to have formed all my bad habits.

BELLA: But you haven't any bad habits.

MARK: The very worst! I'm cantankerous and cold-hearted and disputatious and my hair's getting thin, and worst of all, I'm always right!

BELLA: (*Turning suddenly toward* CASS) Do you hear what he says? Are you going to marry some old Miss Self-Conceit and be cold-hearted and cantankerous and have thin hair and be always right?

CASS: *(Startled)* Why, I—I don't know—

DUNCAN: *(Coming out)* Hey, Mark, come take a hand. We're getting some fancy ones. You ought to see! Let Old Cass keep the lady company.

MARK: *(Rising)* Poor Miss Pedantry won't like it, but— (HE *shrugs and follows* DUNCAN. CASS *reads. There is a gust of rain at the window, and* BELLA *looks up)*

BELLA: I hate the rain. (CASS *looks at her, but does not speak.* SHE *does not look at him*) I hate it when fall comes and the whole world drips and sags. *(Pause)* Don't you hate the rain? *(Pause)* You don't know how I hate it. I'd like to go far away, where it was just sunshine. And flowers. And you never knew what season it was, just day and night, and you slept and woke, and smelt the flowers in your sleep, the way I used to smell the climbing roses under my window when I was a little girl, and the mockers sang all night, for it was moonlight. *(Pause)* Why don't you hate the rain? *(When* CASS *still does not answer)* I said, why don't you hate the rain?

CASS: *(Still not looking at her)* I just remember it differently from you, I reckon.

BELLA: How do you remember it?

CASS: Oh, I don't know.

BELLA: You must remember something.

CASS: In the country when it rains, you can't work, and I would come in late and lie on the floor and listen to the rain. Yes, once, I remember—my mother—I must have been not big then—just barely big enough to go to the field—once my mother sat on the floor and sang to me, and the rain came down.

BELLA: *(After a silence)* You lay on the floor in that—that—

CASS: That shack. Yes.

BELLA: And you were little, lying there, and she sang to you? And the rain came down. *(Pause)* Did you want to curse it?

CASS: The rain?

BELLA: No, the shack. Did you want to curse the shack when you left? The way you said your brother did?

CASS: *(Rising from his chair)* No. No. I didn't want to curse it—for I— *(Groping)* No, for I had lived there, and my mother had lived there, and she had loved me. She had died there. No—no—but— *(Stopping)*

BELLA: But what?

CASS: Nothing. It's just—

BELLA: Just what?

CASS: It's just that everything is so—so different. (ABBOTT, *followed by a young man, comes out of the card room.* ABBOTT *stands behind his sister on the couch, leaning over her, hands on her shoulders, shaking her teasingly*)

ABBOTT: Don't say no, now! Come on, Bella-Girl, say yes.

BELLA: I know it's wickedness.

ABBOTT: Ho, ho, so it's wickedness! *(Coming around the couch, taking her hands, drawing her to her feet, humming, making her dance a few steps with him.* SHE *enters into the spirit of it, flushed and gay, then tries to jerk from him)*

BELLA: Oh, I know it's wickedness. Whenever you start being nice to your old sister, it's wickedness.

ABBOTT: *(Seizing her, twirling her)* Oh, no—it's just that Claude and I are going to town.

BELLA: *(Jerking free, in despair)* You'll go to that Frenchman's. You'll drink too much. You'll play more cards.

ABBOTT: I'll win a thousand dollars, I'll buy you a present. I'll win a million and I'll buy you a thousand presents, because— *(Seizing her again, embracing her, shaking her, tousling her hair, putting his mouth at her ear)* because you're my dear old Bella, my beautiful Bella, and you'll say yes, you'll say yes—say yes—

BELLA: *(Obviously surrendering to his entreaty, but trying to draw from him)* Oh, Abbey, you don't study, you don't do what I say, you—

MARK: *(Who has just come in a moment before, standing there watching the pair. Then seeing that* CASS *is staring at them with a deep, troubled, naked gaze,* MARK *goes to lay a hand on* ABBOTT'S *shoulder and draw him back, in a paternal gesture.)* I'll make him study tomorrow. I'll make his head a pudding of Plato. Won't we, Cass? *(As* HE *turns to* CASS, *the boy flushes, drops his gaze.* ABBOTT *swings toward him, too)*

ABBOTT: Come on, Cass. Let's have some fun. (*As* CASS *hesitates under all eyes, turning unconsciously toward* BELLA)

BELLA: Why don't you go ahead? And take care of my wicked baby brother.

ABBOTT: Ho! Ho! We'll take care of him!

CASS: *(Rising abruptly)* All right. All right. I'll come. (THEY *go out.* MARK *moves restlessly about*)

BELLA: I'm glad he went with him.

MARK: Why?

BELLA: I worry so about Abbott. And Cass is more serious—more grown-up. A good influence, maybe.

MARK: Don't you worry about Abbott being a bad influence on Cass?

BELLA: No—no—he's so—so stuffy. Sometimes. Tonight he got on my nerves. Talking about when he was a child. About that shack. In the pine woods.

MARK: The piney-woods.

BELLA: Well, whatever it was. *(Pause)* What's he like? What's he really like?

MARK: You mean Cass? *(Pause)* I don't know. Not really. *(Pause)* But I know what he will be like.

BELLA: Like what?

MARK: The world.

BELLA: Like the world?

MARK: Of course, dear Bella. For we are the world, and every one of us is trying to make him into our special image of the world. Duncan is trying to make him into another Duncan—a gay, honorable, sentimental gentleman. And Abbott is trying to make him into a charming young rakehell. And Brother Gilbert into a statesman to trumpet Brother Gilbert's glory. And me—

BELLA: And you?

MARK: Yes, me too. I'd make him into a censorious old curmudgeon who peers over his spectacles. And you—

BELLA: *(Soberly)* I think I'll just leave him alone.

MARK: Ah, Bella, that's the one thing nobody can ever do. Leave anybody else alone. *(Ignoring the remark,* SHE *bends over the embroidery for a moment, then speaks very quietly)*

BELLA: Why don't you go back to your game?

MARK: Don't you know Newton's Law? Apples fall and Mark Trice loses.

BELLA: Poor Cousin Mark!

MARK: No female sympathy, Madame. Being on the losing side—that's my proudest boast.

BELLA: Well, it's an awful silly boast. Why are you so proud of it?

MARK: *(Gaily)* Then I know I'm right!

BELLA: Duncan—is he losing?

MARK: Don't you know we are cousins? It's a taint in the blood. But he loses only at cards. In everything else he is on the winning side.

BELLA: You make it sound rather—nasty.

MARK: Not for Duncan, for he is the son of Fortune, so everything comes to him, good looks, dreamless sleep, superb horsemanship, respect of his peers, elegance on the dance floor, and even— *(Pause)*

BELLA: Even what?

MARK: Even you.

BELLA: *(Musing)* Even me.

MARK: Yes, you—and you are his prop and center.

BELLA: *(With a slight edge to her tone)* Don't be silly.

MARK: Oh, yes. If you should crook your little finger in a very special way, the sky would fall. *(During the previous exchange,* HE *has sat down on the couch near her. Now* HE *rises abruptly, and again paces about the room, for a moment seeming to forget her. Then* HE *wheels at her)* The sky is falling every day, anyway. No matter what we do.

BELLA: What?

MARK: Don't you hear it?

BELLA: I don't hear a thing.

MARK: Oh, yes you do. There's a constant resounding crash, like an upset china cabinet. But people have entered into a solemn conspiracy to call it by another name.

BELLA: What name?

MARK: Silence. They call it silence. They ignore it by calling it that name.

BELLA: You're doing tricks with words again.

MARK: Yes. I earn my bread and cheese by twisting words in front of bored and polite young men. But— *(Again turning away)* —a sizeable chunk of sky fell today, anyway.

BELLA: What are you talking about?

MARK: Do you know what day this is?

BELLA: Yes—it's Friday.

MARK: Yes—Friday, the second of December.

BELLA: What's so special about that?

MARK: Just that over in Virginia today they hanged that old man Brown.

BELLA: That murderer from Kansas?

MARK: Yes, that crazy old blood-thirsty murderer from Kansas. If you want to call him that. But the sad thing is that his craziness was dictated by the craziness of the world he lived in.

BELLA: The Abolitionists—yes, and—

MARK: They are just part of the world. Maybe not the craziest part. And a crazy man is dangerous only in a crazy society. Oh, the fool Virginians! *(Rising, pacing about)* Oh, we're all trapped.

BELLA: Trapped?

MARK: Oh, sure—and it's nobody's fault. Not even the fault of the Dutch, or whoever it was brought the first black men to Virginia. Or the fault of the New England skippers.

BELLA: Well, they're here—the black people, I mean—and all you can do is be kind to them.

MARK: Kind? *(Pausing)* Is kindness the same thing as justice? Do you think that is what they— *(Leaning at her with sudden urgency)* Listen, one wrong leads to another, and each wrong worse. And nobody knows how to stop. How to undo the past. How to untie the knot. *(Pausing, striking his right fist into the palm of his left hand)* There must be a way—some reasonable way—

BELLA: *(Tartly)* And what do you propose, Professor?

MARK: Yes, yes— *(Sinking into his chair)* —what do I propose? What does Professor Mark Trice propose? (*Abandoning his self-irony, and smiling at* BELLA) Yes, my dear, you are quite right. *(Suddenly rising again)* But by God, I know one thing. The Virginians are idiots! They are idiots to hang Brown, and their idiocy compounds the idiocy of history. The fools! They make a martyr, they admit their weakness, their bad conscience, their—

BELLA: Martyr!

MARK: Yes, and martyrs don't make themselves. They have to have the cooperation of a whole society. So Virginia made a great show today, marched him out with an army around him—one poor old crazy man—by himself— (MARK *stops, sits down wearily*)

BELLA: That's what Cass said—that first day here—how he was just one old man—alone, by himself.

MARK: Yes, that's the picture that stays after everything else is forgotten. Or lied about. (PHEBE *enters on some household task.* MARK *watches her until* SHE *goes out. Then turning to* BELLA) What happened about her husband?

BELLA: Oh, nothing. Rebecca Hartmann hasn't sold off anything or anybody. *(As* PHEBE *re-enters)* Has she, Phebe?

PHEBE: What's that, please ma'am?

BELLA: Miss Rebecca hasn't sold off anything?

PHEBE: No, ma'am.

BELLA: And Jason—he was home just yesterday, wasn't he? Like usual?

PHEBE: Yes, ma'am.

BELLA: He didn't say anything, did he? Have any news?

PHEBE: No, ma'am.

BELLA: Well, Phebe dear, you be sure to tell me. We don't want to let anything slip, do we?

PHEBE: No, ma'am. (SHE *slips out*)

BELLA: Not a word of truth in it. They just got excited about nothing. You know how colored folks are, they love excitement.

MARK: *(After a long pause)* Will you do it?

BELLA: Buy Jason? Yes, of course. I've been meaning to speak to Rebecca Hartmann, just in case. *(Pause)* Why, you don't think I'd break a promise?

MARK: No—no, you wouldn't.

BELLA: Especially to Phebe. Why, she was a wedding present from my grandmother. She's been with me twelve years. I was just a girl, and Phebe's my age—why, we grew up together. Like sisters.

MARK: If you do buy Jason, what will you do with your present coachman?

BELLA: Oh, with Jim? We don't need two. Sell him, I guess.

MARK: Yes, that's logical. (HE *rises and wanders about*) Bella, I'm tired. If you will excuse me, my dear. *(As* MARK *turns to go, the other men emerge from the card game. There is chaffing and good humor, with goodbyes.* DUNCAN *unsteadily sees his* GUESTS *to the door, then turns back into the room)*

DUNCAN: You never saw such a hand—gad, it was great!

BELLA: Was it yours?

DUNCAN: No—why, no—it was Sam Weatherall's. *(Pouring himself a drink)* Now, Jim Talbutt, he opened for a little something, and— *(Apparently noticing his wife for the first time)* —what was I saying? (HE *comes and leans over her, kissing her hair*) Oh, yes, Jim Talbutt—he opened—

BELLA: And you, poor old tipsy Dunc, you are going to close. (DUNCAN *comes around the couch, avoiding* MARK's *proffered assistance, and reaches out to seize* BELLA's *hand*)

DUNCAN: Dear—dear old Bella— (HE *gets the hand, tries to kiss it, misses, slips to the couch, and then to sit on the floor.* HE *looks up, pleasantly apologetic*) You know—I must have aimed for the wrong hand! (HE *laughs as* MARK *helps him up*)

BELLA: Oh, Duncan, I don't like it when you're tipsy.

DUNCAN: But I like you when I'm tipsy, I like you every way, and— *(Reaching for her hand again)*

BELLA: (*With suppressed anger, and despair, to* MARK) Get him upstairs, please. Oh, please.

DUNCAN: *(As* MARK *is helping him out)* Come on—come on—Bella— *(After* THEY *have gone,* SHE *drops her embroidery, goes to the window and looks out into the dark)*

MARK: *(Re-entering, with forced naturalness)* Well, Jim was up there. He's taking charge of the old vagabond.

BELLA: Duncan—why does he have to do it?

MARK: He's gay, and high-spirited. And it's not—not too often. (SHE *has moved toward him, disconsolately. All at once,* SHE *buries her head in his chest.* HE *comforts her, very carefully and correctly till* SHE *lifts her face)*

BELLA: Listen—life ought to mean something—oughtn't it? Oughtn't it?

MARK: *(Very quietly)* Yes, my dear. It ought. *(Studying her, then stepping back)* You must go up now. You are tired. You are over-tired, my dear. *(Without answering,* SHE *turns and goes out, as* HE *watches her.* HE *notices the embroidery on the couch, picks it up, studies it, then drops it back and goes out. The stage is vacant for a time, the house silent. Then* PHEBE *enters and begins to straighten things.* SHE *begins putting out the lights, leaving only the candles in the seven-branched candelabra.* ABBOTT *and* CASS *enter.* ABBOTT *staggering a little,* CASS *with clothes slightly disarrayed, flushed with drink but steady)*

ABBOTT: *(Slapping* CASS *on the shoulder)* Good old Cass—yeah, I taught you to hold it—yeah, I taught you all you know—but gratitude—has good old Cass any gratitude—no, he goes and takes Molly—little old juicy Molly—takes her away from Abbey-Boy—and is that gratitude— *(Snickers)* It is not gratitude—

and little Molly—she likes it fresh—little Molly, she likes a change, she— *(Spying* PHEBE, *who, with the candle snuffer in hand stands quietly by the table at stage right)* Pretty little Phebe—

PHEBE: *(Very much on the dignity of a well-trained servant)* Good evenin', Master Abbott. (SHE *steps behind the table as* HE *sways at her*)

CASS: (*Quietly, taking a step after* ABBOTT) Hey—hey, Abbott. *(As* ABBOTT *goes toward* PHEBE, *arms out,* CASS *lays a hand on his shoulder)* Listen, Abbott—

ABBOTT: Lemme go! (HE *lays hands on* PHEBE, *who shrinks away*)

CASS: *(Hand more firmly at* ABBOTT'S *shoulder, but his voice friendly)* Hey, old fellow—look here—

ABBOTT: Take your hands off! You think you're so big tonight. Because that slut Molly Jones—

CASS: Come on, Abbott, come on—

ABBOTT: Take your filthy hands off! Oh, because your brother's rich, and I'm not—but I'm Abbott Coldwater—do you hear? I'm still Abbott Coldwater—

CASS: *(Controlling himself with difficulty)* If you weren't drunk! (ABBOTT *jerks away and seizes* PHEBE, *just as* BELLA *appears in the doorway, very white in the face.* SHE *wears some kind of house robe, and her hair is loosely knotted up*)

BELLA: Abbott!

ABBOTT: *(Dropping* PHEBE) I was—was just—

BELLA: You are drunk. You are foul drunk in my house. (SHE *takes a couple of steps toward him, commanding*) Will you please go upstairs? (ABBOTT *obeys, and* CASS, *with a mumbled goodnight, is about to follow*) Wait! *(As* CASS *pauses)* I am sorry you could not have been spared this. *(Seeing that* PHEBE *is waiting with the snuffer in hand,* SHE *turns to her)* I'll put out the candles. (SHE *takes the snuffer from* PHEBE, *then, as the girl goes out, turns back to* CASS) My brother is a wastrel. Did you know that my father was a wastrel? Oh, a great name, but a wastrel! And he died bankrupt. And now my brother bids fair to—

CASS: But he—he's just a boy.

BELLA: Just a wastrel and a fool to boot. He lives off my husband. But Duncan, he's a fool, too, to encourage him to be wild, to be fashionable, to game, to— *(Taking a step toward* CASS, *looking searchingly into his face)* What happened tonight?

CASS: Nothing. Just a wine party.

BELLA: Always just a wine party! And Abbott will always be there. Oh, he's a Coldwater through and through—that handsomeness, that selfishness that looks like something else, that charm that corrupts you. Oh, I know him—I know him because— *(Pause)* —because— *(Suddenly steeling herself to a discovery)* —because I knew my father. Oh, I see it now. I see it for the first time— *(Pause)* Yes, I'll say it. He was a wastrel. He was selfish. He was a bankrupt. Yes—and he wanted me to marry Duncan. Did you know that? (*Leaning at* CASS) He wanted me to. Oh, but he was subtle. He knew how to charm me. He could charm me always, and I— *(Stopping, beginning to work her hands together in a small gesture of desperation)* —oh, that was the only world I knew. The only people I knew— *(Staring at him, as in discovery)* But you—you were in the woods. You were in the piney woods. It was different. It was quiet. You stood in the woods and it was quiet. *(Taking a step toward him, speaking earnestly)* What was it like? What was it like to stand in the woods and be quiet?

CASS: *(Confused)* I—I don't know—I—

BELLA: Oh, I don't mean to embarrass you. It's just I'm upset. I'm worried about Abbott. *(Pause)* I'm worried about you, too.

CASS: Me?

BELLA: *(Retreating to the far side of the table, where the candelabra is, leaning across toward* CASS, *but not looking at him.* SHE *begins to snuff the candles, in a scene reminiscent of Act I, Scene 1, when* SHE *lights the candles.* HE *is staring at her.* SHE *snuffs one candle, and speaks without looking up, in a quiet objective tone)* You must be what you are and not like other people. Listen— *(Looking up, with the snuffer in her hand)* —you told me how you lived in that shack, when you were a—a what?

CASS: A sprig. I reckon I said a sprig.

BELLA: You lay on the floor, in the shack, and you didn't hate the rain. *(Pause)* Whatever it was, don't let them take it away from you. *(Pause, then earnestly)* Don't you see what I mean?

CASS: I'm afraid I don't, quite.

BELLA: *(Extinguishing another candle)* The world—the world is so— (SHE *looks up with the air of discovery, and resolution*) —false. (SHE *pauses, to understand her own words*) False! That is the word. You have no idea, for you haven't lived long enough. Time passes, and it is like a cloud coming over the sun, and the water doesn't sparkle any more and the grass looks gray, not green, and— (SHE *stops, suddenly, and braces herself, then looks attentively at a candle)* That wine party—tonight. *(Suddenly looking at him)* Listen, I'm a lady, and oh, yes, I know nothing of the world. But I heard what my brother said. That you—you and that woman— (SHE *stops short, stares at him, jerks her gaze away, and snuffs out all but one of the remaining candles. The snuffer is still in her hand when* SHE *steps forward from behind the table. But* SHE *does not approach him.* SHE *speaks in a low, demanding voice)* Was it the first—the first time? (HE *cannot answer, confused and embarrassed)* The first time—ever? *(A step closer to him)* Wasn't there a woods-slut in Georgia? Down there where you said everything was so pure and so fine? *(Closer)* Did she come in the shack? And lie on the floor when it rained? Is that why you don't hate the rain? *(Closer)* Oh, why can't you be honest with me?

DUNCAN: *(From above stairs)* Bella!

BELLA: *(At the side of* CASS *now, laying a hand on his arm)* Forget everything I've said.

DUNCAN: Bella! Bella! *(At the voice,* BELLA *lifts her head, and jerks her hand from* CASS's *arm. When the call is not repeated* SHE *turns back to him)*

BELLA: Forget everything I've said. It's just I'm nervous tonight. I want you to have only the best, and not the rotten waste of the world. I'm sorry I've made you unhappy.

DUNCAN: *(More querulous, weaker)* Bella!

BELLA: Forget what I said. For I—for I— *(As* CASS *suddenly looks down at her face)* —I would not—have—you unhappy. (CASS *is staring down at her, his arms stiff at his sides, but a little out from his body, as though* HE *is suppressing an impulse to embrace her*) I would sit in the rain, no matter how much I hate the rain, not to make you unhappy. I would sit in the rain, in the dark, and let it beat down on my head. I would let it beat my hair over my face in the dark, not to make you unhappy.

DUNCAN: *(Very faint)* Bella!

BELLA: *(Flinging her arms around* CASS's *body)* Oh, God. *(Pause)* God help us. (SHE *buries her face in his chest. As* HE *stares down at her, his arms lift slowly and rigidly as though to encircle her, but they do not touch her.* THEY *stand thus, in that abortive embrace)*

DUNCAN: *(Very faint and querulous)* Bella! *(The lights are dimming, as* CASS's *left hand, though his arm is not in contact with her body, has been placed at the small of her back. The other hand, with the same scrupulosity, closes on the hair knotted at the back of her head, as* HE *stares down at her now lifted face)*

Curtain
End Act I

ACT II

SCENE 1

SCENE: *As before.*

TIME: *Early morning in April, 1861.*

AT RISE: GILBERT, CASS, DUNCAN, ABBOTT, MARK, BELLA, *and* PHEBE *are in the drawing room.* GIL *is in travelling clothes, much disordered.* HE *sits in a chair, central and dominant in the scene, his beaver hat on a table beside him, a valise on the floor beside the chair, the others grouped around him.* PHEBE *is in the act of handing him a cup of coffee.* DUNCAN *stands by, the attentive host.* HE *and* ABBOTT *wear uniforms, pale gray, with red slashings and gold braid—the uniform of a local militia command.* MARK *is seated near* BELLA.

BELLA: But you must take some breakfast.

GIL: No, thank you, ma'am. Just your fine coffee. I got some food in Lexington, before I came out.

MARK: And Washington—what's the talk?

GIL: War—and a fool's war. If Lincoln tries to reinforce Sumter. But if it's war—*(Rising abruptly)* —we must win it. It never pays to lose one. *(Laughs)* I'm going back to Mississippi and raise a regiment. In case. And you— *(Turning to* CASS*)* —I'm making you a captain. You've brains enough to parade a company. Few have. *(Turning from* CASS *to touch* DUNCAN'S *fine uniform)* And you—I see you've had some pretty uniforms made.

DUNCAN: Oh, we're raising a little cavalry command. They wanted to make Cass a lieutenant. But that was after your letter about taking him back to Mississippi, so he couldn't accept. But our command—we're having a little muster this afternoon. Hence all this finery.

GIL: *(Stepping to a table where two sabers, in scabbards, lie, and two broad-brimmed gray hats, with plumes, and fingering one of the plumes)* Uniforms don't stay pretty long. *(During this speech* CASS *has slipped out, and idles in the garden house)*

DUNCAN: We just got the uniforms to give the ladies a treat. Yankees—they don't like to fight.

BELLA: I don't want to hear about war. I'll go cut my flowers. *(Slipping out)*

GIL: War is a trade. The Yankees are good at learning a trade.

ABBOTT: But, sir— *(The conversation fades out as* BELLA *enters the garden house.* SHE *drops the basket and shears and steps into her lover's arms)*

BELLA: Oh, Cass—Cass—you're going. (CASS, *not answering, is embracing her more ardently.* SHE *struggles to get away*) No—no—not here. They'll see us.

CASS: *(Grimly)* All right. That would settle something. The lying, the deceiving—at least that would be over and we—

BELLA: *(Pressing her hand over his mouth to stop him)* Don't say it! It's nobody's fault. It just happened. The way things happen. But oh—don't go away!

CASS: I would have gone long back, and taken you with me. Out West, anywhere. Anywhere to be out of this house. I tell you, it's the fact of this house—his house—me a guest in the house. *(Pausing)* But you wouldn't.

BELLA: You know why. I've told you. Abbott—he needs me. Mark—even Mark—he needs me. It was for them.

CASS: Yes. You told me. *(Turning away, sunk into himself)*

BELLA: *(Touching him on the arm)* But oh, I was wrong. I should have gone. But now— *(Seizing his arm)* —I'll go now! Now. Tonight!

CASS: Would you make me a coward?

BELLA: Do you want to wear a uniform, to cut a figure—like— (SHE *glances toward the house*) —like them? Is that it?

CASS: No, I don't want the war. Who does? But what can a man do? I must go with my people.

BELLA: Yes, go with your great brother!

CASS: *(Stiffly)* I would requite his care and affection.

BELLA: You go when he whistles.

CASS: If you will remember, I did not go back to Mississippi last Christmas, though he had insisted.

BELLA: It was very kind of you, Mr. Mastern, to give us the liberty of your time. To celebrate with us the birth of Our Lord—and to commit adultery with the wife of your host.

CASS: All right. I would things were different.

BELLA: *(Reaching to him, in desolation)* Oh, Cass, have you ever been alone? Alone in the wide world?

CASS: Yes.

BELLA: But you—you won't be. You'll be marching with men. But what about me? Day after day, in this house, with these people. And Mark—he looks at me. I think he suspects, but won't speak, just to torture me. Will you leave me here to be tortured? Don't you remember—we love each other.

CASS: *(Savagely)* Don't you think I remember?

BELLA: If you really remembered— *(Closer to him)* Remember how it was when you first kissed me? *(Leaning, almost whispering)* Listen—you leaned over me, and your hand—your left hand—oh, it was afraid but it knew it would do it. Your arm was afraid, your arm didn't touch me, but your hand. Like this— (SHE *places her left hand at the small of her back*)

CASS: Stop it!

BELLA: And your right hand—it took my hair. (SHE *lifts her own right hand to take the hair at the back of her head*)

CASS: *(Huskily)* Stop it! I said, stop it.

BELLA: *(Dropping her hands, but leaning at him)* And then there was nothing, nothing but us, you and me, and it was like falling, falling through fire and through roses. It was like that and I smelled the roses, and it was like dying, for my breath wouldn't come, and I couldn't bear it. (SHE *stops, shakes her head sadly*) What's happened to us now? (SHE *touches his arm, appealing to him timidly*) Haven't we the right just to be us?

CASS: *(Musing)* Us. (PHEBE'S *voice in the distance catches them, and* THEY *stand for an instant,* THEY *pull apart, as the voice is closer*)

PHEBE: *(Entering)* Miss Bella! Miss Bella! *(Seeing her mistress)* Oh, Miss Bella—you promised!

BELLA: What?

PHEBE: You promised to buy him—buy Jason for me.

BELLA: *(Irritated, but with patience, explaining to a child)* But you know perfectly well that Miss Hartmann decided not to go to South Carolina.

PHEBE: But she's gone, gone of a sudden, and they're selling today. Feller come down the road and said how they're selling the people, and never told 'em before, not Jason or anybody—and oh, Miss Bella, you promised! *(Voice rising hysterically)* You promised but you broke it—you broke your promise!

DUNCAN: *(Rushing into the garden house, followed by the* OTHERS, *alarmed)* What's all this? What's all this?

BELLA: *(Now holding* PHEBE *in her arms, trying to comfort her)* It's Phebe—her husband—Jason—

PHEBE: *(Jerking from the embrace)* You promised—you promised—but you didn't tell me the truth!

DUNCAN: Phebe! You're not to say that to your mistress!

PHEBE: *(Hysterically)* But she didn't—she didn't!

DUNCAN: Be quiet!

BELLA: Phebe—Phebe dear—I'll do something!

PHEBE: Too late—oh, it's too late!

BELLA: It can't be—somebody help me! (SHE *is casting wildly about her for help. With her left arm still about* PHEBE's *shoulder, with her right* SHE *reaches out instinctively toward* CASS) Cass! Oh, Cass! (DUNCAN *and the* OTHERS *are staring at her, even as* SHE *seizes* CASS's *arm*) Help me! (CASS *is aware of the eyes of the others.* HE *withdraws from her touch, and* SHE *looks up to find every gaze upon her*)

CASS: *(To her, in an artificially correct tone)* I'll be glad to do whatever I can. Whatever Duncan—whatever Duncan thinks best.

DUNCAN: *(With sudden brusqueness)* There's nothing *you* can do. (*To* ABBOTT) Go to town. Tell Colonel Stauffer I'm detained today. Then meet me at the Hartmann place. Please. *(As* ABBOTT *rushes off,* DUNCAN *steps to* PHEBE, *and speaks in a gentle voice)* Phebe, I'll do the best I can, the very best. (*As* HE *wheels to go, his wife steps to him and seems about to lift her face for a goodbye kiss. But* HE *is gone, and for an instant* SHE *holds that position, then slowly lifts her hand to touch the place on her cheek where a kiss might have been. Then* SHE *realizes that* CASS *and* MARK *are staring at her. Confused,* SHE *turns toward* PHEBE)

BELLA: Phebe— *(Moving toward her, some hint of flight from the eyes in her action)* Oh, poor, dear Phebe! (SHE *embraces the girl and kisses her. When* SHE *releases her, the girl with a long, puzzling, withdrawn look stares after her.* BELLA, *somehow disturbed by this, turns again to face the* MEN, *who still regard her*) Aren't you going to say something? Isn't there something to say?

CASS: *(After a long silence)* I still have some packing. If you will excuse me. *(Bowing,* HE *goes out.* MARK *continues to regard* BELLA. SHE *stoops to recover her basket and shears, dangles them for an instant, then squares herself and faces* MARK. *Without a sound* PHEBE *slips away)*

BELLA: All right. *(As* MARK *makes no reply)* All right. I forgot.

MARK: Poor, dear Bella.

BELLA: Does everything have to go wrong? Oh, I'd buy her a dozen Jasons. Does everything have to go wrong for me? *(Catching* MARK's *gaze upon her)* All right, all right, I let it slip, and I'm going to die I'm so sorry. For I love Phebe, I love her like a sister— *(Again aware of his gaze)* Stop looking at me that way. I didn't mean for anything to happen this way. It's just the way things happen. Oh, the world is so awful. I want to get out, out of it, it's so awful. Stop staring at me, you're always staring.

MARK: *(Sadly shaking his head)* My dear, my dear—I want only your happiness.

BELLA: Happiness! Happiness? What do people mean when they say it? (SHE *drops the basket and shears and rushes out, to the house, across the room, and up the stairs.* MARK *stares after her, then wearily picks up the basket, fingers the few flowers in it, and sets it down on a bench. As* HE *walks meditatively about,* HE *makes an idle snipping motion with the shears,* click, click. HE *goes out, first tossing the shears into the basket. The light changes, shifts, fades, very slowly, the day passing. It gets dusky enough for a* HOUSEBOY *to bring the candelabra into the room. Into the empty room,* DUNCAN *and* ABBOTT, *both very dust-stained and dishevelled, enter, returning from the Hartmann place.* ABBOTT *has entered first, a little ahead of* DUNCAN, *as though trying to elude him.* HE *moves quickly toward the table by the wall where the bottles, glasses, etc. are set out. At the table, pouring a drink,* HE *swings defensively toward* DUNCAN)

ABBOTT: I told you I don't know! Cass was with me at the time. I guess he was. It was months back. How should I know now? *(Holds out the glass)* Here, take a drink. What the hell does it all matter?

DUNCAN: *(Ignoring the offered glass, slapping his boot with a riding crop)* I don't know. I was just curious. I—I just wondered.

ABBOTT: *(With false heartiness)* Here, what you need is a drink!

DUNCAN: No—no, thanks.

ABBOTT: Why be so worried because you couldn't buy that nigger? If that's what's chewing on you. It'll cut Bella up, but she'll forget it. And Phebe—hell, she'll forget it. I'd help her forget it if I had the chance. Here, have a drink.

DUNCAN: No, thanks. *(Pause)* What time is he leaving?

ABBOTT: Who?

DUNCAN: You know. Cass.

ABBOTT: It's *Cass, Cass,* the whole damned day. That, or you're glum as a bear with a burr in his ass-hole.

DUNCAN: I'm sorry I've been difficult. But— *(Stopping)*

ABBOTT: *(Drinking, trying to be casual)* Difficult—my foot!

DUNCAN: *(Bursting out)* But a man's got to know!

ABBOTT: *(Taking a step to him)* Know what?

DUNCAN: You were there. You saw it.

ABBOTT: What the hell are you talking about?

DUNCAN: You were right there and saw her. She put her hand out. To him. To Cass. (ABBOTT *is tense, slightly threatening*) You saw it.

ABBOTT: What the hell are you trying to say?

DUNCAN: She put her hand out, and—

ABBOTT: *(Seizing* DUNCAN'S *coat, bunching it in his grasp)* If you mean—

DUNCAN: *(Looking dully down at the hand)* If I mean—

ABBOTT: She's my sister, do you hear? And I don't care who you are, or how rich you are, if you mean—if you—

DUNCAN: *(Staring down at the hand, softly and bemused)* What made you do that? What made you grab my coat like that? (ABBOTT *draws his hand back, guiltily, and steals a look at the hand, as though it had betrayed him*) What the deuce are we doing, Abbey-Boy? Moping at each other like two constipated owls. Gad, what a day! You know, you're right, Abbey-Boy— *(Slapping* ABBOTT *on the shoulder)* —

what I need is a drink! (ABBOTT *manages a grin, and* DUNCAN *turns to pour a drink, but at that instant* BELLA *enters, followed by* PHEBE)

BELLA: You should have called me. We were waiting. All day, waiting. (SHE *stops short, reading* DUNCAN'S *face*) What? You mean what?

DUNCAN: A man from Tennessee had just bought him. He refused to sell. He absolutely refused to sell. (BELLA *bursts into tears, and puts her face in her hands.* DUNCAN *instinctively starts toward her, then stops*) I did all possible.

BELLA: Oh, why didn't you hurry? I told you to hurry.

DUNCAN: I near wind-broke my horse.

BELLA: Oh, I'll die! *(Rushing to* PHEBE, *embracing her)* Poor, dear Phebe. And I promised you. Oh, I'll die! *(All the while* PHEBE *stands stock still, face somewhat averted from* BELLA, *who now and then punctuates her lament by a kiss on the girl's cheek.* BELLA *becomes aware of her stiffness, and the embrace and the comfort become something else, the necessity to make* PHEBE *respond.* SHE *begins to shake her, just a little, as one shakes a recalcitrant child)* Talk to me—talk to me, Phebe—you've got to talk to me—oh, dear Phebe! *(As the girl does not respond)* But I did my best. You know I did my best. You must talk to me. You must understand! (DUNCAN *has become aware that* PHEBE *is winning a victory over his wife. Now* HE *steps to* BELLA'S *side, and lays a hand on her shoulder*)

DUNCAN: Come, Bella. Phebe may want to be alone. Stop your crying. See how brave Phebe is. *(As her mistress releases her,* PHEBE *moves away, and is about to go, but* DUNCAN *spies her)* Wait! *(Moving to her)* Phebe, I want you to know that I'm sorry. For it was all my fault. Miss Bella, she told me a long time ago, but I was careless. I let things slip.

BELLA: That's not true!

DUNCAN: *(Lifting a hand to block her words)* It is my fault, not hers. And look, Phebe—look how sorry your mistress is. For she thinks a world of you, Phebe. She loves you. *(At his command* PHEBE *looks at her mistress, with an air of obedience. But as* DUNCAN *says that* BELLA *loves her, something seems to crack in the* GIRL. SHE *flings her hands over her face and cries out—for the first time)*

PHEBE: Oh! Oh! (SHE *turns and rushes from the room*)

DUNCAN: Phebe—Phebe— *(Rushing after her, in pursuit)* Listen—I'm to blame—do you hear—it's me—

BELLA: *(Trying to recall him)* Duncan! Duncan! (ABBOTT *has been watching the scene with intent interest, and now, as though* HE *had been biding his time, steps to his sister and seizes her by the wrist*)

ABBOTT: Listen—listen to me!

BELLA: He's lying—Duncan's lying. It's my fault.

ABBOTT: I said, listen to me.

BELLA: What makes him lie? Oh, it's awful—whatever he's doing.

ABBOTT: *(Shaking her)* Forget that buck coachman and listen here; it's about you—you.

BELLA: *(Suddenly frozen)* Me?

ABBOTT: What's going on in this house? *(As* SHE *stares at him)* Forget about that wench and listen to me. I'm your brother—I'm Abbott Coldwater—and I've got a right to know.

BELLA: Oh, Abbey—Abbey-Boy—be good to me. *(Touching him)* You were little and I loved you. Oh, be good to me now.

ABBOTT: But listen here—

BELLA: Hush—oh, hush, Abbey-Boy, for my sake. You were little and I loved you. Don't you remember? (HE *is baffled and distraught, but surrenders to her, anxious to be released from his suspicion.* HE *is standing there, under her touch, even as* DUNCAN *re-enters.* ABBOTT *starts back, almost guiltily—guiltily because, shall we say, the scene reminds him of his own suspicion. And it is clear that it reminds* DUNCAN *of his suspicions, too.* BELLA, *instinctively aware of this, forces herself to face* DUNCAN) What made you lie to her?

DUNCAN: Lie? No, it wasn't really a lie. You had mentioned the matter. Yes, you had.

BELLA: But you're taking the blame—oh, I don't know, but it's patronizing, it's cruel, you are trying to do something to me. I don't know what it is, but— (SHE *hesitates, fumbling into her mind, and feelings)* —oh, yes! When you take the blame, it's a way to accuse me! To blame me worse!

DUNCAN: *(Coming forward to take her hand, gravely)* My dear, I would not blame you.

BELLA: *(Withdrawing her hand)* All right, but it is my fault. I've admitted that. I just don't want any subtle business of blaming me on and on. I admit it's my fault.

DUNCAN: You have no fault in my eyes.

BELLA: *(Bitterly)* Well, you're very blind then.

DUNCAN: No, not blind. I see into your very inside, dear Bella, deep inside, and there is no fault there.

BELLA: Please hush—today has been terrible!

DUNCAN: I remember the first time I saw you. (HE *sits on the couch and looks up at her*)

BELLA: Well, that was a thousand years ago.

DUNCAN: It wasn't a thousand years. It was ten thousand years. It was before the world began, and it is right now. You were a little girl, twelve or thirteen, and your father had brought you out when he drove to see my family. Don't you remember?

BELLA: No.

DUNCAN: *(Reaching up to take her hand, which* HE *holds as* HE *looks up at her)* Your father got out of the carriage, and you stepped out on the carriage block, there was a locust tree beside it then, and you wore a dimity dress, with flowers on it for a pattern, and—

BELLA: I don't believe a word of it. (GIL *has appeared at the door, and stands quietly as* DUNCAN *proceeds*)

DUNCAN: And you wore little black shoes and you set your feet side by side on the gray stone and waited. The locust tree was blooming and the sun came through the leaves. I was a grown man, or thought I was, and knew everything. But I stood there and looked up at you on the carriage block and I didn't know anything. The sunlight was falling on your hair, through the locust, and I didn't know a thing. But your father was saying, "Dunc, this is my daughter Bella, and ain't she a pale little kitten, She won't eat her victuals," and you looked down at me, big-eyed, and said in the smallest voice, "How-do-you-do, Mr. Duncan?" Don't you remember?

BELLA: No, and you don't either.

DUNCAN: No?

BELLA: It's something you dreamed.

DUNCAN: No, it is the only real thing in the world. Everything else has been dreamed.

BELLA: It's not like you—this silliness. (SHE *draws from him, as* CASS *appears behind* GIL *at the door*)

DUNCAN: *(Gaily, rising)* Well, I won't be silly anymore!

GIL: *(Entering)* With your kind permission.

DUNCAN: Come in, come in! (*Seeing* CASS) Come in, boy. Come in and have a drink! (HE *goes to the table, prepares drinks, gives one to* GIL, *then turns with another for* CASS) Well, boy, I reckon this will be our last together for a spell, with you heading off to Mississippi.

CASS: Yes, sir.

DUNCAN: Well, you've given us some pleasant times, boy.

CASS: *(Stiffening)* I'm grateful—oh, sir—I— *(Stopping)*

DUNCAN: *(Waving his hand, gaily)* Nothing to compare to your deserts. Why, boy, you've made a mark here in Lexington. (*To* GIL) You'd be proud, Major. (*Back to* CASS) Yes, you've made a mark. Your professors say you're a master of your studies. And the girls—from what I hear half the fillies in town are looking round their fans at you. (*To* BELLA) Look at him. Hasn't Lexington done this boy good? *(Stepping to* CASS, *and patting his stock)* Why, boy, you even tie a stock right these days. And Greek, too! *(Laying a friendly hand on* CASS's *shoulder)* Forgive me, boy. Don't mind me having a little fun. *(Lifting his glass, just as* ABBOTT *appears)* Come in Abbott. Come in! I was just about to drink a goodbye to old Cass. *(With a quick assessing look, then an air of relief,* ABBOTT *enters)* We've had some good old times with Cass, haven't we, Abbott? Fill up a glass, we'll drink to Cass. *(As* ABBOTT *obeys and fills a glass)* To old Cass!

ABBOTT: *(Coming up and giving* CASS *a friendly punch on the chest, clearly relieved that things go this way)* Good old Cass! Here's to old Cass!

DUNCAN: Here's to you, Cass—to Captain Cass Mastern! (HE *drains his glass, and sets it down*) Lord, I've got to get out of this rig. *(Plucking at the uniform)* Get cleaned up for dinner. Come on, Abbott. You're as grimy as a veteran. You, Cass, you cheer Bella up about this Jason business. She's absolutely not to blame. (*With a gay wave of the hand,* HE *is gone,* ABBOTT *following. On the stairs* HE *sings a snatch. All the while* GIL *has been shrewdly watching him. Now* HE *pats his pocket, somewhat histrionically, as though hunting something, then turns to* CASS)

GIL: Say, Cass, will you kindly get my cigar case from my room? *(As soon as* CASS *is gone)* Mrs. Trice, that man is up to something.

BELLA: *(With cold detachment)* What man can you mean?

GIL: Mrs. Trice, we understand each other, you and I. At least, I understand you, and you will shortly understand me. Your fool husband is up to something.

BELLA: What outrageous—what presumptuous—

GIL: No fol-de-rol, Madame. He is catching on. When a man like him begins to talk the kind of talk I heard there at the door. Dimity and little feet and—

BELLA: So you listened. You eavesdropped, you—you—

GIL: *(With a wave of the hand)* Madame, Madame, I know a gentleman's tricks as well as the next fellow. But I use them and don't let them use me. And now that I'm sure of the facts, I'll tell you—

BELLA: You wretch!

GIL: *(Again with a wave of the hand)* That husband of yours is the kind of fellow that can't face facts, and one fact he can't face is that one woman is made just like another woman in that neck of the woods where it counts most, and so he has had to figure out something extra special for you. And another fact he can't face is that he ought to have broke you to saddle a long time back, but didn't know how, and so has let you get away with general mayhem and murder. And now that you have, as I strongly suspect, got away with murder, he can't face the fact, and so he is working himself up to some grand, high-falutin' gentlemanly nonsense. He has got a spot in him so soft you could punch it out with one finger and he knows it, and that is why he is full of all this nonsense to dress up the rotten spot to seem so Goddamned grand, and a man with that rotten soft nonsense boiling in his guts is as dangerous as a spread-adder. *(During the speech* HE *has, now and then, moved toward her, as* SHE *retreats before him, making broken gestures of protest and outrage. Now* HE *shakes his finger under her nose)* But I warn you, I'll not have any nonsense, his or yours. I was a fool to leave that boy here, just to pick up a few tricks and airs and graces, but now I am taking him away to business, and if you try to make him stay, as I am mortally sure you are trying to do, I shall expose you. I have plans for that boy, and you'll not interfere. Do you hear?

BELLA: *(Struggling for dignity)* I'll summon your brother, and in your presence he shall hear your accusations, and he will denounce you—yes, for he is a gentleman. Even if you are not.

GIL: Call him. *(As* SHE *hesitates)* Call him.

BELLA: *(Moving to the hall)* Cass! Oh, Cass!

CASS: *(Entering)* What is it? (BELLA *does not answer*)

GIL: Mrs. Trice had something to say to you. But it seems to have escaped her mind. (*Bowing to* BELLA) If you will excuse me, Madame. (HE *goes out, and* CASS, *dumbfounded, turns to her*)

CASS: What does he mean?

BELLA: How do I know?

CASS: But you called me.

BELLA: Oh, Cass, Cass, can't you understand? To protect me—that's why.

CASS: To protect you?

BELLA: He suspects, I am sure. He would torture me with hints.

CASS: Torture you? Look here, Bella—

BELLA: Yes, he would. Just like Mark. Like Duncan—

CASS: Mark? Duncan? Duncan would torture you?

BELLA: Do you think he is a complete fool? Even he must have some sense, some feeling, some brains, some—

CASS: *(Lifting his hand in suffering protest)* Don't!

BELLA: But you had better be glad that he is not—intelligent.

CASS: I said—don't.

BELLA: But he is not so stupid as to forget how it once was. How it was between him and me, long ago—before— (CASS *seems to be trying to make another protest but is caught*) Listen, you've had me in your arms, Mr. Mastern. Well, it was like that for him once. Till you came and ruined everything and I could not live in the world any more, and Duncan—poor Duncan—I could not bear him any more, and when he came upon me I averted my face.

CASS: *(Seizing her by the shoulders)* Will you shut up!

BELLA: *(All at once very calm)* Wouldn't you know the difference, Mr. Mastern, if you took me in your arms and I averted my face? *(Whispering)* Wouldn't you know the difference then? *(Suddenly throwing her arms around his body, crying out)* Oh, Cass! *(In pain)* Oh, Cass, don't listen to me. Just put your arms around me, and love me. It's just that the world's gone wrong, the war, and poor Phebe, and Duncan, and oh, I feel so sorry for everybody, I could weep for Phebe, for I love her—and Cass, you are going away! *(His hand is on her hair, trying to comfort her)* Oh, Cass, couldn't we just lie in the dark, like after we've done it, and everything is at peace in the dark. That's all I want—to be quiet in the dark and you hold my hand. *(His arms have come down to embrace her. Her last words have been spoken against his chest. They are standing thus when there is a shot off stage. They stare at each other in dawning apprehension. Then, at a scream above, they break apart. It is* PHEBE'S *scream)*

PHEBE: *(Above)* Miss Bella! Oh, Miss Bella!

ABBOTT: *(Above)* Mark! Mark!

PHEBE: *(Rushing down the stair)* Miss Bella! *(Stopping at the entrance from the hall,* SHE *stares at* BELLA, *and a hard, cunning triumphant look replaces the distress on her face.* SHE *speaks softly now)* Miss Bella, it was just— (SHE *stops, slyly regarding her mistress*)

BELLA: What? Please, what?

PHEBE: Just Mr. Duncan—just sort of cleaning his pistols—you know, cleaning his pistols, I reckon—

BELLA: My God, can't you say it!

PHEBE: Yes, ma'am. I can say it. Just one went off. (BELLA *rushes for the hall, but* MARK *is there to prevent her.* SHE *struggles against him*)

BELLA: Let me go!

MARK: It's too late. It's too late, dear Bella. (SHE *sways for a moment, then slips from his grasp to the floor. Meanwhile,* ABBOTT *has entered, and* CASS. *As* SHE *falls, the two young men lean to assist her, and look at each other across her body.* MARK *is leaning above, solicitously. Behind them stands* PHEBE, *with a deep, avid air of triumph. As* SHE *stands there, the light fades as* GIL *appears, standing to one side, reserved and unperturbed*)

End Act II, Scene 1

ACT II

SCENE 2

SCENE: *As before.*

TIME: *Late at night, after the funeral of* DUNCAN TRICE.

AT RISE: *The drawing room is in shadow, but a little light spills down the stairway in the hall.* CASS *is seated on the couch, head bowed in his hands, not at first discernible.* BELLA *appears on the stairs, and makes her way slowly down.* SHE *stops at the bottom, with her hand indecisively on the newel post.* SHE *has, clearly, been preparing for bed. Her hair is down, having just been combed then loosely ribboned up.* SHE *is wearing a house gown.* SHE *is pale and distraught. At her slight noise* CASS *rises from the shadow of the couch, and* SHE *turns, startled.*

BELLA: *(Huskily)* I didn't know—I didn't know you were here. *(Pause)* I didn't know anybody was here.

CASS: I couldn't sleep.

BELLA: *(Entering hesitantly from the hall)* I couldn't sleep last night. *(Pause, then coming a step closer)* All night, and I lay in the dark and I thought how he—how Duncan, his body I mean—was lying in another room. *(Pause, then closer)* You know, I never could sleep in a strange bed, not even when I was a little girl, and tired out from play, and last night I was in the east room. I was there because I couldn't go to—the old room. I couldn't go to bed in the bed where he—Duncan—and I used to lie. But I couldn't go to sleep in the east room, either. For the bed was strange to me. And I thought—you know what I thought?

CASS: No.

BELLA: It is awful, but I thought it. I thought, "When he is buried, when he is in the ground and not in the house, then I can go back to my own bed. Then I can sleep." *(Pause)* But now—

CASS: He is in the ground.

BELLA: But now Phebe is making up the room—the bed where we always slept. But I can't watch it. I just had to get out. It didn't matter where I went. Oh, I can't—I can't stay in that room. *(Appealing)* Why are things the way they are?

CASS: I wish they were otherwise.

BELLA: I can't bear it.

CASS: What is there to be done, but bear it?

BELLA: Cass, if only—

CASS: *(With a kind of self-directed harshness)* Only what?

BELLA: If only you loved me.

CASS: *(Approaching)* You know I love you.

BELLA: What I know is that you are leaving me.

CASS: There's the war.

BELLA: If you loved me, you'd save me. You'd take me away. Oh, Cass— *(Touching him, in appeal)* —Oh, I can't stay here. In that room. In this house. You know I can't. For I shall die, trapped in this house. Yes, trapped—that's the word. I was trapped here from the start. It wasn't my fault. Take me away, Cass. Then I'd be free. I have never been free—

CASS: There is nothing I want more than your happiness.

BELLA: But— *(with a hint of mimicry)* —there's the war.

CASS: I have a responsibility.

BELLA: Don't you have one to me?

CASS: Yes. Yes, but—

BELLA: You didn't make the war. You didn't make the world. We didn't make things the way they are. It's not our fault that things are so false—and people get lost, and—

CASS: *(Apparently not listening)* Duncan Trice is dead.

BELLA: But it wasn't us. It was—

CASS: Yes. Tell me what it was.

BELLA: It was an accident. Phebe said so. Everybody says so.

CASS: Everybody says so.

BELLA: Yes, and we can go away—just go away and be free. Listen, we can go out West—people go out West—and nothing will ever have happened. Think, Cass— *(Very close to him, and* HE *seems, as in the first encounter, at the end of Act I, to be struggling against his desire to embrace her)* —it would be like starting over, like waking up without any bad dream to remember—for that's all it was, just a bad dream—and I'll wake up— *(Entering his embrace)* —I'll wake up in your arms in the morning, and smile up into your dear face, my dearest, for it will be morning. It will be bright morning. *(Reaching up to take his face between her hands)* And wouldn't you like for it to be morning, and dew everywhere and sun, and everything fresh and bright? Wouldn't you? Wouldn't you?

CASS: Yes. *(As* CASS *buries his face in her hair, there is a slight sound from the stair, and* HE *and* BELLA *jerk apart, as* PHEBE *appears from above)*

PHEBE: *(Slowly scrutinizing them)* Excuse me. *(Pause)* Oh, excuse me, Miss Bella.

BELLA: *(Collecting herself)* What is it?

PHEBE: It's ready. It's all ready. *(Pause)* The bed, I mean, and everything.

BELLA: Thank you.

PHEBE: Do you want me to wait, ma'am?

BELLA: No. No. *(Uncertain)* Yes, I mean, I'm coming. *(Pause)* Get me a glass of milk. A glass of milk, please. Warm it. Warm it please. You see, it will help me sleep.

PHEBE: Yes, ma'am, it'll help you sleep. *(But remaining)*

BELLA: That's all. Thank you.

PHEBE: Just I forgot something. I nigh forgot. *(Watching* BELLA'*s face)* Just something. I was fixing the bed, and I moved the bolster. It was on his side—Mr. Duncan's side, I mean. There 'twas.

BELLA: What? What?

PHEBE: The bed hadn't been touched since—you know, since—since what it was happened. Since he had his accident, Mr. Duncan. Well, I was lifting up the bolster, like you do fixing a bed for somebody, and I saw it.

BELLA: What? What?

PHEBE: Just laying there. He must have put it there. Don't know who else could. Must have put it there before—before what it was happened.

BELLA: What? Put what?

PHEBE: *(Reaching out her hand, slowly opening it under her mistress' gaze)* Just this. *(Softly)* Just his wedding ring. *(As* BELLA *still stares at it)* But no, maybe it wasn't him put it there. Not Mr. Duncan, like I said. Maybe he just happened to drop it on the floor, careless-like, and lost it, and come along Susie or Cissie cleaning up the floor and just found it and laid it under the bolster so he'd find it. Mr. Duncan would. I reckon it was Susie or Cissie who—

BELLA: *(In a harsh whisper)* Give it to me.

PHEBE: *(Putting it into the outstretched hand, then waiting as* BELLA *stares at it)* That glass of milk, Miss Bella—you want it real warm?

BELLA: *(Jerking her head up)* Milk? Milk?—No, I don't want any milk.

PHEBE: Yes, ma'am.

BELLA: I mean I won't need it. I'll get to sleep.

PHEBE: You find you don't get off to sleep, Miss Bella, I'll be glad to get you some. It is awful when folks can't get off to sleep. I'll bring it nice and warm, the way—

BELLA: Please go. Please. *(Pause)* But thank you. Thank you, Phebe. (*With a slow look* PHEBE *withdraws,* BELLA *watching her. When* SHE *is gone* BELLA *swings to* CASS) He never took it off. All his life.

CASS: Before.

BELLA: Before?

CASS: Before he—

BELLA: Don't say it! If you say it—

CASS: *(Pointing at the ring, with difficulty)* You know what that— *(Pause)* —means? (BELLA *turns to stare where* PHEBE *has disappeared, apparently not listening*) We know now. What it means.

BELLA: (*Jerking her gaze from the stairs, swinging desperately to* CASS) She will accuse me. She found the ring, under the bolster, she knows that Duncan put it there—I mean she thinks he put it there—she will think that he—

CASS: What do you think?

BELLA: Oh, I won't abide it! *(Putting her hand to her brow, in a gesture of distraction)* She will look at me. All my life she will be there. She will keep looking at me. That's what they do. They look at you out of the corner of their eyes, they—

CASS: They—they who?

BELLA: Who do you think? The servants, the black people, the Negroes. You know how they look at you. They turn their faces aside, but they are looking. They look from the shadow. From the corner of the hall. They come into the room and their feet are soft. And if you love them—oh, I loved Phebe, I loved her, but she will look at me, she'll spy, she'll— *(Pausing, struck by an idea)* Give me your hand. *(As* HE *uncertainly extends his right hand, confused)* No, your other hand. The left hand. *(As* HE *obeys,* SHE *slips the ring on one of his fingers, then clasps his hand to her bosom, and closes her eyes)* Now take me away. *(Opening her eyes, in an urgent whisper)* Now. Listen—now, tonight. *(Gripping his hand with both of hers, starting up)* We'll go. Now. Nobody will know. They will never know where. Oh, Cass, we can be free. Nothing will ever have happened. *(Pulling at him)* Now! *(Staring at him as* HE *slowly shakes his head)* But you promised. Just a minute ago. Before she—before Phebe—

CASS: That was then.

BELLA: I don't think you love me.

CASS: *(Not hearing, caught in the growing power of his thought)* I don't think we can ever escape.

BELLA: I don't think you ever loved me. (SHE *flings away*) Not ever. (SHE *flees out toward the garden house.* HE *stands for an instant, then follows*)

CASS: But listen— *(Coming up to her, taking her by the shoulders)* Listen—

BELLA: You never loved me. If you had loved me, you'd protect me. You'd accept your responsibility. *(Pausing)* Yes—your responsibility!

CASS: *(Caught, too, by the word)* Responsibility—

BELLA: Yes, but it's like you to dodge it.

CASS: Like me?

BELLA: Oh, yes—and you played so innocent. Yes, you were from Georgia, from the pine woods, the piney woods, and played so innocent, and you made me take the responsibility. Oh, yes, you trapped me.

CASS: What are you saying?

BELLA: You were in this house and you looked at me in secret. You peeped over your book, and I saw what was in your eyes. *(Approaching him)* Tell me the truth, didn't you lie in the dark, in your own room, in your bed, and think what I was doing, I in the dark, in another room? *(As* HE *retreats a step,* SHE *presses her advantage)* Day after day, and you looked at me. It was in your eyes. You were driving me to it. Oh, you'd play so innocent, for that's your game, and make me take the responsibility. And you trapped me. *(As* HE *retreats another step)* Didn't you stand in the hall, in the dark? *(Pause)* Didn't you stand in the dark and look at the closed door? *(Seizing his arm, whispering)* Didn't you?

CASS: *(Dry-lipped)* I—I stood in the dark.

BELLA: And looked at the door?

CASS: I looked at the door.

BELLA: *(With a relief, a gratification)* Ah. *(Collecting herself)* Well, then?

CASS: It's true. I stood in the hall, in the dark, and I thought I would die.

BELLA: Yes, and you made me do it. If I had not known you were in the dark, waiting. It wasn't my fault. It was in your eyes, and you— *(Stops, then with sudden discovery)* You know what I think?

CASS: What?

BELLA: She killed him.

CASS: What!

BELLA: For revenge. To be revenged on me because of that black coachman.

CASS: That's impossible!

BELLA: I don't mean she shot him. But don't you see how? She spied, she told him, she—

CASS: But no—that's crazy!

BELLA: You're crazy not to see it.

CASS: But don't you see? If Duncan knew, if he suspected, it was because— *(Pause)* Remember what you said? *(As SHE shakes her head)* Before. Before he shot himself. That he knew because you were cold to him, because you averted your face when he came upon you?

BELLA: But that is knowing and not knowing at the same time. But it's different when somebody tells you, when—

CASS: But she didn't tell him. You know she wouldn't, she's a servant, a slave—yes, a slave—and—

BELLA: All right, she didn't tell him. All right. But she did worse. She hinted—she asked questions—she made him remember things. Oh, yes—that way the black people know to be so innocent. And Duncan —he thought it was all his own finding out. Yes, that's the way it is when somebody makes you know what you already knew but were afraid to say to yourself. Yes, she—that girl—

CASS: But look here—

BELLA: Don't be a fool! Don't you see it? Say it!

CASS: It simply was not that way.

BELLA: It doesn't matter what way it was. I don't care what way. But she did it some way. And it wasn't all my fault. *(Demanding)* Say she did it. Say it! If—oh, if you love me.

CASS: *(Trying to touch her, but* SHE *suddenly jerks back at his word)* But—

BELLA: So you won't protect me. You'll let her accuse me. You—you yourself accuse me. You want all the fault to be mine.

CASS: That's not what I am saying.

BELLA: What you are saying is that you will not accept your responsibility. That you will not protect me. That you do not love me.

CASS: *(Again moving toward her)* But I do. For listen—if I do not love you, then what—what have I left?

BELLA: *(Coldly)* No. It was Duncan who loved me. *(Withdrawing)* He—he would have protected me. He would have protected me from her. From Phebe. From—*(Pausing, with a gesture of distraction)* Oh, I'll not abide it! (SHE *wheels and flees into the house.* CASS *takes a step after her, his right arm lifted in a summoning gesture, and for an instant* HE *stands thus, as* SHE *disappears.* HE *lets his arm sink, then* HE *reaches to touch the ring on his left hand.* HE *is fingering it, staring down at it, slowly drawing it from his finger, when there becomes visible, beyond him, the glow of a cigar. The voice of* GIL *comes from the darkness*)

GIL: It's just as well she has gone. *(Then, as* CASS *starts, entering)* Don't get excited. It's just me.

CASS: So you listened.

GIL: No, I was simply walking in the garden. I did not want to disturb your—your tryst.

CASS: Well, now you know.

GIL: I was pretty sure already. Only a fool like Duncan Trice would take so long to find out. And speaking of fools, weren't there enough sluts in Lexington? Or do you always demand perfumed sheets?

CASS: You don't understand—

GIL: *(Waving his cigar)* I understand you were taking a damned fool risk. In this house. Under his nose. It was a risk, and may I say that you had no right to take it. You're my brother—Gilbert Mastern's brother, do you understand—and after what I've put into making something of you! If that Trice had killed you, I would have felt like throwing the carrion to the dogs. If he had killed you, I—

CASS: I killed him.

GIL: Listen. There are just three kinds of men in these matters. The kind that kills you. The kind that kills himself. And the son-of-a-bitch who comes around and tries to borrow money off you. Now, in a little experience I once had in Vicksburg—but no matter. But Duncan Trice—you didn't kill him. He was the kind that always kills himself. You were lucky there.

CASS: Yes. Lucky.

GIL: Damned lucky. For one thing, Trice was nearly bankrupt. Couldn't you guess he was the kind that goes bankrupt? *(Flicking an ash from the cigar, with a quick laugh)* He might have tried to borrow money from you, and you're the kind who— *(Pause)* No—no—that wasn't his style. *(Pause)* Anyway, I hope you've learned a little judgment. It's time you learned judgment.

CASS: Yes. Judgment.

GIL: This woman, now. I hope you've learned some judgment there. So proud and correct, but she's the dangerous kind, crazy as a starved cat that smells fish. (*Wagging the cigar at* CASS) So cold and correct, but she's the kind that always makes difficulties. Oh, I don't deny she's a fine looking filly, but I don't like 'em when they can't keep things in perspective. Wants everything her own way, and never enough. Now what she needed was somebody to break her in early. Somebody who wouldn't flinch from using whip and spur. Well, that wasn't exactly Trice's line. Or yours, either, I imagine. *(Musing)* But it would have been pretty task. Such suppleness of thigh, such breasts—

CASS: (*In a burst of pain and outrage, taking a threatening step toward* GIL) In God's name, shut up!

GIL: *(In mild surprise)* Huh! *(Turning from* CASS *to move to stage right where* HE *pauses, not looking toward* CASS, *takes a puff of his cigar and then moves the cigar in a delicate arabesque in the air, speaking meditatively)* Yes—a very fine pair of breasts. *(With a gesture of businesslike dismissal, a flick of the cigar)* Oh, well— (*Turning toward* CASS) Anyway, you've learned something. It's time you learned judgment.

CASS: *(Turning away from* GIL, *caught in a grinding realization)* Judgment. Yes. *(Pausing)* I have learned what judgment is.

Curtain
End Act II

ACT III

SCENE: *As before.*

TIME: *Early afternoon of April 13, 1861, the day after the funeral of* DUNCAN TRICE.

AT RISE: BELLA, *in mourning, moves aimlessly about the room, touching an object here, an object there, stopping now and then to listen, once staring up for a long moment at her own portrait. From outside, very faint at first, comes the sound of the banjo.* SHE *listens, then dismisses it. Then the words become clearer.* OLD ALEC *is singing, as in the First Act, "Listen to the Mockingbird." For a moment,* BELLA *listens, then makes a gesture of displeasure, and steps to the bell-pull. Far back in the house is the sound of the bell.*

PHEBE: *(Entering)* Yes, ma'am?

BELLA: Did John take my message? Has he come back?

PHEBE: Yes, ma'am.

BELLA: Yes, ma'am what?

PHEBE: He's back.

BELLA: Did he deliver the message?

PHEBE: I don't know, ma'am.

BELLA: What do you mean, you don't know? Didn't he go with it?

PHEBE: Had a letter in his hand. That's all I know.

BELLA: Phebe, are you trying to vex me?

PHEBE: No, ma'am. It was just I didn't know. Nobody told me.

BELLA: Oh, don't vex me, Phebe! Oh, please.

PHEBE: *(Studying her)* No, ma'am. I feels sorry, Miss Bella. Sorry for you in my heart.

BELLA: You said John is back?

PHEBE: Yes, ma'am. He said he been to the Phoenix Hotel. He brought you a letter. *(Drawing an envelope from her pocket, with studied slowness)*

BELLA: Oh, you were trying to vex me!

PHEBE: No, ma'am. Just you kept asking things, and I couldn't get a chance to tell you.

BELLA: Well, give it to me now! *(Seizing the letter, reading with evident relief, then lifting her head as the banjo music and song are suddenly close)* Mr. Abbott hasn't come back yet, has he?

PHEBE: No, ma'am. Said he wouldn't be back till round four. After the muster, or what.

BELLA: (*With a movement of irritation, not to* PHEBE) After the Frenchman's.

PHEBE: *(With careful innocence, as though* SHE *had been addressed)* I wouldn't know, Miss Bella. He didn't say.

BELLA: *(With a quick look, trying to assess possible duplicity, then moving on to something more urgent)* Mr. Cass? He hasn't come back?

PHEBE: I heard him tell the Major he was going to be at Mr. Marks's house. To tell him goodbye.

BELLA: *(Stiffening)* Goodbye.

PHEBE: Major Mastern—he's down town too. *(For a moment,* BELLA *studies the letter, then* OLD ALEC, *now in the garden, plays again and sings, the same song)*

BELLA: That noise! Why doesn't he stop?

PHEBE: Just Old Alec. Playing for his coppers.

BELLA: Well, make him stop. Throw him something. Throw him a half dollar. There's a purse. (PHEBE *finds a purse on the table, takes a coin, goes to the window, and throws it out.* OLD ALEC *expertly catches it, doffs his hat, and looks up*)

OLD ALEC: Thank 'ee, thank 'ee! (HE *seizes the banjo and gives a burst of music, singing.* BELLA *presses her hand to her forehead*)

BELLA: I told you to stop him.

PHEBE: *(Out the window)* Don't play any more. My mistress doesn't want any more.

OLD ALEC: She gimme four bits for music! *(Another burst, louder)*

PHEBE: She's giving you four bits to be quiet. (*The Old Man stops, dejected, and squats there, but after a time* HE *begins again to strum, very softly.* BELLA *resumes her pacing about the room, under the watchful eyes of* PHEBE)

BELLA: I have an excruciating headache. Why doesn't he stop that banjo?

PHEBE: *(Looking out the window)* He's moving off now. Nigh out the gate.

BELLA: All I want is a little peace. And he plays that banjo.

PHEBE: Yes, ma'am. *(The doorbell rings)*

BELLA: Answer it. (PHEBE *goes out to return with* M. LARUE, *the slave dealer—the speculator.* HE *is a man of middle age, middle height and build, gray in the face.* HE *is wearing dark clothes, with a sober waistcoat and stock, and a beaver.* HE *carries a heavy, dark stick. His manner is detached, businesslike, almost indifferent, but with a touch of Latin formality.* HE *speaks with a French accent, not too extreme.* HE *makes a bow, over his cane.*)

LARUE: Madame Treece? *(As* SHE *nods)* Monsieur Larue, à votre service.

BELLA: *(Distantly)* How do you do?

LARUE: Vous avez envoyé une lettre?

BELLA: Oui.

LARUE: Bien. Sans doute il s'agissait de—des affaires? Je suis très discret. J'ai fait des commissions pour des personnes très bien placées. Je suis très bien connu, et— *(Pausing)* Perhaps Madame would prefer to speak the English?

BELLA: Yes. Perhaps. *(Glancing at* PHEBE, *who pretends to be occupied adjusting a vase)* Yes. Come. (SHE *moves toward the garden door, the Frenchman following.* SHE *looks back at* PHEBE) Wait here, Phebe. I—I may need you. If anybody comes—my brother, or anyone—say I am not to be disturbed. Under any circumstances. *(In the garden house* SHE *turns and scrutinizes the dealer)* You are a slave trader?

LARUE: I should not say so, Madame. Je suis—shall we say, Madame—a speculator. Very high class.

BELLA: I told the hotel to get a dealer leaving today or tomorrow. When do you leave Lexington?

LARUE: Today, Madame.

BELLA: You are not lying to me?

LARUE: *(Shrugging)* Ask the hotel.

BELLA: Will you buy a—a girl?

LARUE: Ca depend. I have not seen.

BELLA: Yes, you have seen her. *(Nodding toward the house)*

LARUE: But I did not notice well. She is— (HE *hesitates, with the hint of a leer*)

BELLA: *(Coldly)* She would be called well favored.

LARUE: Some people, they like to have the good appearance about them. But some—they— (HE *pauses, shrugging*)

BELLA: You may have her for eight hundred dollars.

LARUE: But I have not examined—I—

BELLA: You will.

LARUE: But I have much expense. And the war—they may make a war.

BELLA: I don't care what they do. I will not haggle with you. You know she is worth twice what I have said. It is merely that I do not want her. She—she bores me.

LARUE: But I have not examined—

BELLA: When you have examined her, you will take her at that price. Immediately, without discussion. Or leave. I have her papers ready.

LARUE: *(With a flicker of calculation)* Oui, Madame.

BELLA: And you will get her out of Lexington. Now. Out of the state.

LARUE: I am très discret, très circonspect.

BELLA: There is nothing to be discreet about. You will take her and leave. *(Pointing off stage as toward a gate in the garden wall)* By that gate yonder. You will simply do as I say. *(Pausing)* You can probably understand that I am not without influence.

LARUE: Oui, Madame.

BELLA: You may see her now. *(Calling)* Phebe! *(As the girl approaches)* Phebe, I have decided to—

PHEBE: *(Lifting her hands in protest)* No! Oh, no—Miss Bella!

BELLA: I have decided.

PHEBE: Oh, I knew it, I knew it— *(Her voice rising to a wailing chant)* Oh, I knowed it—I knowed it—I knowed it—

BELLA: You ought to have known it. After the way you've behaved. After all I've— (ABBOTT *enters from the house, wearing his militia uniform*)

ABBOTT: Hey—there you are! *(Spying the speculator, puzzled and assessing)* What's this?

LARUE: Monsieur Larue—a votre service—

ABBOTT: *(Turning contemptuously)* What's he doing here?

BELLA: He is a—

LARUE: A speculator, monsieur.

ABBOTT: What the deuce is he talking about?

BELLA: He has bought Phebe.

ABBOTT: Bought Phebe!

BELLA: *(Steeling herself, defiantly)* I have sold her.

ABBOTT: Are you crazy? I thought you were stuck on Phebe. You can't sell off a personal servant like that. What will people say?

BELLA: She's my property. I find her presence annoying. (*To the* DEALER) If you are ready?

LARUE: *(Stepping to the girl's side, feeling her upper arm, the back of her neck, slapping her on the buttocks with professional, cold, expertness, while the girl stands in frozen dignity submitting to the examination but somehow beyond it)* Open your mouth. (SHE *obeys*) Wider. (SHE *obeys and* HE *peers in, even putting a finger in to feel her teeth.* HE *turns to* BELLA) C'est satisfaisant, madame.

BELLA: *(Drawing a paper from her bosom)* Here is her paper. *(As* LARUE *inspects the paper, there is the far-off sound of the banjo.* LARUE *is now counting out the bills, laying them on the table, as* BELLA *stares away, trying to detach herself from the process)*

LARUE: *(Taking* PHEBE *by the arm, not violently, but in a firm businesslike grasp)* Vien—we go.

PHEBE: (*Standing firmly, ignoring* LARUE, *facing* BELLA) Miss Bella. Just one thing.

LARUE: *(Pulling more strongly)* Vien!

PHEBE: I just want to say one thing. After what I know now. I know something I just sort of forgot. Forgot in ten years. You know what it was, Miss Bella?

BELLA: (*Slowly giving her attention to* PHEBE) What? What are you saying?

PHEBE: I forgot something but I know it now. I know I'm a slave. I know you can sell me. (*Leaning at* BELLA) And you know what else I know? *(As* BELLA *seems to give ground under her gaze, and* LARUE *tugs)* You always were saying you loved me like a sister. Well, I'm not your sister. And I'm glad, oh, I'm glad!

LARUE: Vien! Mon Dieu— *(Twisting her arm)*

PHEBE: Oh!

BELLA: *(Starting forward with a gesture of protest)* Stop! You'll not do that to her—not here, not in this house—

LARUE: But she's mine—now—

ABBOTT: *(Who had also started forward)* Yours or not, you scum! You'll not touch one of our people, you— *(Threateningly, arm lifting and the* DEALER *with a last vicious twist shoves* PHEBE *to one side so that* SHE *falls on a chair, and begins to draw the blade from what now is discovered as a sword-cane)*

BELLA: He is armed!

ABBOTT: *(Seizing a stool as a weapon)* Armed or not, I'll— *(As* HE *advances upon* LARUE *and* LARUE *crouches with the blade,* PHEBE *cries out and suddenly rises)*

PHEBE: Oh! *(As* SHE *steps forward both men turn toward her, lowering their weapons)* Oh, I'll go. I'll be glad to get out of this house. Away from here! (SHE *retreats a step or two toward the garden gate.* LARUE, *replacing his blade in the cane, follows and touches her. At this* PHEBE *stops, jerks from his touch and turns back toward* ARABELLA) Yes, and I'm glad to be away from you. Yes, you, Miss Bella. For you lied. You lied about Jason. You lie about everything. But I know—oh, I know—I know everything, everything that's happened—and oh, I know what you're like down inside— *(With her hand now on the garden gate, ready to go,* LARUE *following closely)* —and nothing can stop me from knowing— (SHE *goes out followed by* LARUE, *and her voice is heard once more*) —no, not stop me from knowing— (BELLA *has stood with her hands lifted as though about to shut up her ears. Now, with no more sound,* SHE *slowly lowers them, and turns to find* ABBOTT *staring at her*)

ABBOTT: Well.

BELLA: She got on my nerves.

ABBOTT: She must have got on your nerves an awful lot.

BELLA: She got on my nerves.

ABBOTT: Only eight hundred dollars. I saw him count it. She'd be worth fifteen hundred in any market. Two thousand if you got a buyer.

BELLA: Yes—a buyer like you.

ABBOTT: I was drunk that night. You know that.

BELLA: How much money did you say was there?

ABBOTT: You know. You sold her.

BELLA: How much?

ABBOTT: Eight hundred dollars. Why?

BELLA: Maybe it's not what Phebe's worth, but it's still a lot of money. *(Studying his face)* Especially when you're always needing money. *(Suddenly* SHE *picks up the bills and tries to cram them into his hand)* Take it! Take it! And for God's sake stop talking! *(As* HE *hesitates, looking down at the money)* Since when were you so high and mighty about money? You always took it—from me—from Duncan— *(As* HE *pulls away, as from a guilty recollection, staring quickly into her face,* SHE *tries again to thrust the money into his hand. But* HE *turns and goes quickly into the house,* SHE *pursuing)* Wait— *(Overtaking him, thrusting it into his hand, wheedling)* Oh, I'm sorry, Abbey-Boy. Please take it—and forgive—forgive your Bella —take it, you need it— (ABBOTT *has taken the money and stands holding it as* CASS *comes in.* HE *meets the gaze of* CASS, *then looks down at the money)*

ABBOTT: Sure, I always need money. But— (HE *drops the money on the table by the end of the couch*) —maybe I don't need this money. (HE *hurries across the room and up the stairs.* CASS *is staring at the money, then at* BELLA)

BELLA: *(Moving to him)* Oh, Cass—Cass—I'm so glad you've come. Oh, I needed you, Cass.

CASS: *(Not responding to her)* What's happened?

BELLA: *(Closer)* Hush, darling—hush—

CASS: What's that money?

BELLA: Don't talk, darling. Don't talk—it's all over.

CASS: What's that money?

BELLA: Hush—it's all right now.

CASS: Phebe—where's Phebe?

BELLA: *(Laying her hands on him)* Oh, just don't talk. Just hold me and love me. *(As* HE *seems on the verge of drawing away from her)* Oh, I know you've got to go. But be gentle. Don't spoil our last minutes together. Just hold me.

CASS: *(Drawing from her)* Where is she?

BELLA: There's something I must tell you. *(Seizing him, drawing him)* You've got to understand, Cass—understand how I've suffered. You must sit down and be quiet. *(Drawing him to the couch)*

CASS: Where is she?

BELLA: I'll tell you. (SHE *drops to the floor by his knees, her arms across his knees, leaning her head against him*) But I have to tell it right. Try to understand. For you see, I loved Duncan. I mean I loved him as much as I could love anybody before I knew what love is. But you came—yes—and you were so awkward and strange and silent and dark-eyed, and you could stand so still while everybody else moved and talked and talked, and I had never seen anybody like you, and I felt sorry for you, and I made you talk to me, and you told me about the pine woods—the piney woods—and suddenly I saw you standing in the shadow of the pine trees, just a boy, just a sprig, you said, and your face was wet with tears, and all at once I knew I didn't have to feel sorry for you any more, for I was suddenly sorry for all those other people who were talking and laughing and not feeling anything, and sorry for myself and all, all the years gone by, for they looked empty and dry and used up all at once, and I—

CASS: *(Trying to rise)* Where is she?

BELLA: Be quiet, be quiet, and I'll tell you. You see, I was loving Duncan the best I knew and didn't want to hurt anybody, I wanted to be good and make people happy. *(As* HE *stirs, looking about the room)* Oh be quiet! For you see, then everything happened. Oh, why did it have to happen the way it happened? Why didn't I come riding through the pine woods on my mare Celeste, in Georgia, and nothing had ever happened, and I'd see you standing in the shadow of the pines, so awkward and beautiful and silent, and I'd ride up to you, and we'd go into your shack—oh, you don't mind if I call it a shack?—and we'd go in the dark, and nobody would ever accuse me, and—

CASS: *(Rising, letting her slip half to the floor)* God damn it, where's that girl? *(As* SHE *stares up at him)* You sold her! *(As* SHE *scrambles up, retreating under his gaze)* You sold her! *(Picking up the money, looking at it)* No wonder Abbott wouldn't take it. *(Looking again at the money)* Do you know what they'll do with her? In Louisiana?

BELLA: You're so careful of a yellow girl's honor, Mr. Mastern! *(Music of banjo approaching)* Why weren't you so careful of mine? *(For a moment* CASS *stares at her, hit by the accusation. His hand with the money sinks a little.* HE *studies the money)*

CASS: I have been careful of nothing. (BELLA *steps quickly to him, sensing weakness, and lifts the money from his fingers, goes to the window, and throws it all to* OLD ALEC, *who now is crouching there*)

OLD ALEC: *(As the notes flutter down around him, grabbing incredulously at them)* Law-God—Law-God! To 'Lijah—them ravins, they brung it to 'Lijah! *(His voice trails off, and* HE *seizes the banjo and strikes two or three wild glory-chords)*

BELLA: *(Elated, showing her empty hands)* Look! It's gone!

CASS: *(Shaking his head slowly)* No.

BELLA: I have thrown it away.

CASS: No. *(Looking down at his own hands, then at hers)* No, for it's here. *(As* SHE *steals a secret, involuntary look down at her own hands)* What we did, it is here. And you cannot throw it away.

BELLA: No!

CASS: All the things we did— *(Growing, inward awareness)* —They are all one thing, and we cannot throw it away—

BELLA: No—no, don't say it!

CASS: It's all one web, and we spun it. All the lies and deceiving. Jason sold away. Duncan dead. That girl gone to be whored in Louisiana. And that man— *(Gesture toward the window)* —that old man, that old free nigger praising God for that money you threw him. Yes—I see it now, and it's all one. —Oh, don't you see? *(Putting out his hand toward her)* Take my hand. *(As* SHE *looks at the hand, and tentatively lifts her own)* Take it, for if we have ever loved each other. If we have ever loved and not lain together in mere foulness, then we must take hands and say it. Take my hand, Bella. *(As* SHE *touches his hand)* If we can say the truth—take hands and say it—then we can be free—

BELLA: Oh, Cass! *(It is a cry of yearning)*

CASS: We can begin to be free. We can begin to unspin the web. We can begin. Listen— *(As* SHE *lifts her face expectantly toward him)* —I'll get her. I'll find her. I'll bring her back!

BELLA: What? What do you mean?

CASS: Phebe—

BELLA: *(Jerking from him)* Oh, no!

CASS: *(Still in his own excitement)* But she will forgive us—

BELLA: You'll not bring her here!

CASS: —what little she can forgive. Oh, don't you see? If we have said the truth. If we have asked her a little forgiveness—if we—

BELLA: *(Drawing herself up)* I will not be accused. I will not abide it. If you get her she will accuse me.

CASS: *(Pleading now)* But it's not accusation. Dearest, dearest, don't you see? If we are ever to be free—ever to break out of the web we are caught in— *(Stepping back, ready to go)* Oh, don't you see—I'll find her! I'll bring her! *(As HE is at the door)*

BELLA: Wait. *(As HE waits SHE moves toward him)* Do you know what I think? *(Pausing)* I think you love that yellow girl better than me.

CASS: Bella!

BELLA: Yes, I see it. All this time in my house, and you came to me with her spit on you.

CASS: *(In horror)* Can you say that? If you can say that—Oh, don't—for if you do, then what have we? What have we left in the world?

BELLA: If you open that door—

CASS: But you can't believe that.

BELLA: *(With a gesture of distraction)* Oh, it doesn't matter whether I believe it or not. It's just that I suffer so! *(Hardening, getting command of herself)* But if you open that door, Mr. Mastern—

CASS: *(Staring at her for a moment, speaking very gently)* My dear, I know you do not believe it. My dear, I know you could not believe it. (HE *takes a step toward her, his hands close to his body but slightly lifted as though about to come up to take her face between them. As HE leans toward her, SHE closes her eyes, her face going pure and serene with anticipated victory. Looking down at her face, but not touching her, HE fumbles in one of his pockets and draws out a small object in his left hand—the hand toward the audience. Still looking into that calm face, HE takes her left hand in his right, lifts it, and as HE leans to kiss her on the brow, HE presses the object into her hand. As SHE waits, her eyes yet closed, as though for another kiss, HE steps back quickly and soundlessly, and is gone. For an instant SHE stands, as before, then opens her eyes. SHE is frozen there, incredulous, then looks at the object HE had pressed into her hand, holding it up to stare at it. It is the ring. SHE retreats to the stairs, supporting herself against the post, then calls upward*)

BELLA: Abbott! Abbott! (SHE *lets herself sink to sit on the first stair, leaning her head against the post, eyes fixed straight ahead*)

ABBOTT: *(Descending hurriedly)* Yes? *(Seeing her, rushing down now)* Yes, yes?

BELLA: *(Not looking up at him)* He is gone. *(As* HE *leans above her)* He has gone to get her. *(Pause)* That girl.

ABBOTT: Phebe? You mean Phebe? *(Pause)* Well?—Yes, why not. You shouldn't have sold her. It's not—it's not done.

BELLA: She will accuse me.

ABBOTT: Accuse you?

BELLA: *(For the first time looking up at him, but speaking with weariness rather than heat)* Don't be a fool. You know. *(As realization begins to dawn on Abbott's face)* You have known it all a long time. But you wouldn't admit it. (SHE *drops her gaze and again stares out in front of her)*

ABBOTT: *(Almost whispering)* It's true? You—you— *(Looking at her face, withdrawing from her slightly)*

BELLA: *(Again not looking at him, bitterly)* I suppose you think it was my fault.

ABBOTT: And you are Bella. You are Bella Coldwater.

BELLA: Are you trying to be cruel? *(Rising, with an excess of emotion)* Oh, everybody's cruel! He's cruel—I wish I could tell you how cruel. Listen, he will bring her here. Cass will bring her and she will accuse me. *(Suddenly moving toward* ABBOTT, *demandingly)* Listen—she will say I killed Duncan. She will say he shot himself because he knew. Would you like that scandal? Haven't you any pride? *(Studying his disturbed face)* What are you thinking of? *(Pause, as for an answer)* Well, think what your father would have done. Do you know what he would have done? *(Pause)* Are you a coward?

ABBOTT: No—God damn it—but—

BELLA: Well, will you let that yellow slut tell her lies for revenge? Because I didn't buy that black husband of hers? Or do you take her side?

ABBOTT: Look here, Bella. Be reasonable—

BELLA: Reasonable? I suppose you are reasonably prepared to let that Cass Mastern do what he threatens. *(Pushing past him, as though* HE *were not there, entering the drawing room going to the middle, waiting carefully for him to follow, then turning suddenly on him)* I'll explain. Yes, very reasonably. You see, it wasn't my fault. It was an awful accident. And you—yes, you—you had a part in it. It was your fault, too. *(Watching him)* You had gone to the Frenchman's. You and he—that Cass Mastern. And you came back drunk. He pretended to be, but oh, no, he was sober and waiting. Waiting his chance. And you—you were drunk. And

Duncan was drunk. There was no one to help me, and he— *(Putting a hand to her brow as to shut out an image, then reaching out to* ABBOTT *for support with one hand, with the other indicating the couch)* And look— (ABBOTT *looks at the couch, then averts his eyes*) Yes, look! (SHE *suddenly goes hard and factual*) Do you know what he will do now? Can't you guess?

ABBOTT: No—no—

BELLA: He will boast how he did what he did to Mrs. Trice—Mrs. Duncan Trice—to Bella Coldwater. Yes, that's what we get for being civil to people like that. For being kind to them. For taking in a lout from the piney woods—and he hated us all because we were what we were, and now he will have his revenge, and you will let him, you will let him make a joke of your sister by every campfire in the army, and your name— *(Pausing)* Yes, your name is Coldwater? Are you the son of Montgomery Coldwater? Can you answer that?

ABBOTT: Yes.

BELLA: Well.

ABBOTT: Well—what?

BELLA: Stop him.

ABBOTT: Stop him?

BELLA: Challenge him. Find him and challenge him now. Before he brings that girl. And if he refuses—if he is no gentleman—if he is a coward

ABBOTT: *(Struggling with the idea, sinking into a chair)* Challenge him—

BELLA: *(Coming to him, touching him on the shoulder)* You thought he was your friend. But he wasn't your friend. You know what he did to your Bella. Listen— (SHE *leans as though to whisper to him, brushing his hair with a hand. Then, as* SHE *seems to sense a collapse in him,* SHE *takes his head tenderly, caressing it*) Poor Abbey-Boy. Life is so hard, Abbey-Boy. But I love you, Abbey-Boy. Remember—remember when you fell out of the apple tree? And you hurt yourself? It was Bella, your Bella, your big sister—she comforted you. And you— (SHE *leans more closely, her voice taking on a vibrant edge*) —would you let him do what he did to your Bella—

ABBOTT: *(Leaping up, from her touch)* God damn it! *(Staring at her)* What are you trying to do to me? *(Closer, in a near whisper)* Suppose he were dead. Suppose he lay there. *(Staring at a spot on the floor, pointing with his right forefinger, as with a pistol)* Suppose I— *(Staring at his forefinger, withdrawing it)* Suppose I had—

(Turning on her) Is that what you want? Is that what you really want? Look—*(Pointing again at the spot on the floor)*

BELLA: *(For an instant staring at the spot, then covering her eyes with a hand)* No!—No! *(Suddenly reaching out at him, imploring)* Oh, be nice to me, Abbey-Boy. It's just I want somebody to be gentle with me—to love me—not to accuse me—oh, Abbey-Boy—

ABBOTT: Don't call me that!

BELLA: *(Touching him again)* Oh, Abbey-Boy—my Abbey—

ABBOTT: Don't call me that! Not ever again! (HE *jerks from her, rushes from the room, and up the stairs.* SHE *follows, stops at foot of stairs, supporting herself on newel post*)

BELLA: Abbott! *(A couple of steps upward)* Abbott! *(There is the sound of a door above being slammed. For a moment* SHE *stands there, seemingly about to call again, then weakly makes her way upward. The stage is vacant for a time, with light waning as the sun seems to be westering at stage right.* GILBERT *enters from stage left, in a hurry and preoccupied.* HE *marches straight to the bell-pull, gives it a preemptory yank, removes his hat and sets it on a table. The* HOUSEBOY *enters)*

GIL: Mr. Cass—where is he?

BOY: Gone down town, suh.

GIL: God-a-mighty—doesn't he know the war's started?

BOY: I don't know, suh.

GIL: Doesn't anybody in this house know anything?

BOY: Yes, suh.

GIL: Yes sir, what?

BOY: I knows the war's started.

GIL: Well, it's good somebody knows. How did you know?

BOY: Told me in the kitchen.

GIL: *(Snorting)* In the kitchen! Yes, I wager they knew it in the kitchen before the telegraph office. You black folks know everything, don't you?

BOY: No, sir.

GIL: Go to my room and pack my valise. Go to my brother's room. Take one valise—no more, mind you—and pack it for him. You know a gentleman's essentials. Bring the valises down here, ready for us to leave. Have a gig hitched. Ready and waiting. Understand?

BOY: Yes, sir.

GIL: Have some food set out for me. Now. Have a packet of food for Mr. Cass when he comes. We won't wait for him to eat. Understand?

BOY: Yes, sir.

GIL: *(As the* BOY *turns away)* Do you think this war will set you free?

BOY: I don't know, sir.

GIL: God doesn't know either. Though a lot of fools think they know. One way or the other. *(Pause)* Do you want to be free?

BOY: No, sir—I wants to belong here.

GIL: Don't lie, boy.

BOY: I'm not lying, sir.

GIL: You don't know whether you are lying or not. You don't know what you want. *(Pause)* Damned few do. *(Reaching into a pocket)* Here. *(Holds out a gold piece)*

BOY: Thank you—thank you, sir.

GIL: Well, get on with it. It's getting late.

BOY: *(Looking at window where light is failing over the garden)* Sun gettin' on down. Slopin' down.

GIL: Get on with it, I said. *(The* BOY *goes out.* GIL *steps to the center of the room, facing the audience, deliberately extracts a cigar from his case, prepares it, lights it, lifts his head in slow arrogance for the first draw, expels the smoke with indolent relish—the air of a strong active man who knows how to relax. Then* HE *looks about the room with his cold assessing glance, much as at his first appearance.* HE *strolls about, even touching an object here and there, picking up the piece of Sevres, as before.* HE *stops and regards the portrait. Still looking at the portrait,* HE *reaches out and takes one of the sprays of apple blossom from the great vase. Toying with it, gently tapping his leg as with a riding crop,* HE *continues to stare up at the portrait. The boy comes to the door.)*

BOY: It's laid out for you, sir. The something to eat.

GIL: Oh—yes, thank you. *(The* BOY *stands aside for* GIL *to pass, then glances at the western windows, then follows. The room remains empty for a time, the light sink-*

ing. MARK *enters from stage left, hat in hand.* HE *deposits hat, takes quick glance into the empty room, goes to stairs, calling)*

MARK: Bella! Bella! *(After a moment,* BELLA *appears on stairs, coming slowly down, pale, somnambulistic.* HE *goes to take her hand and lead her down)* Poor Bella. Poor, dear Bella. (HE *draws her from hall into the room*)

BELLA: *(In a small, distant voice)* He has gone.

MARK: Yes. He came to my rooms. For an instant. To tell me goodbye. And to tell me—

BELLA: Yes. Yes. So you know.

MARK: About Phebe. *(Pausing)* That Louisiana dealer—he had already left town with her. It was not certain by what road. South. Or to Louisville, for a steamboat. Cass was trying to find what road to take. Perhaps he has found out now. Anyway, he left me to follow. To try to find them.

BELLA: *(Dully, resignedly)* And you let him. *(With a small stir of bitterness)* Yes—you would let him. For you're an Abolitionist. Yes—in secret.

MARK: What if I am—or I were? Oh, I don't know what I am— *(Pausing, taking command of himself)* But aren't you glad that Cass is what he is? That he has gone to find her?

BELLA: Glad? *(Pausing, disturbed)* She will accuse me.

MARK: Oh, aren't you glad—in your deepest heart, in your deepest heart, my dear—that Cass is doing what he has to do?

BELLA: *(Sinking into herself)* Glad? Glad—

MARK: Yes—for if Cass had not— (GIL *appears under the arch, napkin in hand as though just arisen from the table at the sound of voices*)

GIL: Cass? You say Cass? Where is he? *(Pausing)* I'm packed and waiting. Where is he? Doesn't he know about Fort Sumter? *(Looking irritably about)* Doesn't anybody know there's a war?

MARK: Yes. There's a war.

GIL: Well, where's that young fool? What's he hanging around down town for?

MARK: He is not in town.

GIL: *(Taking a step as though to start toward the hall and upstairs)* Oh, he's come! Well—

MARK: No. He hasn't come. *(Pausing)* And he will not come.

GIL: Not come! In God's name, what—

MARK: He has started South. He is—

GIL: You mean he knows about Sumter? Started ahead of me? Why didn't you say so and save all this fuss? *(Makes a motion for his hat)*

MARK: It isn't exactly that way. You see, when he learned that the girl Phebe was being taken South, he—

GIL: That yellow gal?—Well, if Cass wants a yellow gal— (*Turning suddenly to* BELLA) So that was what the row was about? Ho, ho—so he's taken a fancy to your Phebe!

BELLA: *(Starting at him)* No!—No, it's not that. Don't be a fool, it's because—

GIL: Fool? Yes, I was a fool. I was a fool to bring that young fool Cass here for you to work on. I won't be mealy-mouthed, madam. I came into this house, and I saw you. Oh, yes, you were the proud and correct kind, but I saw the way you walked across the room. Yes, I was a fool all right to leave him here. But I figured you had enough to work on with Duncan Trice and— (*Pointing at* MARK) you— *(At this moment* ABBOTT *comes down stairs and enters)* —and you. Well— (*Laughing a quick, hard laugh, turning back to* BELLA) —I was wrong. You worked faster than I thought. You finished off Duncan Trice. You've about finished— (*Indicating* MARK *and* ABBOTT) —these. And you've got Cass off on God knows what foolishness now, and—

MARK: *(Stepping forward)* He has escaped us.

GIL: What do you mean? Escaped?

MARK: He has eluded us— *(With an inclusive gesture)* —all.

GIL: He won't elude me! I've got an investment in that boy—he's my brother, and I'll make him great—he's the brother of Gilbert Mastern, do you hear, and if he thinks he—

MARK: He has escaped you. He has escaped all that you are.

GIL: (*Menacingly at* MARK) If you've filled him full of your Abolition nonsense—if you've Yankeefied him—

MARK: He has escaped all that you are.

GIL: Well, hell's not deep enough to stop me from finding him. For he's mine—do you hear?

BELLA: (*Suddenly coming at* GIL) Oh, no—he will never be yours! *(Striking him on the chest to punctuate her words, a weak stabbing motion, while* HE *stares curiously down at her)* Oh, no, Major Mastern, he'll never be yours—your toy, your thing, your nothing—oh, now he'll never be yours. And I'm glad. At least, I am glad of that. Oh, I am glad! (GIL, *who has been looking down at her with a growing, avid attention, suddenly seizes her by the wrists, twisting them a little.* SHE *goes slack and sways against him, crying out softly*) Oh, oh—

GIL: *(Grinning down at her, in a grating whisper)* It would have been a pretty task, Mrs. Trice. *(Pause)* A very pretty task, to break you in.

BELLA: *(Jerking back, as* HE *still holds her, almost negligently now)* I hate you.

GIL: *(Again grinning at her)* Is it hate, Mrs. Trice? Is that what's going on in your guts right now, Mrs. Trice?

BELLA: *(Toward* ABBOTT, *who has risen from the couch, and who, like* MARK, *is now staring with horrified fascination at the scene between the two)* Abbott! Oh, Abbey-Boy, will you let him? Will you let him do this? To me—to me—

ABBOTT: (*As though released by her words, plunging at* GIL) By God— (GIL *has pushed* BELLA *aside, and* SHE *manages to catch herself and sink again in the chair, nursing her hurt wrists. Meanwhile, with a weary competence,* GIL *has intercepted* ABBOTT *in his plunge, gripped him by one wrist and forced him to one knee.* HE *stares down at him for a second*)

GIL: Sure—all your kind is brave. But— *(Flinging* ABBOTT *aside, to the floor)* —save your strength to kill Yankees. Or get killed by them. *(Adjusting his cuffs)* That takes more strength.

BELLA: Mark! Mark! *(As* MARK *makes no move)* Oh, you coward!

GIL: No, ma'am. Professor Trice isn't a coward, ma'am.

BELLA: (*Still to* MARK) Oh, you coward!

GIL: No, ma'am. It's just he knows the truth, ma'am. *(Locating his beaver on the table, picking it up)* Yes, Professor Trice is the kind of man who knows the truth about everything. He even knows the truth about you. *(Pause)* He even knows the truth about himself. *(Pause)* It's just he never knows what to do about it. *(Pause)* Well, I better get on with what I've got to do. Get back to Mississippi and raise a regiment of rifles. *(Grinning down at* ABBOTT, *seemingly about to prod him with a toe)* Want to come, son? (HE *wheels, and with a heavy military tread moves toward the hall. There* HE *turns sharply, puts his beaver across his heart, speaking with grating politeness, as by rote*) I thank you for all courtesies. (GIL *straightens up, places the beaver firmly on his head and marches out. The* HOUSEBOY *appears, picks up one of the two valises, and follows.* HE *has shoved the other forward, and it is now conspicuous.* BELLA *is still staring at the space where* GIL *has disappeared, unconsciously fondling her wrists. Mark, having watched* GIL *out, turns now toward* BELLA, *with the beginning of a sympathetic, protective gesture. But seeing her in the absorbed fondling of her wrists, as* SHE *still stares at the blank doorway,* HE *stops, and again turns to look where* GIL *has disappeared.* ABBOTT, *pushing himself up partially from the floor, has become aware of her action, and stares at her. All at once,* SHE *finds their eyes on her, and abruptly stops fondling her wrists.* SHE *rises guiltily, and retreats under their gaze.* SHE *moves toward the couch, and suddenly with a cry, flings herself face down on it, under the portrait of herself with the greyhound. The sound of the banjo is heard, distantly. As though summoned by it,* SHE *pushes herself up, listening an instant. Then* SHE *speaks toward* MARK, *in a small, imploring voice)*

BELLA: He's gone.

MARK: Yes.

BELLA: Where—where has he gone?

MARK: *(Studying her now with a sad listlessness)* To Mississippi—to raise his rifles.

BELLA: *(Rising further, agitated)* No—no, not him—I mean— *(Her eyes fix on the valise)*

MARK: *(Following her gaze to the abandoned valise)* Cass?

BELLA: Yes—yes, I mean Cass.

MARK: *(Meditatively, as though to himself)* Cass. Cass Mastern?

BELLA: Oh, why did he go?

MARK: Because— *(Pausing)* —because we all had to try to possess him. To eat him. To destroy him. To make him like us. *(Pausing)* Yes, for he was the living reproach to us—to our dead selves, to our own dead dream. To our own dead innocence. And—we could not abide it.

BELLA: *(Rising farther, agitated)* Abide it—Oh, he's gone—and I can't abide it. Oh, where has he gone?

ABBOTT: *(Rising abruptly, belligerently)* If he's gone to join the Yankees—

MARK: We do not know what he will do.

ABBOTT: Well, if he does—

MARK: Yes, he may join them. We do not know. *(Pausing, going to touch* ABBOTT *lightly on the shoulder)* Abbott, don't you understand? *(As* ABBOTT *stands, not looking at him)*

ABBOTT: But the Yankees—if he joins the Yankees—

MARK: *(Lifting his head as though seeing something far off)* He may not. For I can think of him marching, even yet, with his own people. I can see him—

ABBOTT: *(Turning)* See him?

BELLA: *(Leaning forward on the couch)* Yes?

MARK: *(Not looking at them)* I can see him marching with them, bearing in his knowledge what share he may of the burden they bear in their ignorance. I can see him marching into battle—oh, not Gilbert Mastern's fine captain—only one of the ranks, with a rifle—marching into battle but never firing a bullet. Waiting until some bullet finds him. For if he is to die, perhaps he would die with them. We do not know his last need, and—

BELLA: (*Imploring* MARK) Oh, don't let him die!

MARK: *(Shaking his head, slowly)* We know nothing. Except that he has gone to seek the truth. Whatever truth may be his. To seek—to seek whatever innocence he once ignorantly dreamed life might have. Yes—

BELLA: *(Rising from the couch, moving forward away from* MARK, *lifting her eyes)* Yes— *(Pause)* —oh, I dreamed something, once. *(Pause)* I did. I really did.

MARK: *(Looking at her, as* SHE *stands with her back to him, caught in her thoughts. Then turning toward* ABBOTT, *who is standing with eyes averted)* Yes. Yes. We all did. *(Pause)* Once. *(There is the sound of the banjo, approaching.* OLD ALEC *appears under the window, squats and begins to sing as* HE *plays "Listen to the Mockingbird," in his old, cracked voice.* BELLA *suddenly presses her hand to her brow in a gesture of distraction, then flings herself, face down, on the couch, under the portrait.* ABBOTT *is squaring his shoulders, straightening his military tunic, looking into the distance, as the light dims, but the music continues, muted, as the lights down)*

The End

APPENDIX A

A Robert Penn Warren Time Line

This appendix is based, in part, on facts gleaned from Charles H. Bohner, *Robert Penn Warren;* Joseph Blotner, *Robert Penn Warren: A Biography;* and James A. Grimshaw Jr., *Robert Penn Warren: A Descriptive Bibliography.*

1937: Warren began writing what would become the play *Proud Flesh* on the front porch of a friend's house in Baton Rouge, Louisiana.

A Southern Harvest (edited by Warren) published by Houghton Mifflin.

1938: On a hillside under and olive tree in wheat field in Perugia, Warren continued to write *Proud Flesh.*

Understanding Poetry (edited by Warren and Cleanth Brooks) published by Henry Holt.

1939: Just before Christmas in Rome, Warren finished *Proud Flesh* and sent it to several friends (including Kenneth Burke and Cleanth Brooks) for comment.

Night Rider published by Houghton Mifflin; *An Approach to Literature* published by F. S. Crofts; Warren named Guggenheim Fellow.

1941: Warren wrote to David Clay that he planned to write a novel based on Huey Long.

1942: *Eleven Poems on the Same Theme* published by New Directions; Warren named Professor of English at the University of Minnesota.

1943: Warren pulled out *Proud Flesh* to revise it and saw immediately that it should be a novel. Sometime in either 1943 or 1944, Cass Mastern emerged as a character during the writing of *All the King's Men.*

At Heaven's Gate published by Harcourt Brace; *Understanding Fiction* (edited by Warren and Cleanth Brooks) published by F. S. Crofts.

1944: "Cass Mastern's Wedding Ring" published in *Partisan Review.*

Selected Poems, 1923–1943 published by Harcourt Brace; Warren named Chair of Poetry at the Library of Congress.

1945: "Cass Mastern's Wedding Ring" reprinted in *The Best American Short Stories of 1945.*

1946: *All the King's Men* published by Harcourt Brace; *Blackberry Winter* published by Cummington Press; *The Rime of the Ancient Mariner* (with an introduction by Warren) published by Reynal and Hitchcock.

1947: Eric Bentley put Warren in touch with Erwin Piscator, who began working on a dramatic adaptation of *All the King's Men.*

Circus in the Attic and Other Stories published by Harcourt Brace; Warren awarded the Pulitzer Prize for Fiction for *All the King's Men.*

1948: The Piscator version of the play *All the King's Men* played at the Dramatic Workshop of the New School for Social Research. In the fall of 1948 Robert Rossen suggested that he and Warren collaborate on a play version of the Cass Mastern story.

1949: The movie *All the King's Men* won the Academy Award for Best Picture. March through September Warren worked on the Cass Mastern play with Rossen in Hollywood.

1950: Although dates for specific events cannot be establish with much certainty, Eric Bentley was involved with the development of the dramatic version of the Cass Mastern material from 1950 to roughly 1955. During that time Bentley read an commented on several drafts and hosted a reading of the play in his apartment at 54 Riverside Drive.

World Enough and Time published by Random House; *Understanding Poetry* (Revised Edition) published by Holt; *Fundamentals of Good Writing* (edited by Warren and Cleanth Brooks) published by Harcourt Brace; "Don't Bury Me at All: An Original Story for the Screen" (unpublished screenplay) written by Warren and Max Shulman; Warren named Professor of Playwriting at Yale University and elected to the National Institute of Arts and Letters.

1951: Warren divorced Emma Brescia Warren. Robert Rossen moved to Mexico to avoid the House Un-American Activities Committee investigation of Hollywood.

1952: Warren and David Clay coauthored a television pilot, "The Conway Cabal," for a proposed program titled *This Very Spot.* Warren married Eleanor Clark.

1953: *Brother to Dragons: A Tale in Verse and Voices* published by Random House; *An Anthology of Stories from "The Southern Review"* (edited by Warren and Cleanth Brooks) published by Louisiana State University Press. Rosanna Phelps Warren born July 27; Warrens moved to Fairfield, Connecticut.

1954: *Short Story Masterpieces* (edited by Warren and Albert Erskine) published by Dell Books.

1955: *Band of Angels* published by Random House; *Six Centuries of Great Poetry* (edited by Warren and Albert Erskine) published by Dell Books. Gabriel Penn Warren born on July 19; Warren retired from Yale.

1956: Warren worked with Aaron Frankel (through 1958) on *Willie Stark: His Rise and Fall.*

Segregation: The Inner Conflict in the South published by Random House.

1957: *Promises: Poems, 1954–1956* published by Random House; *A New Southern Harvest* (edited by Warren and Albert Erskine) published by Bantam Books.

1958: Warren worked with Mark Schoenberg on a rewrite of the 1948 (Piscator) version of the play *All the King's Men.* Max Shulman wrote to Warren about their proposed play on John Brown.

Selected Essays and *Remember the Alamo* published by Random House; *Promises* won a Pulitzer Prize, the National Book Award, and the Edna St. Vincent Millay Prize.

1959: The Schoenberg version of *All the King's Men* played for seven weeks at the East 74th Street Theatre in New York City.

The Cave and *The Gods of Mount Olympus* published by Random House; *How Texas Won Her Freedom* published by the San Jacinto Museum of History; Warren elected to the American Academy of Arts and Letters. Warren buys property in West Wardsboro, Vermont.

1960: Warren collaborated with Vincent J. Donehue on a version of "Listen to the Mockingbird" (as the Cass Mastern drama was then known); *All the King's Men* (drama) published by Random House.

You, Emperors, and Others: Poems, 1957–1960 published by Random House; *The Scope of Fiction* (edited by Warren and Cleanth Brooks) published by Appleton-Century-Crofts.

1961: Warren wrote his last draft of a play version of the Mastern material, calling it "An Untitled Play: A Drama of the American Civil War," incorporating the latest revisions suggested by Donehue.

Wilderness: A Tale of the Civil War and *The Legacy of the Civil War* published by Random House; *Understanding Poetry* (Third Edition) published by Holt; Warren appointed Professor of English at Yale University.

APPENDIX B

Correspondence Concerning the Cass Mastern Material

ROBERT PENN WARREN TO DAVID M. CLAY

Atlanta Biltmore
Atlanta, Georgia
November 8, 1941

Dear David:

In accordance with our conversation at lunch today, I am setting down a few facts about my literary work. Here are the things I have published so far.

John Brown: The Making of a Martyr (Brewer and Warren)—1929
essay in I'll Take My Stand (Harpers)—1930—two editions
" Who Owns America—(Houghton Mifflin)—4000 copies (?)
Night Rider (Houghton Mifflin)—4500 copies (?)—1939
(Eyre and Spottiswood)—5000 copies (?) 1940
XXXVI Poems (Alcestis Press)—1936
Approach to Literature (with Brooks and Purser)—(LSU Press, F. S. Crofts)—1936—9000 copies (?)
Understanding Poetry (with Brooks)—(Holt)—1938—14000 copies

Contributions to various anthologies and magazines, such as Literary Opinion in America, ed. Zabel, American Poetry, ed. Untermeyer, the Nation, New Republic, Virginia Quarterly, Scribners, etc.

Here is a list of the things I have in preparation:

And Pastures New[1] (novel) to be published by Houghton Mifflin in March, 1942.

1. This working title was changed to *At Heaven's Gate* (published by Harcourt, Brace in 1943).

Bearded Oaks and Other Poems (poems) to be published by New Directions February, 1942.[2]

Understanding Fiction (with Brooks)—(text book)—to be published by F. S. Crofts, Spring 1942.[3]

Proud Flesh (in collaboration with Francis Fergusson) (play)—entering fourth draft, probably final—conversations with [Paul] Brooks of Houghton Mifflin but no contract—HM could exercise Literary Fellowship option if contract reads "book" and not "novel." Otherwise I am committed to the[m] for one more novel, *I think.* (I'll check contract when I get home.) (New Directions and Atlantic Monthly Press have expressed much interest. AM Press has read it unofficially.)

Selected Poems, including those in XXXVI Poems and Bearded Oaks, and new pieces—verbal agreement with Brooks of Houghton Mifflin, though they'd probably be willing to release it. Word came from Breadloaf [*sic*] this summer that H. was talking about bringing out both Proud Flesh and poems in one volume, but I do not have this information direct from them.

Manuscripts planned, with some work done:

Two novels. Novel one, based on Huey Long situation, but not an exposé—on theme of power versus values, means versus ends—some academic setting, but not central to the novel. I plan to begin work on this next summer. Novel two, very short—an allegorical fantasy, about 50000 words—What Says Don Martin—locale in Mexico.[4] No commitments on either book, unless HM can exercise option on one of them. Will look up contract.

With Brooks I am working on a book on Shakespeare as a poet—the "poetry" of the plays as well as the sonnets. There is no book on this subject. It will attempt to correlate the poetry with dramatic situation, with historical context, with development of Shakespeare, etc. No commitment of any kind.

In addition, I have two novels in manuscript, one which I would not want published, Gods Own Time, under *any* circumstances. The second, But not the Lark, is complete in manuscript but needs drastic revision. If I ever get the right idea for revision it would take about three months to put in shape. Time is 1910, locale, small town in Kentucky.

You have explained to [me] Harcourt Brace's wish to publish all my subsequent books which, after full consideration, I might feel really warrant publication, in trade or text field. I understand that books of a series type are to be ex-

2. This collection was withdrawn from New Directions when Warren went to Harcourt Brace.

3. *Understanding Fiction* was published by Crofts in 1943.

4. This work was never written.

empt from the foregoing provisions and that all textbook ideas are to be discussed with your firm before execution.

The idea of having one publisher permanently appeals to me, and I should be very pleased to be with Harcourt Brace under such an arrangement. I want to give more and more time to writing and that means that I shall want to avoid teaching summer school and shall want to reduce my regular teaching hours and thus my potential earning power, in order to get the writing done. If I do this this will necessitate my having an advance of $750 each summer, with the expectation of my completing every two years a novel or a comparably valuable trade or text book. At my present rate of composition I expect to have a book of poems ready about every three years. I find myself doing fewer short stories. My royalty arrangement with HM on And Pastures New is 10% list price up to 2500 copies, 12 1/2% up to 5000 copies—I don't remember further scaling, but I can check on contract. I would expect a parallel arrangement on my novels and a comparable arrangement on other trade books, and you have explained to me your sliding scale arrangement in your text book department—12% of net wholesale in any year up to a fixed number, 15% net wholesale on increase, and 18% in any one year at a still greater number to be fixed—this on books written rather than collections edited. I agree with you that a permanent association with Harcourt Brace would advantageously be conducted without the use of an agent for film, second serial, and foreign rights, but only if HB conducts a department for systematically handling such business, and exhausts the possibilities before publication of any given item.

I'll send you any other information as soon as I can get it together and in so far as satisfactory details can be worked out at both ends, this letter can be said to constitute a tentative arrangement depending on satisfactory releases and satisfactory agreement on trade royalty.

Very sincerely,
RPW

P.S. I forgot to mention that in conjunction with Allen Tate and Cleanth Brooks I am under contract with Scribners to do a critical and analytical anthology of modern poetry. But this contract has been in force some six years, and I am inclined to believe that the facts of separation of the collaborators from each other (Tate is in Princeton now) and of more pressing interests will probably prevent the fulfillment of the contract. Tate received an advance on the book, but I waived an advance, and so have no financial obligation. Brooks, too, has had no advance for the book. Tate, being a Scribner's author, has his own arrangements with them. I don't imagine I would have any difficulty in getting a release from the contract, if it seems desirable.

And another matter, which involves my personal situation. I have a note falling due October 1, 1942, for extra payment on a house I am buying, the sum of $600. I have an opportunity of going to Iowa for the summer term, it seems, with a light schedule (several days a week free for writing) at a very good salary, good enough to see me through the summer. But I would like, for next summer, to be able to take the Iowa job, *if* it can be arranged so as to give me at least three uninterrupted days a week for writing, and take a reduced advance from HB—$600 to take care of the note. This would enable me to avoid burdening myself with a loan in the fall to handle the note. Then, after that time, I would avoid regular summer teaching, though I would like to feel free to take a short lecture appointment, say up to two weeks, if such an opportunity should present itself.

ROBERT PENN WARREN TO LAMBERT DAVIS

2740 West Lake of the Isles Boulevard
Minneapolis, Minnesota
November 24, 1945

Dear Lambert:

First, many thanks for handling the matter of the hotel reservation. I am enormously grateful, and I shouldn't have trouble[d] you with the matter if I had had any hope of being able to arrange the matter by letter.

Second, I am delighted by the view you take of the novel. I have been waiting with breathless anxiety to hear from you. As for the things you mention: Check on the matter of the deception about the relationship of Cass Mastern to Jack. This is easily remedied. I can simply state the relation of Cass to the Scholarly Attorney and then let the chips fall where they will. Check on removing bits of the smart alecky style. I'll try to do that. Check on the matter of language to mother. On the matter of going back to the story of Cass Mastern in the end, I may have to let the matter ride. Some verbal changes which may help make the thing more plausible may be possible. I'll give this my attention, but I don't believe I can see my way clear to drop the thing. But you may convince me when we meet face to face. Meanwhile, I have had Joseph Warren Beach, whose instinct for and knowledge of fiction is very great, to go over the manuscript. He has suggested a number of detailed changes, all very small, matters really for proof or on manuscript at the last minute (I'll bring my notes on them with me and try to make them there in your office), and two or three bigger changes. Two of the larger changes had to do with tying in the Cass Story and the Anne story (chapter vi) more closely *at the time of the actual narration.* So I have written some new stuff to be inserted in the manuscript you now have. Just pull out the pages with the same numbers and put these in, please sir. I have another notion of his which I want to talk over with you when I see you. It's not very big, nothing drastic.

I am also enclosing here a new story, one I wrote after winding up the novel to sort of taper off on. Will you let me know what you think of this? And will you add it to the manuscript of stories which you all have there and add the name to the table of contents? Many thanks.

Jimmy Reid was here. I had a very pleasant session with him.

As ever,
Red

ERIC BENTLEY TO ROBERT PENN WARREN (1950)

Sept. 12

Dear Red:

I'll jot down a thought or two about Version A without precise relation to their practical use. For one thing it is no hard to know which comments, if any, will be the useful ones, so I'll give all that occur to me and you do the choosing and rejecting.

I think all the re-shaping has been to the good, tho am not surprised to learn from yr latest letter that the present re-shaping has suggested yet another one—which, incidentally, sounds just right. The whole latter end of the play was a nest of possibilities and will become much more than a latter end. Am sure this is right.

When I think of staging the play, a couple of problems jump to mind, and forgive me if I state them in the inadequate critical language of the practical theatre. One is "an unsympathetic heroine." The trick with, for example, the Tennessee Williams ladies is that they aren't really unsympathetic but are symbolic representations both of the author and his audience: all have their neuroses together. You are attempting something much harder: namely, candid moral criticism instead of psychological excuses. This is what makes yr heroine what the theatre call unsympathetic. Problem: if the part is played by a highly sympathetic actress, yr play may go out the window, but if it is not, no audience will come in at the door. I state it bluntly to provoke thought. Maybe nothing can directly be done about it. The one possibility might be that Arabella seem quite sympathetic until, later on, we really get wise to her.

The innocence of Cass is something that has possible theatrical values, but I don't know that Version A shows it off enough. When Mark gives his fine summary on p. 3-3-42, it somehow does more for Cass than the actor of the part wd have been able to do for him (again, forgive exaggeration). Suggestion: cd the innocence be given more of a chance to be acted? Cd we for example see Cass as something besides an adulterer—in the earlier part of the play—(Am not sure there'd be time of course.)

Mention of Mark reminds me that he is still a problem, because there is so little to him besides his function in the dramatic structure—that of raisonneur. And the "old beau of the heroine" archetype seems to limit rather than liberate you (and him).

You speak of juice, and it may be that both Mark and Gilbert (who now trouble me a little) will be okay when the juice is injected. I bring in Gilbert too, because he also often seems to dwindle to the *idea* of the Machiavellian. I know the problem because am myself currently trying to write dialogue for an Inquisitor!

I liked all new elements in the story esp. Phoebe pointing the accusing finger instead of anybody's getting stabbed and killed. Perhaps, however, Cass shdnt just be got rid of in a speech by Mark esp. if that speech has to carry so heavy a burden of thematic content. (Otherwise he seems to go down the river simply because RPW's theme sends him there—and not on his own steam.)

Style. All that you have done to eliminate diffuseness is good, and there is perhaps more to do. What can crudely be called the Poetry of the dialogue is certainly its hardest feature for the performer and spectator, and am not sure the hardness always justifies itself. For example, an extreme case is such a speech as at bottom of II-1-6. I know how this speech is meant, but perhaps chiefly because I know your poetry and yr novels. The sudden bursting-out of such a style in a prose play is going to baffle any audience, tho. It reminds me of the verse in PROUD FLESH, but it is more problematic because in this case not seeming part of the scheme of things.

It still bothers me, tho I may be wrong, that passages of narrative in the dialogue, when the characters relate incidents from years back, are done in an incantatory style which certainly has atmosphere but which make us lose the thread of the narrative itself, so that if you asked me what has just been related, I cdnt always tell you. This was why, for example, when you told me about the family background of Gil and Cass in conversation, I caught on a lot quicker than I had when reading the play itself.

Sometimes, what you have here is naked theatre, then it will slip away into reverie. The passage of reminiscence are the best examples of this, tho I think also in this category are bits of love-talk, or any talk that you try to push beyond the moment, as it were (for an extra dimension of poetry). I think the extra dimension will finally just *emerge* from yr structure and story, and will not need deliberate stylistic features.

(Example of this love talk that I thought not "sharp" enough—in focus, so to speak—is when Duncan tries to recapture the romance of his courtship.)

A mere detail: the rhapsodic vein which I think is a carry-over from yr work in other mediums and is not quite right for theatre shows in a couple of tiny things that almost become mannerisms in the play. One is the tendency to apostrophe—too many "Oh, ..."'s. Another is the constant use of the word *for* (the conjunction) in the elegant, old-fashioned use of the word (in cases where the word in modern conversation is simply omitted).

I think the use of the picture symbolically is quite successful now. Possible that some of the lighting and pantomime you suggest wd need movie cameras to give to the audience (effects with a lit cigar, or suddenly focusing on one person only, or showing that a doorway is suddenly *filled* by a person). But all this cd be discovered in due time.

I *think* Arabella's giving herself to Gilbert, or being prepared to, is now convincing, tho I wd like the reaction of someone who comes new to the story. Even now there may be too much stress on the conscious reason why Gilbert wd like her, his *theory* of her (that she needs breaking in etc.), and too little direct attraction. I don't know that even Gilbert cd achieve and verbalize quite the attitude of a slave-dealer to the contour of breasts etc., maybe I'm wrong.

I think Abbott now justifies his place in the proceedings, tho am wondering if you bring out as clearly as you want to the idea (mentioned more than once) of making over other people in one's own image. Is that, as it were, the second theme of the play, the first being refusal of responsibility? Or is it (I state the danger) a notion thrown in for good measure with a status that we (or you) never become quite clear about? It might take a whole play to dramatize that idea.

Detail: a place where we feel we have missed something is where Mark says he loved her the best of all of them. If the remark is meant pretty much as a commonplace, its truth is evident: he has loved her longest and we knew it. But you must have meant more? And if so what? In what sense, best?

The war now seems worked in well. Only problem (and probably we needn't bother about it) is that the period between Harper's Ferry and Sumter is just a vague blob in most minds, and since all that anyone knows in New York is that there were two armies, the stuff about the local uniforms etc. may be slightly confusing. A British spectator, for instance, might say: is the war off or on? What is that the uniform *of?* How can Cass go off down the river if he's in the war? (In a modern play of war-time you'd explain that yr hero for some reason wasn't drafted if you needed to keep him in civilian dress.)

That's all for now. we plan to return to NY tomorrow, so perhaps the meeting we need to have when yr Version A is ready cd be in the City? Best time to reach me by phone is usually around lunch time or early evening. Joanne is in the phone bk if you lose our number.

So sorry about Eleanor's illness and trust it is now only a memory

As ever
Eric

have done a confused first draft of Galileo

ERIC BENTLEY TO ROBERT PENN WARREN (1955)

54 Riverside Drive
March 28

Dear Red:

David Clay gave me the tape recording, and I heard two of the three acts, but didn't bother about the last: the reading is quite bad, I finished the play reading to myself.

I am still deeply interested in the work but would not wish to direct it as it stands or even with minor revisions. Therefore if you and the Stevens office wish to go ahead now, you should feel free to do so without me. Naturally, though, I owe you an explanation. Here it comes.

There is a play here, once the first act is rather severely cut down to size. And if you go ahead with it, I wish you all the luck in the world. I myself lack confidence in this play because—

Well, first, the rhetoric. If I prune your dialogue, you will presumably feel that I have not understood the intention of your style, the nature of this sort of speech, the idea of poetic prose and poetic drama. I should have to retort that I don't think this rhetoric is succeeding. For example, Cass's dying speeches. To me, there is a lack of dramatic progression in the long speeches. They hang in the air. I say this after a certain experience with your work. You were right to detheatricalize DRAGONS, because your mind tends to a philosophical poetry, rhetoric which is non-theatrical. Some of the passages in PROUD FLESH were non-theatrical in the same way. They didn't have the drive and thrust *forwards into the action* which I require from theatre-poetry. Please make allowance in these statements of mine for the oversimplification and dogmatism that come from trying to set down opinions and impressions too briefly. I feel that the rhetoric of WEDDING RING cd be worked on until it *is* theatre, but I am not sure that *you* wd like the result, or that you really want to push it in that particular direction. In urging you, I may be urging you against the grain; so I don't urge, but, instead, write you this letter.

Next, your presentation of Arabella. You have a character, but not a role; that is, you don't hand your character on a silver or other platter *to an actress.* For example, in the early scenes she seems just a bit-part actress for a while, whereas on stage the leading role must always be that from the actress's first entrance—or rather from the build-up *for* that entrance—and must be that consistently from then on. (I am not thinking of the star's ego, but of the very nature of a lead performance.)

If I push the critique of Arabella further on this line, I come to a criticism of more than Arabella, namely, of your method in the play in general, which I wd characterize as too *abstract.* You have a marvelous idea. But it is only an idea, and it pushes your characters around, *they* are victims of your idea, they can't quite become human beings. The point at which this is most strongly felt is the moment when Gil has his "love scene" at the end. Your simple audience will shriek: What?! And I think I am in sympathy with that shriek. Don't reply that this is the intention—theatrical surprise. The surprise, even when absorbed, is not convincing—except abstractly intellectually. The idea, I take it, is that since Arabella flouts truth she shd take up with a man you represent as flouting truth, a sheer Machiavellian. But the jump here from sex to politics, as it were, is too big a jump. Or rather, though what you say is logical, it is not psychological, it is not natural or human. I don't deny that an Arabella might become the mistress of a Gil, but there is a prima facis case against it, and it is your job as dramatist-attorney to break that case down, to show us that it would and must happen. Instead, you jump the gun. I feel that the whole ending of your play is particularly wrong, because this gun is jumped right on top of a lot of rhetoric which also would be all but impossible to put across.

Another place where I catch you with your ideological slip showing is in your using a raisonneur. I don't say you can't use one. But I do feel that such a character represents for you, Red Warren, a lure, a temptation. (I am thinking back to the chorus-doctor in Proud Flesh, and also, in a way, to Jack Burden. You always express a certain embarrassment over these creations which shows itself in little jokes at their expense; jokes against being professorial or journalistic etc. But I won't let you use these jokes as an alibi. The problem remains.) The quick way of taking care of Mark is to cut down on his lines in act one. I question if that is enough. Such a character is an *idea* thru and thru, isn't he? And isn't that a fault? In a play that might be as human as Anna Karenina?

Anyway, just as I find you drowning your characters in ideas, I'm afraid I find you drowning your ideas in rhetoric. No, this is unfair, or at least an exaggeration. (How hard to be accurate in such matters!) But I do mean that though your ideas are, I think, clear to me, who have studied your collected works and am a dabbler in philosophy, I would despair of making them clear to almost any audience you cd mention. As for the Broadway audience, it wdnt begin to know what you are talking about. It is so disposed to sympathize with the lies an evasions of those Southern ladies, that your stern almost religious condemnation wdnt be understood—thus rendering yr ending doubly impossible.

Mind you, I would strike out this last paragraph of mine if the play were right in all other respects. I would say: well, it will be hard to put this over, but it's worth the effort. In short the Broadway public is not my primary interest. On the contrary, I not only understand your attitude to Arabella, but share it: I should positively *enjoy* trying to convey your idea to a public. It gives me only the greater pleasure that your play says, as it were, the opposite of what we are used to from Tennessee Williams et al. I am *your* fellow traveler, not his.

But, as things are, I feel your point would not get made and that the play would prove bewildering and profoundly unsatisfactory.

Possibly this only means it would prove bewildering and unsatisfactory if directed by me. The alternative is to get someone else. It all depends, first, how you feel about it and, second, if you shd agree with me at all, whether you feel you can and will do anything about it. Please realize that I have not said in this short space all that I think about the play either for or against. I have tried to set down just my main misgivings. That I owe to you. I should not have ventured to be so blunt except that I bank greatly on our friendship, and I trust you to remember that the admiration expressed in my essay on your novels still exists, undiminished.

You can either go ahead with another director and my blessings on yr head; or drop the project; or take it up with me as a longer-term affair.

yrs as ever
Eric

VINCENT J. DONEHUE TO ROBERT PENN WARREN

Schary Productions, Inc.
434 North Rodeo Drive
Beverly Hills, California
March 11, 1960

My dear Mr. Warren:[1]

Here are my notes about LISTEN TO THE MOCKING BIRD. They have basically to do with problems of stagecraft. In connection with two of the characters however, the notes are intimately involved with making more manifest your basic themes. Concerning Bella, I told you in New York that any more specific characteristics, either inner or outer, would be helpful all through the play. That she carries the theme of irresponsibility most heavily in the play, and therefore can too easily seem a symbol rather than a vibrant, specific person, I wish to call again to your attention. The more specific she can be all through the play, the more interesting she is as a human being, the better it is in terms of theatre story. In the notes that follow, you will also notice that I have suggested at several points in the play that her turning away from realization and ignoring responsibility be made more overt and more dramatised.

Mark, besides being a very vivid character within the story, seems to me to function as a somewhat removed commentator or Chorus. I specifically feel that at the end of the play, since it is Mark who best understands the spirit of Cass, it is he who should have the final control, or as it were the last word. I think that Mark would round out the play better, rather than the less important relationship between Gil and Bella. I do not feel that the penultimate thing to be said in the play is what Gil contributes, but rather the spirit of Cass, and no one understands that spirit except Mark.

Some of the following thoughts, as you will see, are minor craft problems. Others would take some reorganization of your planning.

1. In the whole beginning of the play in Scene 1, I have a feeling that the horse-riding guests should be reduced to possibly two or three specific guests. These guests should be very definite characters that can reoccur in the play, particularly in the cardplaying scene. I do not feel that they should come on the stage until your are really ready to use them, and once they are on they must be used and be

1. Though this letter is among the holdings of the Beinecke Rare Book and Manuscript Library, Yale University does not claim ownership of it as intellectual property. The editor's efforts to find an owner of the letter have been unsuccessful.

part of all the conversation. I do not think it best, this early in the play, to have a distracting group around the punch bowl. In brief, I feel the guests should not come on until you really want to use them on the stage, and once they are on the stage they must be part of the entire conversation.

2. On Page I-1-11 and 12, I do not feel that the Bella-Phebe scene can be played with a lot of people on stage, and that a way should be found to have it played alone. It is much too important a moment to be dissipated. I feel further that the relationship between Jason and Phebe should be more specific. Are they a closely married couple? Have they lived together or does Phebe wait for the days and nights that they can spend together? How aware is Bella of their lives together? Has she at all been involved in making it possible for them to be together? I feel that the whole Jason-Phebe-Bella background and story should be more specific.

3. I feel that Wilton's arrival and his news all seems too fortuitous. Perhaps his arriving should be prepared for in previous dialogue. Could we have more of a sense of waiting to hear about what has happened at Harper's Ferry or could the people be wondering about whether the Army or Robert E. Lee would step in? Who is Wilton? Could he be made a character to serve throughout the play? I would like to think about the simple construction here. It is not good that first Mark arrives with news, and then in a very similar way, shortly after, Milton [*sic*] arrives with news.

4. Why is Gil going to Washington?

5. It seems to me that by Page I-1-18, the guests should have concretely left. I do not feel that the Gil-Cass scene should be interrupted.

6. In Scene 2 on Page I-2-32, I suggest again that there be specific characters for these guests—that they might be those from the first scene and that exact dialogue in terms of their characters, both for their entrances on Page 32 and their exits on Page 39, be developed so that both their coming and their leaving makes more point.

7. On Page I-2-43 and 44, please think about the possibility of the dialogue about John Brown taking place in front of and involving Cass. I think a further point concerning Cass' primitive humanity could be made in relation to this dialogue. As the scene now stands, it is merely a statement of Mark's views and it does not advance the dramatic conflict or growth of the play.

8. I-2-45: I think this dialogue should be revamped so that Phebe is on stage and part of the conversation. You might stress here her continued anxiety about her husband, despite the reassurance that the lady is not selling him. You might also make a further statement about her close relationship to Jason. Further,

I think we might have another chance to have a reflection of Bella's lack of responsibility.

9. The dialogue on Page I-2-46 could be used for the exits of the guests, for which there is now no existing dialogue. I feel also, with the guests present, it would point Bella's embarrassment about Duncan. I feel also that Mark should be very much a part of this scene. And again I feel that after Duncan has gone upstairs, that in Bella's scene with Mark she could again reveal herself further by her pointedly being unaware of any personal responsibility for Duncan being the way he is as a man.

10. In Act II, Scene 1, Pages 6 and 7, the scene between Phebe, Bella and Cass: I feel that this scene should be extended and more fully investigated, particularly if the suggestion for a prior opening up of the relationship between Phebe and Jason and Bella has been followed.

11. I again feel, in relation to the same story, that the scene beginning II-1-12 between Duncan, Bella, Abbott and Phebe is too short, too quick and too easily passed over.

12. I feel, on Pages II-1-16 and 17, that Bella possibly recovers from the Phebe business too easily. I mean only that it annoys her rather than profoundly bothers her.

13. Page II-1-19: It seems to me that the line from Duncan "You, Cass, you cheer Bella up about this Jason business" is too blatantly "on the nose."

14. The end of Scene 1, Act III puzzles me because of its emphasis. Why do we go to Gil and an interest in him instead of staying with the Bella-Cass problem and the split because of her failing to understand her responsibility and his really understanding it? Why does not the scene end with a foreshadowing of the possibility of her going to make Phebe the brunt of her guilt?

15. III-2-22: What does Bella do while waiting for Monsieur Larue to enter? This seems to me an uninteresting stage wait unless you have something specific in mind.

16. Would it not be more interesting for M. Larue to be a less obviously villainous character? It seems to me that the "mechanics of his slave buying" would be the more horrifying if they were practiced by an unvillainous man who practiced them without seeming evil or without sadistic feelings but merely as a "modus operandi."

17. Would it be interesting for Phebe to continue to have her dignity and to hold on to it despite M. Larue, so that even her handling of this frightful situation could only increase Bella's uncomfortableness and guilt?

18. In New York we talked of a change in construction of Act III, Scene 2. It seems to me that a scene between Gil and Cass might be possible, with Cass actually stating his intention and freeing himself of Gil. It also seems possible to consider that Gil might not come back at all. As it stands now, I do think there is faulty construction in first Gil coming back, immediately following Abbott and Mark coming back.

19. I am not convinced of the necessity of Gil's dialogue on Page III-2-48.

20. Page III-2-50: This is the material of Mark's which I should like to consider as the basis for the end of the play. I feel that it might be further pointed by Mark's pointing out that Cass is facing his responsibility in the world as he has found it or as he has caused it to be. That he is taking the responsible step. As I said earlier, I feel that it is the spirit of Cass in contrast to the broken Bella that should dominate the end of the play. Gil's scene only obliquely supports this situation, and should be used only to reduce Bella "to ashes." I do not feel that the final impetus should be Gil's; it should be from Cass through Mark, stating the positive action, contrasted as it is with the visual image of the negative (i.e., Bella).

21. The inbalance between the three acts of the play is a problem. At this stage of the work I have only one suggestion and that is the possibility of having a second scene in Act II which would use all of the present Act III up to Act III-1-16, ending with Cass' line "I have learned what judgment is."

I realize that my notes are somewhat lengthy, and in certain cases would require rather large areas of work. As I told you in New York, these thoughts do not in any way affect the thematic strength of the play, nor do they in any way lessen my basic profound admiration for the work.

My home address out here is 24620 Malibu Road, and the telephone is Globe 62859.

I send you my warmest wishes.

Sincerely,
Vincent J. Donahue

APPENDIX C

James A. Perkins Interviews Eric Bentley

I interviewed Eric Bentley on Saturday, October 18, 1997, in his apartment on Riverside Drive in New York City. I had sent him copies of letters he had written to Robert Penn Warren over the years and told him in advance that I was interested chiefly in discussing his work with Warren as a dramatist. The interview lasted for more than three hours and ranged into many very interesting topics unrelated to the scope of this volume. I was forced by a lack of space to edit the interview and focus on Bentley's comments on Warren as a dramatist and on Cass Mastern. I sent a transcript of the entire interview to Michael Bertin Heinlein, who is working on a biography of Eric Bentley. Bentley is a fascinating individual. I look forward to seeing Heinlein's completed work.

P: When you reviewed the Piscator version for *Theatre Arts* ["All the King's Men," *Theatre Arts* 31 (November 1947): 72–73] you ended the discussion with a paragraph that I quoted to you in a letter, I believe: "How good a play is *Proud Flesh* (the University of Minnesota used the title *All the King's Men*)? In moments of enthusiasm or straining after a slick superlative, one might exclaim 'Here at last is *the* American play.'"

B: Yeah.

P: "On the lowest estimate, it's very brilliant and meaty and suggestive. It shows that Warren, potentially at least, is as much a playwright as he is a poet or a novelist."

B: Yeah.

P: "As a first play, it is astonishing." And then this last sentence, "I know of no single fact that gives me more hope for American drama."

B: Yeah.

P: Now, I read a lot of your criticism, at about this time, and you were grousing pretty much about what was going on, on Broadway especially . . .

B: Yes. Yes.

P: . . . and you must have been attracted to Warren because he dealt with ideas or . . .

B: That was certainly part of it. But what hit me when I read *All the King's Men* was its powerful dynamics and its extraordinary tempo. The most noticeable difference between Warren and the other southern novelists is the *speed* of his prose. Faulkner's prose is rather leisurely. . . .

P: Slow as molasses at times.

B: Warren seems to be driving one of these fast cars that swerve around the corners with a screech of brakes. Drama! Theater! However, Cass Mastern was something else again, and there I thought, going over the pages that you sent me, the kind of prose he uses there is *not* theatrical.

P: Well, isn't the problem with Cass Mastern that, OK, when we find out about him, he's dead . . .

B: Yeah.

P: . . . and he's being interpreted by another character . . .

B: Yes.

P: . . . and then we only have his letters and his diary and the suppositions.

B: Yes.

P: Now, diaries and letters and suppositions have a hard time getting up and walking.

B: Well, there's a lot of that, almost that, in Ibsen, isn't there? Of old documents, and mysteries about people's backgrounds?

P: Yeah.

B: For me, the problem was with the prose. I ran into the same thing with Joseph Conrad. When you read Conrad, a great part of the pleasure is in this melancholy, beautiful language. It gets you in the mood, and you go with the long sentences. There's very little dialogue—in Conrad anyway. So that when they take a Conrad piece—I saw one on television, *The Secret Agent*—and they have to write their own dialogue, because he didn't write much dialogue, and they don't use his prose, the paragraphs of narrative and description, you've missed the part of Conrad that you relish, and you are only given the bare bones of his story. It isn't anything like as rich an experience as reading his book. I think the same is true of Cass Mastern—it's a beautiful piece of writing and you enjoy that beauty. Also the melancholy tone that carries you through—lost when it's all dialogue.

P: Well, in the version that you saw, I'm trying to remember, I think it ends with Mastern being killed by the man, by a slave owner, because he [Mastern] goes to try to find the octoroon that she [Arabella] has dismissed and sees him [the slave trader] mistreating another slave and intervenes and gets stabbed by a sword cane?

B: Yes.

P: OK, well, in the final version, he's marching off to Mississippi to join the rifles, which he does in the book, . . .

B: Oh.

P: . . . but it's just sort of a letdown.

B: Yes, yes.

P: All of the business of him going out to look for his death by carrying a rifle and not even firing it . . .

B: Yes.

P: . . . all of that's lost and I guess the high point of the drama, such as it is, is when she confronts him with the ring and says "you know what this means." I have problems with it too as a drama. The reason that I want to bring it out is that I think it completes *All The King's Men.*

B: There was a reading of the play at my apartment, not this apartment, but one lower down Riverside Drive. I can't remember who was in it. Some well-known actress? Who was it?

P: I don't know.

B: If it was a friend of mine, it would have been Uta Hagen. But I'm not sure we got her, though she did read a couple of plays for me around that time.

P: Well, that leads me to another thing because there's some of your handwriting in here.

B: I can remember the evening. I can remember Red and Eleanor arriving at the apartment, but I can't remember the reading at all.

P: You were evidently thinking about—now here's where you may need glasses—you were evidently thinking about casting this.

B: Oh, that's my handwriting.

P: Yeah. And this says, "Arabella Trice says 'Tandy.'" Were you thinking about Jessica Tandy?

B: It must be. If I'm going to have to look at things I need my reading glasses. [At this point Bentley went off on an unsuccessful trip to find his reading glasses.]

P: And then Cass says "Burton" and then it says slash "Dean" then slash "Mendez" or "Mendy?"

B: *Mendy* Wager. That is Michael Wager.

P: Then you have Arabella Trice out this way, it says "Geraldine."

B: Geraldine Page. No. Geraldine Fitzgerald, probably.

P: And then, Duncan Trice, who's the man who kills himself, "Gales?" *G-A-L-E-S*?

B: *G-A*? Oh, *D-A-L-E-S?*

P: No, this is a *G*. Oh, Gates. Gates. Does that make sense?

B: Is it a man?

P: Yeah.

B: Yes, there was a Larry Gates. Yes, Gates is one of the many derivatives of Katz.

P: OK. In the *Theatre of Commitment* you wrote, "Sometimes I think all our poetic and fictional talent today is dramatic talent scared away by the idiocy of the theater."

B: Yes.

P: "Certainly if Ernest Hemingway or Robert Penn Warren could devote ten years to theatrical work, he would write even the best of our playwrights off the stage."

B: Yes.

P: And there are so many things I want to know about this quotation.

B: Yes?

P: What was the idiocy of the theater at that, what did you have in mind?

B: Broadway dialogue is slick: slick "commercial" dialogue, machine made. You could get much better dialogue from a real writer. Mind you, I'm no longer as sure as I was in those days that the novelists can do it. But I did think that the more talented writers did the novels and the professional playwrights were second rate, bottom drawer. Which made me think that if people like Hemingway would try the drama they'd be better at it than the playwrights, being better writers. However, as early as 1940, I had seen Hemingway's play *The Fifth Column* on Broadway, and I couldn't help noticing that, though it had some good dialogue in it, it isn't a good play. Hemingway seemed to have no talent for *building* a play, although he wrote very clever dialogue, which did "work" in the theater. Am I unfair? *The Fifth Column* was a Hemingway story adapted by someone else. . . . I saw, later, the one play that Faulkner ever had on Broadway; was it called "Requiem for Someone"? [Faulkner's *Requiem for a Nun* is a novel written as a play in three acts. Ruth Ford produced and acted in it in New York beginning in January 1959.] I was rather taken with it, but it had deficiencies as theater. . . . So probably the novelists were right to stick to the novel. As for Red Warren, when he writes speeches for Willie Stark, those speeches do "work" theatrically—they are truly dramatic speeches—but when he writes speeches for the characters in Cass Mastern, well, he doesn't create theatrical *roles* from which the speeches should derive. It's literature, maybe, but it's not drama, it's not spoken dialogue, not what an actor needs to have control of. Tennessee Williams used southern speech so that it *works* with audiences—southern, northern, east or west. In Cass Mastern it's *Warren* writing prose it's not these characters talking. I let him know something of what I felt on this matter, but I never learned what he made of my criticisms. He didn't argue back and defend himself but he didn't say I was right.

P: I can tell you to some extent because I've read—you sent him quite a lengthy letter [containing suggestions for improving *Cass Mastern's Wedding Ring.* The text of this letter can be found in Appendix B] . . .

B: Yes?

P: . . . and the subsequent versions of the play attempt to move in the direction that you were trying to get him to move.

B: Nice to know.

P: But I'm not convinced that it ever made a good drama. You know it's still way too much something about ideas and not about people.

B: Oh, I wanted to mention—this is jumping a bit—but Allen Tate and Red Warren—you have Allen Tate quoted quite accurately saying "Warren was the most talented person" he'd ever known. Allen was a drinker, as you know, and would say all sorts of things. I've also heard him talk against Red in a certain way, not personal, but against his writing. I thought it was rather strange so it stuck in my mind. He said, "Red Warren has no ear." We were talking about Red's poetry and he repeated it: "Red Warren has no ear, has no ear." He felt the rhythms were all wrong. Well, Allen was a far keener critic of poetry than I am, but I don't know that anyone else ever felt this about Red. Maybe Allen wasn't serious; he loved to make preemptory judgments and didn't always stand behind them. He was aggressive. Had you heard . . .

P: . . . that Red had no ear?

B: That Allen could be naughty.

P: Oh, yes. . . . You said in the later years you and Red lost touch with each other?

B: Oh, yes, completely. I never even found out how the Cass Mastern story ended . . . what happened after I stopped making those criticisms.

P: He kept at it and in fact the last version, which I also have here, is one that he had sent to somebody named Vincent Donehue.

B: Oh, yes, the director. He was a very successful Broadway director.

P: And Vincent Donehue did the same thing you did—he sent him page after page after page of suggestions, and again he redid it and incorporated those changes. [The text of Donehue's letter can be found in Appendix B.] But at that point, it seems to have just died. There's no further work on it. And this is 11-1-60.

B: Well, there go the nineteen fifties!

P: Yeah.

B: Donehue was a well-established director. If he'd wanted to direct it, he'd have raised the money, and it would have been a Broadway show.

P: And the other person involved here is Lawrence Langner.

B: Yes, well he was the head of the Theatre Guild for decades.

P: OK. Yeah, this is the Theatre Guild copy.

B: I had many dealings with him. An old bore, but he was a very powerful figure in the theater for a while, mostly back in the twenties and thirties. He did all Shaw's plays in the twenties. The world premiere of *St. Joan* on Broadway and so forth. Very narrow-minded, but that wouldn't have stopped him doing Cass Mastern. I remember in my book *The Brecht Memoir* I quote a letter from him as to why he won't do Brecht's *Mother Courage.* Because it's gloomy. A strange reason, considering how many plays are gloomy.

P: Let me tell you how it ends. This is the last couple pages of the last version. Cass Mastern has marched off to Mississippi to join the rifles, and this character Mark, who does not appear in *All the King's Men* at all—Mark Trice, who is the teacher at Transylvania . . .

B: Yes?

P: . . . and he's evidently just pulled in there to get Cass to say some things . . .

B: Yes?

P: . . . that he otherwise wouldn't. He's a stage device for the most part. And Mark says, "I can see him marching with them, bearing in his knowledge what share he may of the burden they bear in their ignorance. I can see him marching into battle—oh, not Gilbert Mastern's fine captain, only one of the ranks, with a rifle, marching into battle but never firing a bullet. Waiting until some bullet finds him. For if he is to die, perhaps he will die with them. We do not know his last need. . . ." And then Arabella says, "Oh, don't let him die," which she would. And Mark says, "We know nothing except that he has gone to seek the truth, whatever truth may be his. To seek whatever innocence he once ignorantly dreamed life might have." And Arabella says, "Yes." And then she says, "I did. I really did." And Mark says, "Yes. Yes. We all did—once." Then, fade.

B: So it ends with original sin: there's no such thing as innocence.

P: Yeah.

B: We have sin in us *from the beginning.* Which may be a little stronger than having him stabbed by the slave owner.

P: And you know one reason Cass Mastern never made it anywhere? It started out with Robert Rossen, the director of the movie. He and Warren were collaborating on this thing, and he had changed movie studios—he wasn't with Columbia . . .

B: Rossen was interested in Cass Mastern?

P: Yeah. They started out working together on it.

B: I didn't know that.

P: And he had changed studios, but Columbia still had the rights, for the length of the copyright, of the whole book, and that chapter four was part of it. So he and Red couldn't go ahead.

B: I remember that Red got mixed up with Rossen's life, but he had as little understanding of the Hollywood communists as they had of him. Piscator had no understanding of Red Warren, and Red had no understanding of Piscator. Rossen was breaking loose from communism at the time. Red kind of knew that he was involved in "all that" at the time when he should have been concentrating on the film.

P: Yes, I believe so.

B: You may have caught the allusion to Rossen in my book *Thirty Years of Treason.*

P: Yes.

B: I first read "Cass Mastern" in *Partisan Review.* I think I got more out of it in splendid isolation than in the book.

P: It wasn't in the first two British editions.

B: Because the editors over there couldn't see the relevance?

P: Well, they were just asking for a shorter book. Because of paper shortage, I think, after the war.

B: Yes. Well, it's pretty wild to stick it in the middle of *All The King's Men,* though there's a point to that.

P: When Warren finally put it back, he wrote an introduction and said that he always thought it was central to the book and he was very glad to have it returned.

B: Warren thought thematically, but most novel readers don't.

APPENDIX D

Listen to the Mockingbird: Some Production Notes

Kay L. Coughenour and James A. Grimshaw Jr.

"The Gods who live on high have decreed that wisdom comes to man alone through suffering" . . . and wisdom does not come easily when the smell of blood is in the air.

—Aeschylus, *Oresteia*

Change from fiction to drama necessitates corresponding change in structure of the plot. As Warren learned, "If you begin to alter, however casually, a form . . . you are bound in the end to alter meaning. For form is meaning."[1] By pursuing his continued interest in playwriting, Warren found a style, a voice that blends modern narrative with the realistic dialogue of early-twentieth-century American drama. *Listen to the Mockingbird,* his own adaptation of chapter 4 of *All the King's Men,* alters meaning and creates in the leading female role an antihero, Bella, who dominates the action of the story. That shift is captured most explicitly toward the end of the play when Cass Mastern, who is more the focus of the fictional story, leaves to find Bella Trice's personal servant, Phebe. In the novel Cass joins the battle in the Civil War, is wounded, and dies in a hospital, thus

Listen to the Mockingbird was first produced by Texas A&M University–Commerce Performing Arts Theater, directed by Kay Coughenour, October 7–11, 1998. These production notes refer to this production.

1. Robert Penn Warren, "Playwright's Column," in program for performance of "Willie Stark: His Rise and Fall; A Play in Three Acts" at the Margo Jones Theatre, Dallas, November 25, 1958, quoted in Aaron Frankel, "Working in the Theater with Robert Penn Warren," in *RWP: An Annual of Robert Penn Warren Studies,* vol. 2, ed. William Bedford Clark and James A. Grimshaw Jr. (Bowling Green: Western Kentucky University, 2002), 2.

finding redemption for his complicity in guilt. However, in the play Cass tends to romanticize his atonement for his sins, an act that undercuts his stature and leaves unanswered the question of his redemption.

The result of that shift in focus is a very powerful story of betrayal and survival and of southern values. The shift in focus also reveals a potentially powerful playwright whose "insight into the theater," Aaron Frankel notes, "was unique and original, a native American style a-borning."[2] Producing *Listen to the Mockingbird* carried with it the zest of being in the presence of something new and exciting.

BACKGROUND OF THE CASS MASTERN STORY

Robert Penn Warren worked with the Willie Stark story from 1937 to 1960: *All the King's Men* was published as a novel in 1946, but it began as a play, "Proud Flesh," and was published as a play, *All the King's Men,* in 1960. It has also been produced as a film (same title) and as an opera, titled *Willie Stark.* The play produced in October 1998 at Texas A&M University–Commerce was based on a 1959 dramatic version of the Cass Mastern story, which appears in chapter 4 of the novel and which William Faulkner considered the best part of the book.[3] Warren apparently revised that 1959 version and smoothed out some of the difficulties anticipated in a March 11, 1960, letter to Warren from Vincent J. Donehue, who had been considering directing a production of the play. The Cass Mastern story parallels some of the motivations and the pragmatist-idealist dialectic in the novel, a parallel the British publishers missed when they excised chapter 4 from the first British edition. Perhaps because of Faulkner's comment or perhaps because of the Shakespearean elements with which Warren was intrigued or perhaps because of his continuing interest in the ideas of hope, love, and endurance, Warren continued to grapple with this story as drama. And years after he had first adapted *Listen to the Mockingbird* from the novel, he was still concerned with the background influences on the story and with the control people of power and position exert over others.

2. Ibid.

3. Robert Penn Warren, "Listen to the Mockingbird," June 1959, typescript, carbon corrected (Draft P [marked "version D"]), YCAL, MSS 51, Box 158, F.2852, Beinecke Rare Book and Manuscript Library, Yale University; William Faulkner to Lambert Davis, July 25, [1946], in Joseph Blotner, ed., *Selected Letters of William Faulkner* (New York: Random House, 1977), 239. Specifically, Faulkner wrote: "The Cass Mastern story is a beautiful and moving piece. That was his novel. The rest of it I would throw away."

In a 1978 interview for the *New England Review,* Warren made the following comment about the Cass Mastern story: "Cass Mastern's story had a germ. A lot of the details are historical—it's based on the Jefferson Davis story. His father, Sam, came to Kentucky, to our country, where Jeff was born. Old Sam Davis was so feckless! In our country there's a river valley and rich land to raise horses in. But Sam went up to the northern part of the country, to the Knob section, and tried to raise race horses where the soil is two inches thick over the limestone cap! Instead of five feet thick down our way."[4] About Jefferson Finis Davis, Warren provides some biographical background such as his birth in Todd County, Kentucky (Warren was also born in Todd County), June 3, 1808; that his father, Sam Davis, was born of Welsh immigrants; that Jeff was the tenth child; that Joseph Davis, an older brother who became a successful lawyer and owned a plantation, Hurricane, "assumed the paternal role and defined the character and aspirations" of Jeff; that Jeff Davis attended Transylvania University before receiving an appointment to West Point, where he graduated twenty-third in a class of thirty-three; that Joseph gave Jeff a plantation, Brierfield, adjacent to Hurricane; and that Jeff, "with no date of emancipation perceptible in the drift of history [in the early 1830s], did organize Brierfield for a kind of training that would help protect the black man, once freed, from being exploited by ruthless white competition."[5] From even these sketchy details, Warren's use of the Jefferson Davis background in this play is evident. Another biography of Jefferson Davis was written by Allen Tate, a friend of Warren. They surely exchanged ideas about Davis.

Earlier, in 1974, Warren, prompted by a producer who wanted to stage it, told Marshall Walker about the development and later phases of the play *All the King's Men:*

> [O]f course, there was my own dissatisfaction with the original version of the play ["Proud Flesh"]—a verse play then—that preceded the novel by some eight years. . . . The original version of the play was a tight play about the dictator, the Huey Long figure, and the people around him. Now the theory of that play was that the dictator, the man of power, is powerful only because he fulfills the blankness and needs of people around him. His power is an index to the weakness of others. In other words, his power lies in the defects of others rather than a thing existing in itself, and so he

4. Robert Penn Warren, "Interview with Eleanor Clark and Robert Penn Warren," in *Robert Penn Warren Talking: Interviews, 1950–1978,* ed. by Floyd C. Watkins and John T. Hiers (New York: Random House, 1980), 276.

5. Robert Penn Warren, *Jefferson Davis Gets His Citizenship Back* (Lexington: University Press of Kentucky, 1980), 40.

> fulfills the needs of people around him. The idea that gradually developed in the course of writing the play was the contrast between the "hero" as a person and the "hero" as a reflex of history.[6]

Knowing that rationale helps in relating to Gilbert Mastern and to Bella (Annabelle in the novel) in the dramatic version of the Cass Mastern story. That version is also enhanced by knowledge of other aspects of Warren's writing.

Warren's first book-length publication appeared in 1929, titled *John Brown: The Making of a Martyr,* in which he portrays Brown as a hero on one hand and as a fanatic on the other. In *Listen to the Mockingbird,* Cass expresses some empathy for John Brown, not as a fanatic rebel but as a lonely human being who is trapped at Harper's Ferry. *John Brown* is but one expression of Warren's lifelong interest in the Civil War, an interest kindled early in Warren by his maternal grandfather. Warren described his reaction to Grandpa Penn's stories in an interview with Edwin Newman in 1971:

> At the first, of course, a small boy of six or seven hearing about battles, it's all very romantic because he doesn't understand blood, but I do remember very distinctly the shock of discovering that the old man, my grandfather, who had fought battles, wasn't romantic about it. I remember that shock very distinctly. It was a story, an important story to tell, but it wasn't romantic. This was a great shock, because I wanted to make it all very romantic in my childish way. This shock was quite real. I even wrote a poem about it, called "Court Martial"—about that moment when the old man was not romantic at all, and I had been romantic, and suddenly he was realistic about it.[7]

Cass arrives at the Trices' house a romantic idealist.

In 1974, responding to a question from Marshall Walker about slavery, Warren commented:

> In the whole question of the Southern story this split [over slavery] is deep, from Thomas Jefferson right on down—to take it at the grand level—to Robert E. Lee, who was an emancipationist; and Grant held the last slaves legally held in the United States, I think. There are no *morals* in this, it's just part of the comedy of our history; but segregation was a very late development in the South, it only became legal quite late, and the old people had been *against* segregation because they didn't have that kind of racial

6. Robert Penn Warren, interviewed by Marshall Walker, "Robert Penn Warren: An Interview," in Watkins and Hiers, *Robert Penn Warren Talking,* 180.

7. Robert Penn Warren, interviewed by Edwin Newman, "Speaking Freely," in Watkins and Hiers, Robert Penn Warren Talking, 163. For more information about Warren's grandfather, see Joseph Blotner, *Robert Penn Warren: A Biography* (New York: Random House, 1997).

> antipathy. They might be the boss but they had no racial antipathy. It was a question of the structure.[8]

Warren goes on to talk about two of his other novels which deal with the Civil War, *Band of Angels* and *Wilderness.* The subject runs deep and is expressed more privately three years earlier. In a 1971 letter to his friend Cleanth Brooks, Warren wrote:

> The C[ivil] W[ar] did "commit" the US to centralization etc., was a 'turning' point; but it strikes me as very important to distinguish between the "symbolic" importance of this and the "literal." As symbolic—as the enactment of ideas—it is focal for our history, it seems to me, a definition of issues, etc. AND of the issues in a marination of ironies of all sorts. But some of these ironies, those that would put the Southern values into other perspectives, did not function because defeat raised those values into another dimension: they were spared the test of the future-become-history. The Northern values were, God knows, put to this test with a vengeance and are still being put to it with pollution, Attica, etc. What I am getting at is this: I feel that there is a very strong probability that if the South had won, they would have embarked socially and economically on much the same course. First they would have learned that you have to industrialize. They were at the moment trying their best to industrialize, to catch up, in order to win a war. If they had won, in one way, or another, they would never have settled for the plantation team—and many defenders of the Southern system were already aware of the industrial needs. Fitzhugh. Furthermore, there was a strong imperialistic, expansionist psychology in the South, which was expressing itself, of course, in terms of expanding the plantation system. Cuba, Central America, etc.—but it wouldn't have confined itself to that; it would have been soon geared to a new psychology.[9]

This speculation on Warren's part is interesting from the standpoint of the various ways certain roles might be played, e.g., Gilbert, Duncan, and perhaps a mix of opinions among the guests at the Trice house (act I).

In *The Legacy of the Civil War,* Warren states that the Civil War gave the South the Great Alibi, by which southerners explain, condone, and transmute everything; they turn defeat into victory, defects into virtues, and even their great virtues into absurdities. The war gave the North the Treasury of Virtue, which be-

8. Warren interviewed by Walker, "Warren: An Interview," 186.

9. Robert Penn Warren to Cleanth Brooks, October 6, 1971, in *Cleanth Brooks and Robert Penn Warren: A Literary Correspondence,* ed. James A. Grimshaw Jr. (Columbia: University of Missouri Press, 1998), 330.

stows on northerners a feeling of redemption by history, even if history is rewritten to suit them, and allowed them to feel they had earned "grace abounding, for the least of sinners."[10] Notwithstanding Warren's later view, the Cass Mastern drama ends on the afternoon of Duncan Trice's funeral, April 13, 1861, with Cass's departure to attempt to find Bella's personal servant and slave, Phebe.

OVERVIEW

Interestingly, Warren seems to have shifted his focus from the naïve Cass Mastern to the seductive temptress, Bella Trice; added Abbott Coldwater, Bella's younger brother and Cass's guide into the more sensual world of Lexington; added Mark Trice, Duncan's cousin and a professor at Transylvania University who provides the moral backdrop; and allowed Gilbert an explicitly stronger role as "the 'hero' as a person and the 'hero' as a reflex of history."

Bella is seen early as adventuresome, a risk taker in riding her horse Celeste; manipulative, as she controls Abbott (Abbey-boy), Duncan, and up to a point Cass; fearful of the rain, of anything restrictive in her life; and disloyal, ultimately true only to herself. Her presence on stage, her motivation of plot, and her boldness of character qualify her as protagonist, the main character against whom Gilbert, the antagonist, contends for Cass's future. Another title for this play could have been "The Education of Cass"; Mark Trice summarizes that motif best. In response to Bella's challenge to Mark's claim that he knows what Cass will be like, he says that "we are the world, and everyone of us is trying to make him into our special image of the world. Duncan is trying to make him into another Duncan—a gay, honorable, sentimental gentleman. And Abbott is trying to make him into a charming young rakehell. And Brother Gilbert into a statesman to trumpet Brother Gilbert's glory. And me . . . Yes, me too. I'd make him into a censorious old curmudgeon who peers over his spectacles" (I.ii.41).[11]

Cass's "darkness and trouble" mentioned in the novel includes his discovery "that there is an education for vice" in the world—the gaming table, the bottle, the racecourse, the "illicit sweetness of the flesh."[12] Abbott does entice Cass to go

10. Robert Penn Warren, *The Legacy of the Civil War* (New York: Random House, 1961), 60–64.

11. References to *Listen to the Mockingbird* cite the 1959 version by act (I), scene (ii), and manuscript page (41).

12. Robert Penn Warren, *All the King's Men,* 2nd Harvest edition, with a foreword by Joseph Blotner (San Diego: Harcourt Brace, 1996), 164. Hereinafter, references to this edition are cited parenthetically in the text.

into town and "have some fun" (I.ii.39). They return drunk, Abbott tries to make a pass at Phebe, Cass intervenes, and Bella enters to see what the commotion is about. She chastises Abbott and sends him to bed. The stage is now set for Bella, who has been curious about Cass's impoverished childhood in Georgia when he was just a "sprig," and Cass to have an intimate dialogue. To Bella, however, "the world is so—false" (I.ii.52–53). She is also curious about Cass's evening with Molly, about whom Abbott has teased Cass earlier. Perhaps Bella is a little jealous of Molly's having had Cass. Her life, she feels at the end of act I, is without hope and love. At that point she embraces Cass.

Act II opens in April 1861, about sixteen months later. Preparation for war dramatizes better the chaos that reigns in the Trice household. Gilbert has returned to collect Cass, whom he expects to fight for the cause. Bella senses that she is about to lose Cass and tries desperately to keep him. A subplot also thickens with the loss of Jason, Phebe's husband, who had belonged to a neighboring plantation owner but, we learn in this act, has now been sold. Bella has thus betrayed Phebe, whom she had promised to buy Jason to prevent his being taken away, and Duncan discovers Bella's betrayal of him when Bella pleads with Cass to save Jason. Duncan, however, is willing to forgive Bella, who aggressively attacks Duncan for lying to Phebe about Jason. Gilbert, who overhears the accusations about Cass, is not upset about Bella's unfaithfulness but about her involving Cass: "But I warn you, I'll not have any nonsense, his [Duncan's] or yours. I was a fool to leave that boy here, just to pick up a few tricks and airs and graces, but now I am taking him away to business, and if you try to make him stay, as I am mortally sure you are trying to do, I shall expose you. I have plans for that boy, and you'll not interfere. Do you hear?" (II.i.21). Duncan commits suicide at the end of this act.

Act III opens after Duncan's funeral. Up to this point, Cass has been the pawn of his "educators." His change manifests itself in his decision to seek Phebe, thus defying Bella and Gilbert. After Phebe finds Duncan's wedding ring under his pillow, a clear implication that his death was not an accident, Bella sells her—her second betrayal of Phebe. True to her character, Bella blames Cass for dodging his responsibility by not protecting her (Bella), that is, if he really loved her (III.i.10). But in the climactic scene, Cass explains to Bella: "It is all one web, and we spun it. . . . If we have ever loved and not lain together in mere foulness, then we must take hands and say it. . . . If we say the truth—take hands and say it—then we can be free—" (III.ii.34).

Cass leaves to find Phebe, whom he believes will forgive them. The play's denouement is left to Bella and Gilbert after Mark, perhaps Warren's voice in the play, says that Cass has gone South to seek the truth and that they are all responsible for trying to possess him. Gilbert has the last word when Bella calls Mark a coward for not standing up for her. Gilbert says that Mark is not a coward: "No, mam. It's just that he knows the truth, mam. Yes, Professor Trice is the kind of man who knows the truth about everything. He even knows the truth about himself. It's just he never knows what to do about it" (III.ii.53). Gilbert will endure.

The dramatization of the Cass Mastern story written by Warren in 1959 came thirteen years after the publication of the novel, and in the same year the stage version of *All the King's Men* was produced off Broadway. The play retains the focus on the moral implications associated with the virtues of hope, love, and endurance and the vices of despair, apathy, and instant gratification that is discernable in the novel. If we believe Mark, then Cass would represent hope in seeking the truth; if we believe Gilbert, the South and its struggle are the hope of the future. Cass's love is idyllic, notwithstanding his adulterous affair with Bella. Bella's love does not rise above self-serving control; in that sense Bella is apathetic about others' feelings of love. Gilbert, the pragmatist, will endure as will Mark, the one wed to Truth (I.ii.35). That Warren continued to revise this play reminds us of his fascination with the story and all that it implies about the use and abuse of power. Producing *Listen to the Mockingbird,* even with some knowledge of the play's background, still created a variety of challenges.

BACKGROUND TO THE PRODUCTION

In an article based on his experience directing *Willie Stark: His Rise and Fall,* an adaptation by Warren of *All the King's Men,* for the Margo Jones Theatre in Dallas in 1958, Aaron Frankel quotes Warren's notes for a "Playwright's Column" written for the production. A shortened version is cited above; the complete quotation follows: "There was a moral to this story. If you begin to alter, however casually, a form—which was what Aaron Frankel and I started out to do—you are bound in the end to alter meaning. For form is meaning. That is the moral to this story—an old moral, but one that I had been relearning in my long association with Willie Stark."[13] Just as Warren had altered the meaning when he developed *Willie Stark: His Rise and Fall* out of *All the King's Men,* he similarly alters his emphasis, if not his whole meaning, in the writing of *Listen to the Mockingbird.* In addition to separating the Jack Burden story from the Cass Mastern story, *Listen to the Mockingbird* also abbreviates the time frame for the Cass Mastern story,

13. Warren, "Playwright's Column," quoted in Frankel, "Working in the Theater," 2.

deletes some of the characters found in the original story, and adds new characters. In making those changes, Warren is able to make the adaptation a drama rather than a documentary.

Staged adaptations of chapter 4 of *All the King's Men* seem to produce documentaries rather than drama. Two examples will illustrate this conclusion. The first is Adrian Hall's 1990 adaptation, *Prologue to "All the King's Men,"* which was staged in the Dallas Theater Center's basement theater. Hall was founder of the Trinity Repertory Theater in Providence, Rhode Island, which was one of the first regional theaters to receive a grant from the National Endowment for the Arts. Known for taking new approaches to Shakespeare and for producing postmodern plays, Hall was trying to produce works that were, while not exactly meant to shock the audience, on the cutting edge of contemporary theater. He was trying to return the Dallas Theater Center to a time when it was known for doing avant-garde material, sometimes shocking, sometimes exciting, but not theater done to appeal to the masses, not theater done for little more than escape or pure entertainment. Hall's production of chapter 4 was enjoyable, but outside of the creative staging of the story, he had used much of Warren's dialogue and many of his situations. The play was a fast-paced production and, in a sense, could be accused of making its point the hard way. Hall had staged this production as a somewhat shocking documentary. Hall may have been privy to a March 16, 1954, letter that Frankel had written to Warren. Frankel had alluded to documentary drama: "There is a strong journalistic vein in *All the King's Men,* though of a high order, and I think the play would be best cast in the mold of a documentary. I myself see the form of the play coming out of such combined roots as the 'Living Newspaper' style of the Federal Theatre of the Thirties and the rapid fire, audience-centered style of the Group Theatre's *Waiting for Lefty.*" Earlier in the same letter, Frankel also fingers the difficulty in adapting the novel to the stage: "One central problem in making a play of the novel I have found paramount, however. In the novel Jack Burden it seems to me is the central focus and this works because the novel form allows you to develop the story out of Jack's introspection. This, however, is not as easy to apply on the stage." Thus one of Frankel's "main suggestions" is that Willie Stark should be the central character.[14] In adapting the Cass Mastern story, the problem is similar: it is Cass's story, not Jack's.

The second example of adaptation becoming documentary drama comes from a staged reading in 1992 at Texas A&M University–Commerce. Kay

14. Quoted in Frankel, "Working in the Theater," 9.

Coughenour adapted the Cass Mastern story as a play for a graduate seminar. Trying to eliminate the Jack Burden element, he attempted to remain otherwise faithful to Warren's version, starting with Cass in the hospital, dying from his wounds and writing a letter to Gilbert. Flashbacks were introduced to reveal Cass's journey, and Cass had an opportunity that Frankel describes Warren's characters as having: to "step outside the action of the story to observe, comment on, and justify [himself] to us." Behind the readers in the production was a projection screen upon which video clips and slides depicting scenes of the Civil War were shown. The reading turned out to be an episodic biography of Cass Mastern, a documentary in ways similar to the Hall production and, incidentally, to Erwin Piscator's production of *All the King's Men* in the New School Dramatic Workshop in 1948. The experiences that led to this realization, and the realization itself, were excellent preparation for the 1998 production of *Listen to the Mockingbird* as an entry in the Kennedy Center American College Theater Festival.[15]

THEMATIC THRUST

Aaron Frankel comments that southern writers "tend to cultivate the lust for violence, pain, and darkness as inborn, permanent, dominant, inescapable, from generation to generation. Sin is original with man (indeed). In Warren it is more than an idea, it is felt, a stench, an intuition made fact by belief. Goodness is only a hope. Evil is a conviction. It even becomes a principle, a cause."[16] A refrain in *All the King's Men* reminds readers of man's predicament: "Man is conceived in sin and born in corruption and he passeth from the stink of the didie to the stench of the shroud."[17] In *Listen to the Mockingbird,* after Cass discovers that Bella sold Phebe, he struggles to correct his sinful ways by following Phebe in an effort to save her from a fate worse than death. He says to Bella: "You sold her! You sold her. No wonder Abbott wouldn't take it. *(Looking at the money.)* Do you know what they'll do with her? In Louisiana?" (III.ii.32). Cass cannot articulate

15. Further background, so necessary for the actors' understanding of the life and times of the historical period of a play, was kindly provided by historian Don Reynolds, whose specialty is the American Civil War. He covered such areas as (1) the life of a field slave versus the life of a household slave (2) the role of the wife on the plantation (3) considerations in freeing the slaves (4) intimacy with household slaves (5) the place of Kentucky in the Civil War; and (6) the events that took place during some of the various battles.

16. Frankel, "Working in the Theater," 15.

17. Warren, *All the King's Men,* 49.

the details of the horror that lies ahead for Phebe. In his essay Frankel observes that Warren's primary subject, perhaps his obsession, is the premise that, "Confronted by evil, good must be created out of it. It is the definition of a man." It is, Frankel notes, "in allegory form the history of the South." [18]

A major supporting image is the powerful spider web metaphor that appears in the novel and is partially retained in the play. Cass tells Bella:

> It's all one web, and we spun it. All the lies and deceiving. Jason sold away. Duncan dead. That girl gone to be whored in Louisiana. And that man *(Gesture toward the window)*—that old man, the old free nigger praising God for that money you threw him. Yes—I see it now, and it's all one.—Oh, don't you see? *(Putting out his hand toward her)*. . . . Take it, for if we have ever loved each other. If we have even loved and not lain together in mere foulness, then we must take hands and say it. Take my hand, Bella. *(As she touches his hand)* If we can say the truth—take hands and say it—then we can be free. . . . We can begin to be free. We can begin to unspin the web. We can begin. Listen—*(As she lifts her face expectantly toward him)*—I'll get her. I'll find her. I'll bring her back. (III.ii.34–35)

Beekman W. Cottrell considers the spider web metaphor to be "the major philosophical image of the novel" and accurately points out Cass's explanation of it in the novel: "It was, instead, the fact that all of these things—the death of my friend, the betrayal of Phebe, the suffering and rage and great change of the woman I had loved—all had come from my single act of sin and perfidy, as the boughs from the bole and the leaves from the bough. Or to figure the matter differently, it was as though the vibration set up in the whole fabric of the world by my act had spread infinitely and with ever increasing power and no man could know the end." [19] The play, of course, does not provide the entire spider web metaphor, in terms of which Jack Burden is able to see Cass's life from an outside perspective. But the thematic demand for "accepting responsibility" is, as Cottrell has found, inherent in that metaphor: "Cass did not brush the Spider web voluntarily. Chance threw him with Annabelle [Bella] Trice, and the vibrations of the web began. Their intense affair was wrong—sinful—in every way and Cass knew it." [20] Cass is the only character in *Listen to the Mockingbird* to accept responsibility for his sins.

18. Frankel, "Working in the Theater," 11.

19. Warren, *All the King's Men,* quoted in Beekman W. Cottrell, "Cass Mastern and the Awful Responsibility of Time," in *Twentieth-Century Interpretations of "All the King's Men,"* ed. by Robert H. Chambers (Englewood Cliffs, NJ: Prentice-Hall, 1977), 116, 118.

20. Cottrell, "Cass Mastern," 119.

CHARACTERS AND CASTING

Georg II, Duke of Saxe Meiningen, in the late 1800s pioneered the idea of making every character in a play important. Since that time, directors of plays with many minor characters have encouraged the actors to create individual identities for their characters. While characters in crowd scenes often need to react as one voice, they also need to be individuals in a group. During early readings of the script, the characters "First Guest," "Second Guest," and "Third Guest" were assigned to specific actors and given names derived from those of guests who are mentioned in the dialogue. Additional roles were identified by assigning wives to these guests, and other women were identified as relatives of some of the guests.

Identifying one or more characters whom the audience can relate with and admire proves a difficult task in *Listen to the Mockingbird.* Certainly, religious and moralistic audiences are not willingly going to admire someone who commits suicide, someone who commits adultery, someone who achieves wealth at any price, someone who lives off the wealth of others, or someone who is corrupted by power. Duncan Trice, instead of fighting for the woman he loves, is so heartbroken and weak that he commits suicide. Furthermore, he seems to be a person who did not come by his wealth the old-fashioned way. The wealth that he inherited he has almost lost; he is near financial ruin. Other human frailties that audiences might not admire are his excessive drinking and gambling. In dealing with Bella, however, he is simply weak.

Warren expands the character of Annabelle (Bella) Trice, making her a much stronger character in the play than she is in the novel. Bella's character was, indeed, sufficient reason for producing this play. She comes from a moneyed family that had fallen on hard times before she married Duncan. Bella apparently has never forgiven her father. In the first act, after Cass and Abbott return from drinking in Lexington and Abbott is caught trying to seduce Phebe, Bella tells Cass that her brother, like her father, is a wastrel: "Oh, a great name, but a wastrel! And he died bankrupt" (I.ii.50). She continues: "Just a wastrel and a fool to boot. He [Abbott] lives off my husband. But Duncan, he's a fool, too, to encourage him to be wild, to be fashionable, to game, to . . . " (I.ii.50). Mr. Coldwater gave Bella in marriage to Duncan Trice, perhaps in hopes that he might benefit from their marriage and certainly knowing that his daughter would benefit from the marriage. Bella seems terribly self-centered, spoiled, and reckless. She is definitely assertive. But even if assertiveness, daring, and recklessness might appeal to an audience today, Bella surely carries the daring too far when she seduces Cass in the Trice house. Bella and Duncan's marriage appears on the surface to be good; they seem happy, gay, and attracted to one another. Duncan is undoubtedly attracted to Bella. Using the novel as a source, interpreters of Bella's character may conclude that her seemingly nonchalant attitude about her affair with Cass is of no significant consequence or that she is able to maintain a remarkable charade when they are in Duncan's presence. Her adultery and self-centered nature do not make her a likeable character for the audience.

By introducing the character of Mark Trice, a college professor, Warren was able to keep his "voice" in the play—Mark Trice's *raison d'être.* Mark Trice also replaced the character of Mr. Lawson in the novel, the tutor whom Gilbert Mastern had provided Cass in Mississippi and who provided Cass with his firm grounding in Latin and Presbyterian morality. Viewers might even see him as empathetic, but he, too, is not without shortcomings. Although he can take the moral high ground philosophically, he does not really take any actions himself. He is cerebral, but he seems to lack courage to act on his beliefs. His "objectivity" enables him to understand Cass better than any other character in the play. He philosophizes about the effects of power and the search for truth and observes to Bella that people, including himself, are attempting to shape Cass in their own image. Bella turns on Mark in the last scene of the play and calls him a coward for not defending her honor against Gilbert's accusations. A sense of honor may, however, be in the ethical background of the beholder. Some audiences might not see anything admirable in Mark because he lacks heroic qualities.

On the other hand, audiences tend to favor a strong man who has succeeded in life against all odds. Willie Stark might serve as an example at the beginning of the novel. Gilbert Mastern is a man who has pulled himself up by his own bootstraps and might clearly deserve an audience's admiration. They might even applaud his success as an exemplum of the Protestant work ethic. From nothing Gilbert amassed a fortune, including seven or eight plantations in Mississippi. In Warren's descriptions of Gilbert's ascendancy in the novel, one finds a somewhat overbearing, self-confident son who stayed away until his parents died. He rescues his brother and sister, Lavinia, who is not mentioned in the play, from poverty. In the play Gilbert's plans for Cass are fairly obvious, and Gilbert appears as a manipulator who is willing to use his own brother to further his political ends. Even Gilbert's apparent generosity in sending Cass to Transylvania University, where Jefferson Davis attended classes, seems to have political undertones. Clearly, Gilbert is shrewd. If Cass acquires the skills of society, skills that perhaps Gilbert lacks, Cass, too, might enter the political arena, under Gilbert's influence, of course. Though his purpose is kept secret, Gilbert's sudden departure for Washington, D.C., is enough to suggest some political design. Two tragic flaws might keep Gilbert from being admirable to an audience: hubris and greed. He is a survivor, a practical man of action (not unlike Willie Stark toward the end of the novel), and an opportunist. In act I, scene I, Gilbert makes clear those characteristics when he remarks that no institution is sacred and once an institution stops getting things done, it should be replaced. Like Willie Stark's, Gilbert Mastern's appeal may be short lived.

Abbott, Bella's brother, lives off Duncan's money in return for being a companion to Duncan when they go carousing. When "Abbey-Boy" refuses the money Bella received for selling Phebe, she rebuffs him: "Since when were you so high and mighty about money? You always took it—from me—from Duncan—" (III.ii.30). She twists the insult to an appeal, a tactic that had apparently worked in the past when she wanted to manipulate her brother. Abbott is a contrast to Cass; he is the worldly side and lends a certain degree of experience to the innocent Cass. He teaches Cass the ways of manhood in Lexington and in that role might be seen as a corrupter of innocence. As a brother, a brother-in-law, a student, and a peer, Abbott lacks admirable qualities.

Even though audiences might not empathize with any of these characters, would they find Cass an admirable person? Perhaps to a certain extent they can forgive Cass, who, one might assume, at the age of twenty-two probably lacks experience in sexual escapades. In fact, Abbott introduces Cass to "little old juicy Molly" (I.ii.48), a woman of the night, the same evening that Bella seduces Cass, and this might be seen as a catalyst for Cass's unseemly act. Nevertheless, if one person in the play deserves the audience's admiration, compassion, and empathy, it is Cass Mastern. Cass Mastern is the only one in the play who tries to right his wrong, to take responsibility for his action, and to unspin the web of deceit and betrayal. Cass confesses his sins and wants to atone for them. Bella, on the other hand, denies them and does not want to accept responsibility for Duncan's suicide, his wedding ring notwithstanding.

Warren replaced the blind Negro singing "Old Dan Tucker" with the character of Old Alec, a freed slave who sings the haunting song *Listen to the Mockingbird.* Old Alec represents an idea prevalent in the antebellum South that the Negro, once freed, would be worse off, a sentiment expressed by Cass in the novel. Old Alec represents those freed slaves and seems to have no reason to rejoice until Bella gives him the eight hundred dollars gained from the sale of Phebe. However, casting the role of African Americans is not always an easy one, as Frankel commented in a November 22, 1967, letter to Warren about a production of *Brother to Dragons:* "I have to report one strange problem, so ironic, and a product of the inflammations of this year of I hope our Lord, 1967. Negroes don't want to play Negroes."[21] Several explanations are possible but, in fact, only one African American male showed up at auditions for *Listen to the Mockingbird* though the play has one female and three male parts for African Americans. Even appeals to the campus minority affairs director for help produced no new prospects. After recruiting an African American female to play Phebe, the two roles—Old Alec and the houseboy, a slave who was given the name John for the Texas A&M–Commerce production, were played by the same actor. Given the historical time period and the play's subtitle, "A Drama of the American Civil War," an audience should not feel that the roles are demeaning for the actors; Phebe is adequately developed as a character. Yet these roles depict Negroes in the plantation South before and during the Civil War, a historical situation that most African Americans, it seems, would choose not to relive. The character Phebe seems to be reasonably true to life and is not depicted as an evil person. She does nothing wrong but is caught in the web because she finds fault with her mistress for having an affair that resulted in her husband's death. She implicitly accuses Bella by presenting Duncan's wedding ring to her, a symbolic message left by Duncan for his wife, telling her that his death was not accidental; in telling her mistress where she'd found the ring, Phebe insinuates that she understands its meaning. However, Phebe remains loyal to Bella and does not reveal her discovery to anyone else.

Old Alec represents the slave who has been freed but, having no job skills, is left to panhandle to stay alive. John, the houseboy, also voices a southern belief that generally slaves were treated well and preferred living on the plantations under the protection of the land owners. The appearance of these characters is brief, but they are important to the play's depiction of the relations of household slaves to their masters.

Larue, a slave trader from Louisiana, is a dark-skinned person of Indian and French decent. He must always be aware of people who detest his occupation. Although slavery was accepted as an economic necessity and a way of life at the time, Larue's profession was still viewed as unpleasant at best. His character could be played as an evil figure or as a man making a living in a legitimate trade in 1861. The Texas A&M–Commerce production depicted Larue as the latter. Once the actor began searching for the reasons behind Larue's behavior, his actions were viewed as truthful and honest, not villainous. Larue was simply acting in a professional manner, a manner and a profession that were accepted in that region

21. Aaron Frankel to Robert Penn Warren, November 22, 1967, quoted in Frankel, "Working in the Theater," 14.

during those times. Once Larue has paid for Phebe and has received her papers, he is simply defending his property.

Casting and interpreting roles were based largely on the historical background of the period, on information from the novel about the characters upon whom the dramatic characterizations are based, and the playwright's presentation of them. That Warren's ongoing interest in the Cass Mastern story continued well beyond this 1959 version leads to the conclusion that these characters were still being developed; consequently, roles had been and were being altered, ever so slightly, to accommodate nuances and shifts in emphasis. Use of the Keirsey Temperament Sorter, a test which "types" personalities and assists in determining how one's personality can affect emotions and reactions in various situations, enabled actors to make decisions about their movements on stage and about their emotional reactions to other characters in the play. The actors responded to the test as if they were the character whom they were playing and used the results to interpret and to assimilate those personality traits.

SET DESIGN

Warren converted the sprawling, episodic story of Cass Mastern by reducing the number of locations and the time span covered in chapter 4 of *All the King's Men.* Instead of painting the broad landscape of Cass's life from his childhood in Georgia to his adulthood in Mississippi and Kentucky and in the Confederate army and ultimately to his death in an Atlanta hospital, Warren confines the physical action in the play to one location—the home of Duncan and Bella Trice, the drawing room Warren describes at the beginning of the play. Below are excerpts from the concept statement prepared by the set designer, Rosanne K. Coughenour:

> My concept of designing *Listen to the Mockingbird* came from various sources, and I took many things into consideration. *Listen to the Mockingbird* is based prior to and including the Civil War period. I wanted a realistic set, but wanted imagery and suggestion in the design. My primary goal was functionality on a limited budget. I wanted to set the period through the selection of furniture and architectural units.
>
> After discussing how the set needed to be used to accommodate the action, . . . the director and I decided to use a scrim for the wall between the foyer entrance area of the house and the drawing room. We did this to permit the audience to see all of the action, such as the eavesdropping during private moments. Originally we had a single entrance door, but because of the costuming and the skirts, we made double doors to accommodate the period skirts. Cass Mastern's line about a spider web inspired a cres-

> cent shape window above the door with a spider web design; the actor portraying Cass gestured toward the window during his blocking.[22]

The precise placement of furniture within the house and the location of some of the entrances and exits evolved as the blocking evolved (see Appendix E). This flexibility made it easier to establish the location of offstage areas of the house, such as the kitchen and the area where guests would be received as they exit their carriages. The scrim permitted the audience to take note when a character was eavesdropping on action that was taking place in the drawing room.

In addition, Warren selectively condenses the time frame of events in the Trice home from several years in *All the King's Men* to a span nineteen of months in the play, from October 1859 to April 1961. The historical time frame of Duncan's death is moved from 1854 to 1861, and details of the early years of Cass Mastern's life are related through exposition. In the play Warren does not follow Cass on his journey in search for Phebe, no onstage action takes place in Lexington or Paducah or on Cass's trip to visit Lewis C. Robards's barracoon to witness the selling of a comely female slave.

Other aspects of the set design helped eliminate problems with exchanges between Bella and Phebe, Gilbert and Cass, Cass and Bella, and Abbott and Alec. An outside area with lattice and a bench stage right just off the drawing room created an image of a garden and summerhouse or gazebo that helped prevent several awkward moments on stage. For example, one difficult piece of staging requires Abbott to give Old Alec some money and tell him to go around the house to the kitchen. Stage directions call for Abbott to throw the money out a window. This window might cause some problems if placed in the fourth wall. The solution was found collaboratively with the lighting designer by projecting light in window patterns to indicate front windows. This solution, however, still presented blocking complications, but having Abbott go through French doors from the drawing room into the outside summerhouse area to speak with Alec proved more effective and diverted the audience's attention from the party. During such diversions in act I, the background noise of the party was lowered, and guests were moved upstage into an entry foyer represented by a scrim wall just inside the main entrance doors before entering the drawing room. The scrim between the two rooms created the semblance of a party while still allowing the main dialogue to be heard.

22. Rosanne K. Coughenour, "Concept Statement," prepared for exhibit of set design at the 1999 Region VI Kennedy Center American College Theater Festival, hosted at Texas Woman's University, Denton, Texas, February 23–27, 1999.

THE DONEHUE LETTER

In a March 11, 1960, letter to Warren (Appendix B), Vincent J. Donehue described the "problems of stagecraft" he encountered in the script of *Listen to the Mockingbird.* His twenty-one "notes" also address concerns about two characters, Bella and Mark, and encourage Warren to make his basic themes "more manifest." A comparison of Donehue's notes to the 1959 manuscript indicates that Donehue was indeed working from that version. Interestingly, without prior knowledge of the Donehue letter, many of the same difficulties with stagecraft were identified and solved in the 1998 production.[23] Donehue's comments seem to demonstrate a lack of confidence in Warren's script and in the ability of actors to convey the necessary moods and feelings that can be created through the actors' imaginations. To illustrate that claim, a few observations on Donehue's notes and our production experience follow.

Donehue suggests that Bella "carries the theme of irresponsibility most heavily in the play," and therefore "the more specific she can be all through the play, the more interesting she is as a human being." However, the script contains sufficient hints to provide an experienced actress ample clues to develop Bella's character through action as well as dialogue. Though Abbott may seem more irresponsible generally, Bella's "irresponsibility" is more seriously ethical in nature. The theme of betrayal seems to be more heavily emphasized, and Bella's actions—her affair with Cass and her selling Phebe—speak louder than her words. The specificity that Donehue calls for would only diminish the role of the actress in bringing the character to life.

The opening scene is Cass Mastern's arrival at the Trice house and his introduction by Gilbert. Several people dressed in riding habit are chatting gaily at the celebration after a hunt or an exhilarating ride. Although Donehue suggests that the number of guests be reduced to two or three specific guests (in note 1), an increase in number by including spouses and other escorts allowed for distractions necessary for the foreshadowing exchange between Bella and Phebe. Phebe reveals to Bella that her husband, who works on a neighboring plantation, might be sold. Bella agrees to buy Phebe's husband should that occasion arise. Donehue recognizes the importance of that exchange and suggests that it be lengthened and played with only the two characters on stage (note 2). With the distractions in the background, however, Bella can reassure Phebe without effort or commit-

23. A handwritten note at the top of the Donehue letter suggests that his critique was preliminary to his directing the play, but in fact the production Donehue was considering never came about.

ment. Set design facilitated the staging of this scene. The set simultaneously depicted both the interior of the Trice house and an indication of a summerhouse or gazebo outside the house. The dialogue between Bella and Phebe took place outside, just off the drawing room. A lighting crossfade was used to draw attention away from the chatter of the attending party guests and focus attention on Phebe and Bella outside without making their conversation seem too intimate. Specific guests at the gathering were provided names that appear elsewhere in the dialogue—Jim Talbutt, Sam Fairlea, and Colonel Allen—and were assigned speaking parts that were identified anonymously in the script. Phebe is a marvelous character. Donehue's suggestions for further development are understandable, and Warren's script provided enough material for her character to come alive on stage without additional lines.

Some of Donehue's notes seem to be one director's preference rather than corrections of indisputable errors, but a close reading of Warren's manuscript reveals how subtly he has woven this story. In note 9, Donehue suggests that the guests be present to hear the intoxicated Duncan act foolishly in front of them. The moment in act I, scene ii, is more intimate, an intimacy that Bella and Mark understand. That moment lets the audience know that all is not well between Bella and Duncan. Warren's stage directions indicate Bella's sadness: "*All at once she buries her head in his [Mark's] chest. He comforts her, very carefully and correctly till she lifts her face*" (I.ii.47). Earlier in the quiet exchange between Bella and Mark, Mark reveals that Duncan loses only at cards and wins at everything else. From that moment we learn that Bella might have a need for another man in her life, and we also learn that Mark might envy his cousin but has the restraint not to be that other man. The scene works better if the guests are not present.

Gilbert Mastern's role is yet another concern, and Donehue questions the need to have Gilbert return at the end of the play (note 18) but suggests that a scene between Gilbert and Cass be added in which Cass declares his independence from his big brother. The story in the novel makes clear Cass's independence and his death; Warren chose not to make that point in the play. In not magnifying the character of Cass in the final scene, Warren leaves the audience with a broken Bella. The dominance of her character at the end shifts the focus from Cass to Bella, a fallen woman, and more clearly identifies the play's tragedy.

In his last note (21), Donehue refers to the imbalance in the three acts of the play. It is true that there is an imbalance in the lengths of the three acts. The brief second act in which Duncan commits suicide is the pivotal point in the play. Brevity becomes it. Gilbert, whose political aspirations are subtly alluded to, asserts himself in act III. Donehue it seems would have liked to reduce Gilbert's role; however, the audience responded well to Gilbert's revealing to Cass that he has been listening and to his expressing an animalistic lust for Bella. He rightfully and dramatically points out the inevitability of Bella's role. Thus Gilbert helps prepare the audience for the final scene of the play. The tragedy is Bella's tragedy. She brushed the spider web and is caught. If indeed Bella—not Cass—is the protagonist of this play, then Aristotle's commentary on the protagonist's inability to control his or her destiny is apropos; fate does play a role in her destiny. Bella has become who she is because she was born attractive and through heredity and/or environment has the innate need to control others. The denouement is left to Gilbert. Mark seems to understand what Cass is seeking and why the others have abandoned their quest for the truth. Gilbert reduces Bella by accusing her of everything she has done, and he makes her acknowledge her actions. He may even be seen as virtuous in the Socratic sense that "virtue is knowledge and nobody can teach you what virtue is. You remember it from the time before you were born, when you were not of this world" (I.ii.31). If not, he clearly is a man of action who seems to know who he is and what he is about. When he departs, Bella, Mark, and Abbott are left in an empty house to lead empty lives.

Each director sees a script differently. If Donehue did, indeed, direct this play, it may have been closer to the 1960 version. But Donehue expressed in his letter his "basic profound admiration for the work" and the thematic strength of the play, and Warren was clearly intrigued by the story for a number of years.

CONCLUSION

The Cass Mastern story should have another life. It should be a movie or an opera. The potential is definitely there. But, in which story—the story in *Listen to the Mockingbird* or the story in chapter 4 of *All the King's Men*? Rewrites of chapter 4 by Hall and by Coughenour produced documentaries, but Warren rewrote the story and created an exciting drama. He did so by changing many facts and by inventing new characters. His ability to rearrange and condense the events, to make them take place in one location, to move pieces of the story and have them take place at different times, and to invent new characters reflects his skill as a diverse and talented writer. Warren admitted altering the meaning when he adapted the novel *All the King's Men* as the play *Willie Stark: His Rise and Fall.* In changing the form of the Cass Mastern story from prose fiction to drama, Warren also altered its meaning. After working with both the story and the play, one discovers the temptation of directing the story although the play is Bella Trice's tale.

APPENDIX E

Blocking and Motivational Units for *Listen to the Mockingbird*

Kay L. Coughenour

Blocking is the method directors use to reveal the story and theme of a play by suggesting choices for actor movement, stage picturization or arrangement of actors, and the subtleties of body posture and gesture. In a play that is representational, the director attempts to ensure that the actors have motivation for their actions, whereas in a presentational play, the impetus for movement and the creation of stage picture is less necessary. Actors also contribute to blocking by making choices about movement, posture, and gesture. The director approves of these choices and/or suggests alternatives.

Choices made in blocking are restricted by the confines of the stage setting and the specific scenic elements (placement of various locations including furniture, physical or indicated walls, and entrances/exits) placed on the stage. The scenic designer and director consult the script for cues in the stage directions and dialogue to determine the placement of scenic elements. Because a previously unproduced play presents challenges that have not been addressed in past productions, a careful analysis of the stage directions and other hints found in the script is necessary. Choices about the location of stage elements are often modified during the rehearsal process as discoveries are made and inspiration suggests changes. These suggestions may come from the director, the actors, or the designer.

The director leads the actors toward an understanding of their respective roles by engaging them in character analysis. Eventually, perhaps the actor understands the character portrayed better than the director; however, the director has helped the actor arrive at this clearer understanding. The director understands how one character in a play influences another and how a characters are used by the playwright to reveal theme or to cause an action. Warren's

> characters relate as directly to the audience as to each other—that is, the actors "narrate" as well as "play" their roles, much as we do when we tell a story to friends. On cues supplied by Warren, they will step outside the action of the story to observe, comment on and justify themselves to us. The illusion on the stage, while still sought after, counts only so long as the characters may argue about its meaning, making not merely the stage but audience and entire theater into a tribunal, forum.[1]

Through conversations with the director, the actors begin to understand what motivates their characters to make a specific movement on stage, whether that movement is a facial expression, a hand or arm gesture, or a physical cross from one location on the stage to another. The challenge in directing *Listen to the Mockingbird* was to help the actors distinguish between the representational moments and the presentational moments—between the need at times to create the illusion of realistic characters and situations and at others to step out of character to narrate.

While directing *Listen to the Mockingbird,* I employed the Keirsey Temperament Sorter, which "types" personalities and offers insight into how one's personality can affect emotions and reactions to situations. The actors were asked to take this test as if they were their characters, to read the description of the personality and temperament type identified by the test, and then to reflect on the findings. I had used this test previously when directing other representational dramas *(The Glass Menagerie* and *Cat on a Hot Tin Roof).* My discussions of the test results with the actors contributed to their ability to make decisions regarding their movement on stage and their emotional reactions to other characters in the play.

Blocking is thus the result of a collaborative process between the director and the actors. The director often provides a framework of movements that the actor is asked to follow. As the process of rehearsal moves from the initial blocking of scenes into the uninterrupted running of scenes, the actor may suggest alternative movements or gestures. Indeed, the actor may spontaneously change her/his blocking by "becoming" the character—reacting as a result of another actor's

1. Aaron Frankel, "Working in the Theater with Robert Penn Warren," in *RWP: An Annual of Robert Penn Warren Studies,* vol. 2, ed. William Bedford Clark and James A. Grimshaw Jr. (Bowling Green: Western Kentucky University, 2002), 2.

movement or line reading. The director is the eye of the audience member. In this role, the director decides whether the actor's alternative blocking should be used or the original blocking maintained.

Listen to the Mockingbird Motivational Units

UNIT	PAGES[a]	CHARACTERS	DRAMATIC ACTION/KEY REVELATIONS
ACT I, SCENE I. *Late afternoon, October 1959. Gil is bringing Cass to Lexington to attend college, stay with the Trices, learn their genteel ways, and become refined in his manners and appearance.*			
1	1–3	Cass and Gil	Gil convinces Cass to stay at the Trices. Why doesn't Cass wish to stay?
2	3–5	Cass, Gil, Bella, Abbott, Duncan, Talbutts, Allens, and Fairleas	The Trices compliment and welcome the Masterns. Bella rides a horse and takes chances.
3	5–8	Cass, Gil, Bella, Abbott, Duncan, Talbutts, Allens, Fairleas, and Mark	Mark enters and tells us about Harper's Ferry. We discover that Mark has arranged for Cass's education at Transylvania College. Perhaps some metaphor is revealed about looking at slavery as a labor system worth defending until it is no longer useful or until a better system comes along. For Bella, is Duncan her slave until Cass comes along?
4	8–9	Cass, Gil, Bella, Abbott, Duncan, Talbutts, Allens, Fairleas, Mark, and Phebe	Foreshadowing and laying the foundation—Phebe gets Bella to agree to purchase Jason. What do I do with others standing around? What do they talk about? Obviously, Mr. Wilton could enter earlier than noted to tell Duncan the news about Robert E. Lee.
5	9–11	Cass, Gil, Bella, Abbott, Duncan, Talbutts, Allens, Fairleas, Mark, Phebe, and Mr. Wilton	John Brown will be captured at Harper's Ferry. Gil has been in the military and knows R. E. Lee. Bella draws Cass away; their lines reveal how sensitive and compassionate Cass is and also his sense of fair play and ethical values. Bella must find this gentleness attractive.
6	11–12	Cass, Bella, Gil, Abbott, Duncan, Talbutts, Allens, Fairleas, Mark, Phebe, and Mr. Wilton	Cass and Bella are left downstage as Duncan leads the others beyond the arch. We learn that Gil is a friend of Jefferson Davis. We learnthat Mark has similar leanings regarding Abolitionists.

UNIT	PAGES[a]	CHARACTERS	DRAMATIC ACTION/KEY REVELATIONS
7	12–15	Cass, Gil, Bella, Abbott, Duncan, Talbutts, Allens, Fairleas, Mark, Phebe, and Mr. Wilton	Abbott returns first. Duncan, Gil, and Mark follow; perhaps the others have moved *out on the porch.* Abbott, Mark, and Duncan are trying to accommodate Gil's desire to leave immediately and talk to Cass in privacy. This is prompted by Harper's Ferry, but Gil had told Cass that he would stay for a few days. This unit will take time to block. I want to overlap dialogue. Gil tells Cass that "fools" live in this house but a strong man can learn from "fools." Gil has plans for Cass. We learn that Bella is adventuresome and her horse is Celeste.
8	16–19	Bella, Cass, and Mark	The "idyllic" life in the piney woods is revealed; Cass is homesick. In Cass, Bella finds a lost puppy to care for. The spider web has brushed both of them. Mark has not left with the others.
9	20	Mark, Bella, and Cass; Duncan and Abbott also return	The plot thickens. Mark's "Yes, of course" can have several meanings. The past has begun to affect the present and the future.
			ACT I, SCENE II. *Two months later—evening, early December 1859 (100 years before Warren is writing this play). It is raining outside. Evidently, the rain is preventing the men from having fun in town.*
10	21–25	Duncan, Bella, Mark, and Cass	Mark and Cass temperament versus Duncan and Abbott temperament. We discover Socrates' idea of virtue as "knowledge," and Cass believes that you must remember it from the time before your were born (the gods). Bella answers, "But that's what's important! The opinion of people." Cass says the gods must inspire you. Bella becomes intrigued by the possibility of remembering the "time before you were born."
11	25–26	Duncan, Bella, Mark, and Cass (four guests enter: Jim Talbutt, Sam Fairlea, Colonel Allen, Sam Weatherall, and Claude?)	Who lets in the guests? Phebe? The guests are going to town for "a little congress" or to drink and be merry, play cards and? Duncan suggests they play cards in his house. Duncan leads the guests into another room to drink and gamble.

Listen to the Mockingbird Motivational Units (*continued*)

UNIT	PAGES[a]	CHARACTERS	DRAMATIC ACTION/KEY REVELATIONS
12	26–28	Cass, Bella, and Mark; later Duncan calls	Light conversation. This is a humorous scene where we learn about Mark. We discover that Mark is a bachelor married to "Truth"—not the homely sister of "Truth," Miss Pedantry/Self-Conceit. And she is not very good in bed. Bella shifts the conversation to Cass. Mark leaves to join the other men.
13	28–30	Cass and Bella	The rain picks up, drawing Bella to the window. Bella hates the rain because it is confining and depressing, and she yearns for "sunshine and flowers." Whereas Bella views the rain as restrictive, Cass sees the rain as an opportunity to escape work and dream and be with his mother. Even the shack has positive memories.
14	30–31	Cass, Bella, Abbott, and Mark	Abbott comes in with a friend to entice Cass into going to town to drink, gamble, and indulge with the ladies. The others are still playing cards. Mark is left with Bella.
15	31–37	Bella and Mark	One of the play's messages is revealed by Mark who is the voice of Robert Penn Warren. Mark excuses himself to leave.
16	37–38	Bella, Mark, Duncan, and guests, who are leaving	Must block the guests leaving and Duncan coming down to engage in conversation with Bella. Duncan is drunk. He wants intimacy with Bella. Bella rebuffs his advances and asks Mark to help Duncan upstairs. The stage is left silent as Mark takes Duncan up to "Jim" (a servant? or Talbutt?). Bella allows her façade to slip and cries on Mark's chest. Mark does not take advantage but suggests that she is tired and should take her leave. Mark picks up Bella's embroidery and exits.

Listen to the Mockingbird Motivational Units (*continued*)

UNIT	PAGES[a]	CHARACTERS	DRAMATIC ACTION/KEY REVELATIONS
17	38–39	Phebe, Cass, and Abbott	Cass and Abbott return as Phebe is putting out the lights and straightening up the parlor. Abbott seems jealous that Molly preferred Cass to himself. He sees Phebe and attempts to have his way with her. Cass attempts to reason with Abbott, but Abbott releases his pent-up anger about Molly and allows his pride to raise the stakes. Bella hears the commotion and enters.
18	39–40	Bella, Cass, and Abbott	We see Bella's strength as she humbles Abbott and sends him to bed. Cass starts to leave, but she stops him to apologize for her brother's behavior. This is a transition to talking about Cass.
19	40–43	Bella and Cass; Duncan with lines offstage	Bella is fascinated with Cass and his idyllic world in the piney woods. She is rebounding from Duncan's being drunk. She is perhaps envious of Cass's being with Molly. She is also very cognizant that her youth and beauty are slipping by; she says there is "a cloud coming over the sun, and the water doesn't sparkle anymore." Bella finds Cass attractive, pure and innocent. She tries to resist but cannot. Cass cannot resist Bella's advances. They move toward an embrace, which is interrupted by Duncan calling Bella. But we know Duncan will fall back asleep as the two will fall into each other's arms on the sofa. The attraction of the forbidden fruit is too great for both of them to resist.
		ACT II, SCENE I. *Four months later—early morning, April 1861. Gil has returned from Washington. The war is about to erupt.*	
20	44–45	Phebe, Gil, Duncan, Bella, Abbott, Cass, and Mark	Gil is on his way to Mississippi to raise a regiment and has stopped to pick up Cass on the way. Duncan is putting together a cavalry command with spiffy uniforms that he and Abbott are wearing. Abbott and Duncan have a false sense of the Yankees' commitment to the war. Gil has a clearer understanding. This scene must freeze as we crossfade the lights as Bella exits into the garden.

Listen to the Mockingbird Motivational Units (*continued*)

UNIT	PAGES[a]	CHARACTERS	DRAMATIC ACTION/KEY REVELATIONS
21	45–47	Cass and Bella (the others are on stage but frozen in position in the parlor)	The war is about to separate them. In the last four months they have become secret lovers. Bella is now, apparently, devoted to the excitement of being with Cass. She is controlling Cass and now losing this influence because Cass has to leave with Gil.
22	47–49	Phebe, Cass, and Bella	Jason is about to be sold, and Phebe comes to get Bella to hold her to her promise to buy him. Bella tries to calm her wailing but to no avail. Phebe's screams bring the others from the drawing room. Bella, distraught and unable to quiet Phebe, seeks someone to help her solve this dilemma and keep her promise to buy Jason. She turns to the one she loves and trusts the most—Cass, not Duncan. Duncan sees this, shuns Bella's kiss, and leaves to solve the problem. Bella is left speechless yet tries to comfort Phebe. The other men are staring at Phebe and Bella. Eventually, all leave except Mark.
23	49–50	Bella and Mark	Bella is distraught. Mark tries to tell her that all want only her happiness and are not accusing her of anything.
24	50–52	Houseboy, Abbott, and Duncan	Time passes; it is now evening, and a Houseboy comes into the drawing room with a candelabra and lights some lights. As he leaves, Abbott and Duncan return from the Hartmans'. Duncan has been interrogating Abbott about Bella's relationship with Cass. Abbott, in auditions, has used getting a drink as motivation for his entrance. Duncan dwells on the importance of Bella seeking the assistance of Cass in her moment of need.
25	52–53	Bella and Phebe enter; Abbott and Duncan remain	We learn that Duncan did not accomplish his task of purchasing Jason. Bella pleads with Phebe to understand that she tried to keep her promise. Duncan tells Phebe that it is his fault; he lies about a previous conversation with Bella. Phebe rushes from the room in tears and Duncan follows.

UNIT	PAGES[a]	CHARACTERS	DRAMATIC ACTION/KEY REVELATIONS
26	53–54	Bella and Abbott	Abbott confronts Bella and demands to know what is going on with Cass. Bella treats him like a little boy who needs comfort.
27	54–56	Bella, Abbott, Duncan, and Gil	Bella's best defense is to attack. Therefore, upon Duncan's return, she attacks him for lying, thus changing the subject/parrying the thrust of Duncan's accusation with one of her own. Bella tries to take the blame. But Duncan tells her she is blameless in his eyes—for this and any other transgressions. He does not want to lose her. He tries, as best he can, to tell her how much he loves her by recalling when they first met. We see Gil entering to hear Duncan's last words and perhaps even earlier words. Duncan is unaware of Gil's presence.
28	56–57	Bella, Abbott, Duncan, Gil, and Cass	As Cass enters and Duncan becomes aware of his and Gil's presence, Duncan's mood shifts. He tries to save face and to conceal his suspicions. Duncan and Abbott leave to change clothes. Gil asks Cass to retrieve his cigar case from his room.
29	57–59	Bella and Gil	Gil confronts Bella with the truth. He is stronger than she is strong. This is a foreshadowing of Duncan's suicide. Gil is pragmatic and talks in his gutter vocabulary. He knows that Bella understands. Gil is not upset about Bella being unfaithful to her husband, only about her involving Cass.
30	59–61	Bella and Cass; Gil leaves after one line	Cass enters to find Bella distraught. Bella uses her manipulative ways to try to get Cass to turn on her brother and to support her, to protect her from an enemy who tortures her. She tells Cass that everybody knows of their affair and all are staring at her, accusing her. She tries to shift the blame to others. She selfishly tries to get Cass to embrace her. She is on the verge of succeeding when we hear a gunshot and a scream, the inciting incident/turning point for the play. The dice have been thrown.

Listen to the Mockingbird Motivational Units (*continued*)

UNIT	PAGES[a]	CHARACTERS	DRAMATIC ACTION/KEY REVELATIONS
31	61–62	Phebe, Abbott, Mark, Bella, and Cass	A quick denouement for the inciting action. The consequences of sin. Phebe and Abbot are heard; then Phebe enters as the messenger of Duncan's death. She is followed by Mark, who stands in the path of Bella, who starts to rush upstairs. (Doorway or steps? Read 62 and 63 stage directions for set.) Cass returns with Abbott to support Bella as she slips to the floor in front of Mark. We fade to blackout.
ACT III, SCENE I. *Late at night, after the funeral of Duncan Trice.*			
32	63–66	Bella and Cass	Reminiscent of Lady Macbeth after the killing of Duncan, Bella has a difficult time erasing the her part in the crime—she and Cass were responsible for Duncan's committing suicide. Unlike Lady Macbeth, she did not encourage Cass to kill Duncan, but she did encourage Cass to have an affair. She tries to convince Cass and herself that Duncan's death was, as everyone has said, an accident. Cass sways between his desire for Bella's happiness and his responsibilities for the war. Bella wants her own happiness, selfish and new and fresh happiness.
33	66–68	Phebe, Bella, and Cass	Phebe enters to give Duncan's ring to Bella and thus remove any doubt that Duncan committed suicide. Several things are revealed—Duncan never took his ring off. Yet Phebe tries to make an excuse by saying that maybe Susie or Cissie (other servants) picked the ring up and put it under the bolster on the bed. Bella is obviously unnerved because she forgets that she wanted a glass of milk. Phebe's remembering the milk and offering to get it can be taken on several levels.

Listen to the Mockingbird Motivational Units (*continued*)

UNIT	PAGES[a]	CHARACTERS	DRAMATIC ACTION/KEY REVELATIONS
34	68–69	Bella and Cass	Bella admits that Duncan never took off his ring to Cass, who confirms the meaning of the ring's being found under the bolster. Bella starts with her fear of being "looked at." She refers to having "loved Phebe" in the past tense—significant because she no longer loves her. Again, Bella wants to escape, but when Cass will not go away with her, she questions whether Cass ever loved her.
35	69–71	Bella and Cass	Bella goes on the offensive and accuses Cass of ducking his responsibility, of being manipulative by playing innocent. She almost gets him to believe it is true: "he did stand in the dark and stare at her door."
36	71–72	Bella and Cass	A new attack for Bella. She now accuses Phebe of killing Duncan for revenge. Is this a way of getting Cass close to her after blaming him? Cass does not accept her accusation against Phebe.
37	72–73	Bella and Cass	She wants Cass to believe her and prove he loves her by agreeing with her accusation against Phebe. He should protect her and live up to his responsibility. He says he loves her and that is all he has. This is not good enough. Bella says that Duncan was the only one who truly loved her; he would have protected her. Bella exits into the house, leaving Cass outside.
38	73–75	Gill and Cass	Gil, who has been standing in the background, says he was walking in the garden. Gil's message is "Learn from your transgressions." He tells Cass that he was lucky. Gil expresses his lust: his frank, unrefined admission that he would have enjoyed the pleasure of "breaking Bella in early." As an audience, we should find this offensive.

Listen to the Mockingbird Motivational Units (*continued*)

UNIT	PAGES[a]	CHARACTERS	DRAMATIC ACTION/KEY REVELATIONS
ACT III, SCENE II. *Early afternoon, April 13, the day after the funeral of Duncan Trice.*			
39	76–77	Phebe and Bella	A character named "John" is mentioned. This could be the "Houseboy." Suspense is created as Bella questions Phebe as to whether John has delivered a message in town. We discover that Phebe does have a return letter but is not forthcoming in her responses to Bella's inquisition. Was Phebe trying to "vex" Bella?
40	77–79	Phebe, Bella, and Old Alec	Bella is agitated, nervous, and apprehensive. She questions the whereabouts of Abbott and Cass. She is annoyed/upset about Old Alec playing the banjo and singing. Even though she instructs Phebe to give Old Alec money to quit, he continues to play, annoying her further. Finally, the doorbell rings. Phebe answers the door and admits Larue, a speculator/slave trader.
41	79–80	Larue, Bella, and Phebe	Uncomfortable situation. Bella cannot tell Larue why she requested him to come to her house. Bella gets agitated because Larue speaks in French. They exit to the garden where they can talk in private.
42	80–82	Larue and Bella	Bartering over the sale of Phebe, Bella is anxious and does not wish to quibble; yet she knows she is selling Bella for far less than she is worth. Larue is perhaps not used to dealing with a woman and sees, perhaps, an opportunity to swindle her and make a big profit on buying Phebe. Bella simply wants to be rid of Phebe as quickly as possible.

Listen to the Mockingbird Motivational Units (*continued*)

UNIT	PAGES[a]	CHARACTERS	DRAMATIC ACTION/KEY REVELATIONS
43	82–84	Larue, Bella, Phebe, and Abbott	How far will Bella go to relieve her conscience? The idea to sell Phebe is challenged by Abbott. Bella watches Phebe suffer the indignity of being examined as an object of property and perhaps realizes the consequences of what she is doing. Yet Bella remains resolved. Still, even after handing over the papers to Larue, she chastises him for his treatment of Phebe. But Larue has exchanged the money. Abbott, perhaps, gains a little stature in our eyes because he tries to protect Phebe. But Phebe has the last word, saying, "I know. . . ." This makes it easier for Bella in a way to watch Phebe go; she now tells Bella to "Be quiet!" Phebe can only say, "I knows what I knows."
44	84–85	Abbott and Bella	Abbott questions Bella's decision to sell Phebe. She instinctively lashes out at him. She is like a caged, wild cat one moment and a weak, pleading, injured animal the next. Abbott, perhaps because Cass enters, does not give in to Bella's manipulative ways.
45	85–87	Bella and Cass	Bella and Cass will suffer consequences for their illicit affair, which caused Duncan to commit suicide. Bella tries to hang on to Cass, but at the same time she blames him for her transgressions. She says "I didn't want to hurt anybody, I wanted to be good and make people happy." She wants desperately for someone to be able to comfort her, to be able to escape, to find that moment of extreme calm and comfort which occurs after making love.

Listen to the Mockingbird Motivational Units (*continued*)

UNIT	PAGES[a]	CHARACTERS	DRAMATIC ACTION/KEY REVELATIONS
46	87–89	Cass, Bella, and Old Alec	The final climax of the play. Cass will not save Bella, will not protect her. For him Socrates' definition of "Virtue" is the correct one. He cannot accept that Virtue is merely the "opinion of people" (see unit 10). Bella throws away the "30 pieces of silver" to Old Alec, who ironically thanks God. He refers to the ravens bringing it to him. The spider metaphor that all things are one and inseparable and have ultimate consequences is discussed. Cass realizes they have sinned and wants to atone for those sins, to try to unspin the web. Bella will not admit her sins.
47	89–90	Cass and Bella	Bella's last attempt to keep things together fails as Cass, shocked by Bella's accusation that he has been unfaithful to her by having sex with Phebe, leaves to try to unspin the web. Bella is without hope.
48	90–93	Cass and Abbott	Bella does not give up. She calls for Abbott and tries to send him out to avenge her honor by challenging Cass to a duel. She artfully uses several different approaches and finally gets Abbott to go look for Cass, to go avenge her honor. She savors her triumph of control over Abbot and her anticipated victory over Cass.
49	93–96	Houseboy and Gil	For Gil, the time has come to move on with life and leave the past behind. Ever the pragmatist, Gil tells the Houseboy to pack a bag for Cass—just the essentials. The Houseboy voices one of the arguments against abolition: "No, sir [not wanting to be free]—I wants to belong here." Gil sees the "system" (slavery) changing and claims that "damned few" know what they want.
50	96–97	Bella, Mark, and Abbott	Abbott admits that he is glad he could not find Cass and challenge him to a duel. Mark asks Bella to agree, but before she can answer, Gil enters. Will we find out whether Bella can forgive Cass?

UNIT	PAGES[a]	CHARACTERS	DRAMATIC ACTION/KEY REVELATIONS
51	97–98	Gil, Mark, Abbott, and Bella	Gil discovers that Cass is gone. He makes lewd comments about Cass wanting a "yellow gal." Bella, indirectly, comes to Cass's defense by admitting that she sold Phebe. Gil accuses Bella of pulling the strings of everyone around her, of consuming them, finishing them off.
52	99–101	Mark, Gil, Abbott, and Bella	Mark, ever the philosopher, says that Cass has escaped all of them. He envisions Cass marching into battle with the knowledge of having the burden of original sin. Mark believes he has won and that Cass will "seek the truth." Mark states that they have all taken away Cass's innocence. "Abide it" is a phrase that stays with Bella. Gil will not admit that Cass has escaped him.
53	101–2	Gil, Bella, and Abbott	The protagonist and antagonist confront each other. Bella finally says that she is "glad" that Cass has escaped, if only because Cass has escaped Gil's clutches. Gil leers at her, insults her with "A very pretty task, to break you in." Bella uses her pawn, Abbott, to step in front of Gil's attack. But Gil brushes him aside. She next tries to get Mark to do battle by calling him a coward. But even Gil admits that Mark is not a coward; however, he does note that, in effect, the "truth" is useless unless one "knows what to do about [knowing] it."

[a]Page numbers refer to Draft P, version D, of "Listen to the Mockingbird," YCAL, MSS 51, Box 158, F.2852, Beinecke Rare Book and Manuscript Library, Yale University, on which the Texas A&M–Commerce production of the play was based.

Bibliography

Bentley, Eric. Review of *All the King's Men,* by Robert Penn Warren. *Theater Arts* 31 (November 1947): 72–73.

———. "The Meaning of Robert Penn Warren's Novels." *Kenyon Review* 10 (summer 1948): 407–24.

Blotner, Joseph. *Robert Penn Warren: A Biography.* New York: Random House, 1997.

———. *Selected Letters of William Faulkner.* New York: Random House, 1977.

Bohner, Charles H. *Robert Penn Warren.* New York: Twayne, 1964.

Brady, Thomas F. "Columbia Will End Pact with Rossen." *New York Times,* May 29, 1952.

Brooks, Cleanth. "*All the King's Men:* The Local and the Universal." Typescript of speech (n.d.). In Robert Penn Warren papers, YCAL MSS 51, Box 102, F.1886.

Cottrell, Beekman W. "Cass Mastern and the Awful Responsibility of Time." In *All the King's Men: A Symposium,* 39–49. Carnegie Series in English 3. Pittsburgh: Carnegie Institute of Technology, 1957.

Coughenour, Kay L. Adaptation of "Cass Mastern's Wedding Ring," by Robert Penn Warren. Department of Communications and Theatre, Texas A&M University–Commerce, September 1, 1992. Photocopy.

Coughenour, Rosanne K. "Concept Statement." Prepared for exhibit of set design at the 1999 Region VI Kennedy Center American College Theater Festival, Denton, TX: Texas Woman's University, February 23–27, 1999.

Fisher, Ruth. "A Conversation with Robert Penn Warren." In Watkins, Hiers, and Weaks, 170–89.

Frankel, Aaron. "Working in the Theater with Robert Penn Warren." In *RWP: An Annual of Robert Penn Warren Studies,* vol. 2, edited by William Bedford Clark and James A. Grimshaw Jr., 1–16. Bowling Green: Western Kentucky University, 2002.

Grimshaw, James A., Jr. *Cleanth Brooks and Robert Penn Warren: A Literary Correspondence.* Columbia: University of Missouri Press, 1998.

———. *Robert Penn Warren: A Descriptive Bibliography, 1922–79.* Charlottesville: University Press of Virginia, 1981.

Grimshaw, James A., Jr.,and James A. Perkins, eds. *Robert Penn Warren's "All the King's Men": Three Stage Versions.* Athens: University of Georgia Press, 2000.

Hall, Adrian. "Prologue to *All the King's Men.*" Unpublished play based on chapter 4 of *All the King's Men,* by Robert Penn Warren. Directed by Adrian Hall. Dallas Theatre Center, "in the basement," Dallas, TX, January 2–21, 1990.

"Interview with Eleanor Clark and Robert Penn Warren." In Watkins and Hiers, 260–77.

Justus, James H. *The Achievement of Robert Penn Warren.* Baton Rouge: Louisiana State University Press, 1981.

Kimball, Sue. "The Many Dramatic Lives of *All the King's Men,* the Play." Unpublished essay written in the NEH Summer Seminar conducted by R. W. B. Lewis at Yale University in 1989.

Krieger, Murray. "The Assumptions of the 'Burden' of History in *All the King's Men.*" In *Robert Penn Warren's "All the King's Men,"* edited by Harold Bloom, 71–90. New York: Chelsea House, 1987.

Newman, Edwin. "Speaking Freely." In Watkins and Heirs, 158–72.

Perkins, James A. "Racism and the Personal Past in Robert Penn Warren." *Mississippi Quarterly* 48, no. 1 (winter 1994–95): 73–82.

Perkins, James A., Patrick C. McCarthy, and Frank D. Allen Jr. "Human Genetics and *All the King's Men:* The Case of Jack Burden's Paternity." *Mississippi Quarterly* 56, no. 1 (winter 2002–03): 65–75.

Robinson, Forrest G. "A Combat with the Past: Robert Penn Warren on Race and Slavery." *American Literature* 67, no. 3 (September 1995): 511–30.

Sale, Richard B. "An Interview in New Haven with Robert Penn Warren,"in Watkins, Hiers, and Weaks, 179–80.

Walker, Marshall. "Robert Penn Warren: An Interview." In Watkins and Heirs, 173–95.

Warren, Robert Penn. *All the King's Men.* New York: Harcourt Brace, 1946.

———. *All the King's Men.* 1st English edition. London: Eyre and Spottiswoode, 1948.

———. *All the King's Men.* 2nd English edition. London: Eyre and Spottiswoode, 1960.

———. *All the King's Men.* 1st English paperback edition. London: Landsborough, 1960.

———. *All the King's Men.* 3rd English edition. London: Secker and Warburg, 1974.

———. *All the King's Men.* 2nd Harvest edition, with a foreword by Joseph Blotner. San Diego: Harcourt Brace, 1996.

———. *All the King's Men.* Restored edition. Edited by Noel Polk. New York: Harcourt, 2001.

———. *All the King's Men, A Play.* New York: Random House, 1960.

———. *At Heaven's Gate.* New York: Harcourt Brace, 1943.

———. "Cass Mastern." In This Is My Best, edited by Whit Burnett. Garden City, NY: Doubleday, 1970: 389–413.

———. "Cass Mastern's Wedding Ring." *Partisan Review* 11 (fall 1944): 375–407.

———. "Cass Mastern's Wedding Ring." In *The Best American Short Stories 1945,* edited by Martha Foley, 303–43. Boston: Houghton Mifflin, 1945.

———. "Cass Mastern's Wedding Ring." In *200 Years of Great American Short Stories,* edited by Martha Foley, 701–31. New York: Galahad Books, 1975.

———. "Cass Mastern's Wedding Ring." In *A Robert Penn Warren Reader,* edited by Albert Erskine, 98–130. New York: Random House, 1987.

———. Correspondence. Harcourt Brace Editorial Archives, Orlando, Fla.

———. *Jefferson Davis Gets His Citizenship Back.* Lexington: University Press of Kentucky, 1980.

———. *John Brown: The Making of a Martyr.* 1929. Reprint, Nashville: John Sanders Publishers, 1993.

———. *Legacy of the Civil War: Meditations on the Centennial.* New York: Random House, 1961.

———. "Listen to the Mockingbird." Unpublished play (1959). YCAL MSS 51, Box 158, F.2852, Beinecke Rare Book and Manuscript Library, Yale University.

———. *Night Rider.* Boston: Houghton Mifflin, 1939.

———. "A Note to *All the King's Men.*" *Southern Review* 61 (summer1953): 476–80.

———. Papers. Yale Collection of American Literature (YCAL), MSS 51. Beinecke Rare Book and Manuscript Library, New Haven, CT.

———. "A Poem of Pure Imagination: An Experiment in Reading." In *Selected Essays,* 198–305. New York: Random House, 1958.

———. "Proud Flesh." Unpublished play (1940). YCAL MSS 51, Box 96, F.1786–87, Beinecke Rare Book and Manuscript Library, Yale University.

———. *Segregation: The Inner Conflict in the South.* New York: Random House, 1956.

———. "An Untitled Play: A Drama of the Civil War." Unpublished play (1961), formerly "Listen to the Mockingbird."YCAL MSS 51, Box 158, F.2856, Beinecke Rare Book and Manuscript Library, Yale University.

———. "Willie Stark: His Rise and Fall." Unpublished play (1958). YCAL MSS 51, Box 105, F.1945–48, Beinecke Rare Book and Manuscript Library, Yale University.

Watkins, Floyd C., and John T. Hiers, eds. *Robert Penn Warren Talking: Interviews, 1950–1978.* New York: Random House, 1980.

Watkins, Floyd C., John T. Hiers, and Mary Louise Weaks, eds. *Talking with Robert Penn Warren.* Athens: University of Georgia Press, 1990.

Index

"Cass Mastern's Wedding Ring," "An Untitled Play," and "Blocking and Motivational Units for *Listen to the Mockingbird*" are not included in this index.